The stench of uncontrolled greed is engulfing all our once-admired institutions. Top business bosses pocket millions for even the most dismal performance. Bureaucrats pay themselves eye-watering amounts, while wasting billions of our money. Bankers lie, steal our savings, rig interest rates and wreck our banks and our economy. Politicians fiddle even more from their expenses than before the expenses scandal broke.

Everything that once made Britain admired in the world – our sense of fair play, our decency, our tolerance, our trustworthiness, our democracy – seems to have been cynically trampled into the mud by our self-serving, grasping ruling elites. But while our masters loot ever more of our money for themselves, they hypocritically preach to us about the need for austerity, cutbacks and sacrifices.

Greed Unlimited exposes how our voracious, selfish, immoral elites have made fools of us all and looks at how we can fight back against the rapacity of those who have so much power over us.

David Craig spent most of his career working for some of the world's best and worst management consultancies. After writing two whistleblowing books, *Rip-Off* and *Plundering the Public Sector*, about how consultants take millions from businesses and government departments while delivering little of value, he was blacklisted and so left the profession. Since then, he has written several books about government corruption, incompetence and waste, including *Squandered: How Gordon Brown is wasting over one trillion pounds of our money* and *Fleeced: How we've been betrayed by politicians, bureaucrats and bankers*, both of which won the Hammond Whiteley journalism award. He is also the author of *The Great European Rip-Off* and *Pillaged! How they're looting £413 million a day from your savings and pensions.*

Praise for *Squandered*

"This is a terrifying book, but a brilliant and necessary one… Please read it." *Daily Telegraph*

"The most illuminating political book to date this year." *Evening Standard*

"Prepare to weep." *Daily Telegraph*

"Impossible to read without becoming angry." *New Statesman*

Praise for *Plundering the Public Sector*

"This is a good topic and Craig knows his stuff. He writes with passionate disgust and with rich detail." *Management Today*

"The first serious book to deal in a thorough fashion with the incompetence, nepotism and waste that have defined New Labour in government." *Spectator*

"Racy yet well-researched….gripping and important." *New Statesman*

Praise for *Rip-Off*

"The most shocking book of the year." *Independent on Sunday*

GREED UNLIMITED

How Cameron and Clegg protect the elites while squeezing the rest of us

"A declaration of war against the people running and ruining Britain"

David Craig

The Original Book Company

The Original Book Company
Unit E2, Kings Walk,
19a Knyveton Road,
Bournemouth BH1 3QZ
www.snouts-in-the-trough.com
email: originalbookco@yahoo.co.uk

First published in the UK by The Original Book Company

A copy of the British Library Cataloguing in Publication Data is
available from the British Library

ISBN: 978-1-872188-09-6

Written, printed and bound in Great Britain (part of the EU)

CONTENTS

Part 5 – Fightback

Introduction

Rise of the raptors

The stench of gluttonous greed and rampant corruption seems to be engulfing all our once-respected institutions.

While squeezing the wages of their employees, leading company bosses pocket millions however excellent or dismal their performance.

As they spend and waste hundreds of billions of our money, top bureaucrats have been quick to jump on the big salaries and rewards for failure gravy train.

Our bankers, many of whom have received knighthoods and other honours, have been rigging interest rates, stealing our savings, laundering drug money and wrecking the banks they ran, confident that if they got caught, they could waltz off with their bags stuffed with millions of ordinary people's cash.

Pension companies and unit trust managers have been robbing their customers blind with seemingly endless hidden fees, penalties and other charges.

Our EU rulers in Brussels take and squander ever more of our money, while forcing crippling budget cuts on those who pay for the eurocrats' luxury lifestyles.

Bankers, business leaders, sports stars, celebrities, musicians and many others have been hard at work with their accountants hiding their huge earnings from the taxes that the rest of us have to pay.

And in the centre of it all are our politicians. When they're not fiddling even more from their expenses than they did before the expenses scandal first broke, our politicians are busy grovelling to business bosses and bankers in the hope of scoring a few lucrative side jobs to add hundreds of thousands of pounds a year to their already generous MPs' salaries and pensions, and are busy networking to prepare well-paid sinecures for themselves, ready for when they voluntarily, or otherwise, quit Parliament.

Everything that once made Britain admired in the world – our sense of fair play, our decency, our tolerance, our trustworthiness, our democracy – seems to have been cynically trampled into the mud by our self-serving, grasping ruling elites. And while our masters loot ever more of our money for themselves, they hypocritically preach to us about the need for austerity, cutbacks and sacrifices.

Greed Unlimited exposes how our voracious, selfish elites have made fools of us all and looks at how we can fight back against the rapacity of those who have so much power over us.

Part 1

What a mess

Chapter 1

The NIMBY 'cuts'

Playing the Austerity game

When the Coalition came to power, they were very clear about why they were elected - to sort out the horrific mess left by New Labour's unprecedented profligacy with our money. David Cameron told us, 'if markets don't believe you are serious about dealing with your debts, your interest rates rocket and your economy shrinks.'[1] George Osborne clearly saw eye to eye with the PM, 'we need to tackle the deficit so that our debt payments don't spiral out of control'.[2] David Laws, briefly Chief Secretary to the Treasury, explained, 'the years of public sector plenty are over, but the more decisively we act the quicker and stronger we can come through these tough times' while personally doing his bit to increase the deficit by possibly pocketing a bit more of our money than he really should have done. His successor Danny Alexander gave us the same story, 'it is fair that we tackle our debts today so that we don't burden our children tomorrow'.[3] But apparently these weren't just the usual empty politicians' promises. Two years into the Coalition, Cameron seemed proud to announce the Government's supposedly remarkable progress in reducing public spending, 'in just two years we have already cut the deficit by over a quarter' and 'we have taken some pretty tough action on the deficit'.[4]

Since the Coalition began work in 2010, we've been treated to a right old slanging match between the Coalition and the Opposition, both in Parliament and the media. On the one side, there have been almost endless appearances by Coalition members talking about 'tough decisions' and 'necessary cuts' and 'reductions in the bloated state'. Meanwhile, Labour have howled in outrage about 'cutting too deep and too fast' and repeated the superficially convincing mantra of 'a recession made in Downing Street' because of supposedly 'savage cuts' in public spending.

This narrative of deep cuts in spending has been enthusiastically supported by the media, ever eager to find something dramatic to report. On the Right, the government has been praised for seizing the nettle of the country's disastrous financial situation, while from the Left there has been a flood of vituperation, with articles having titles such as 'as the cuts bleed harder, the cruel Tory truth will emerge'.[5] The employers' organisation, the CBI, said it was 'encouraged' by the Government's 'painful but necessary' actions. And, of course, the public-sector unions pitched in with their furious opposition to the Government's supposed cuts, 'the scale of the cuts promised means there will be real suffering. People should be very afraid'.[6]

This has all been highly entertaining. But it has also been a ridiculous charade, a well-paid game in which all the participants have a wonderful time getting worked up about something that simply isn't happening. As for our politicians, they have resorted to the most brazen lies – the Coalition in order to make us and financial markets believe that they are getting a grip on the massive increase in spending caused by Gordon Brown's and Ed Balls's apparently incurable financial incontinence and Labour in the hope that if they throw enough mud at the Coalition, then we'll forget whose mind-blowing economic incompetence and managerial failures got us into the current mess in the first place.

Going up, up, up

Unfortunately for us ordinary taxpayers, whatever the politicians and the leaders of the various self-interest groups claim, as they act out their chosen parts in the great 'cuts' drama, the reality is that regardless of whoever has been in government over the last fifteen years – Labour or the Coalition – public spending just keeps on going up, up, up (see Figure 1).

Figure 1 – Looking at actual and forecast spending, it's difficult to spot any cuts

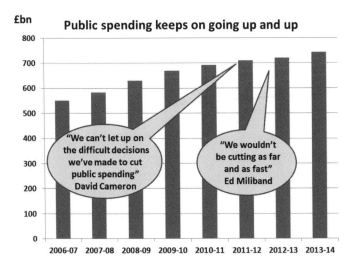

So what is actually happening? How can all our leaders witter endlessly on about 'cuts' when public spending continues its seemingly effortless upwards trajectory? Why are the unions protesting about cuts, if there aren't any? And how can a recession be caused by Downing Street cuts, if the Prime Minister and Chancellor have allowed an increase in spending and are planning for further regular increases in the years ahead?

Keeping a straight face

To get an understanding of how supposed 'cuts' actually, and usually, lead to ever-increasing public spending, we just need to look at some 'cuts' that were made by our tough-talking Prime Minister himself. Before the 2010 general election, David Cameron accused Labour of wasting millions of pounds funding 'a cushy lifestyle for politicians' and pledged he would 'cut the cost of politics'. He could not have made his intentions clearer than when he gave a speech announcing that under his government 'the gravy train would well and truly hit the buffers'.[7] Cameron was, he informed us, going to reduce the number of MPs, cut the number of cars available to ministers, cut ministers' salaries and lower subsidies on food for MPs. All this was very laudable and had ordinary people commending Cameron – 'at last a politician saying what we all know' one person commented; 'it's a good first step' wrote another; 'Dave is right. You have to start with small cymbolic (sic) cuts' agreed a third; and 'cannot wait till Mr Cameron is installed as the new PM of the UK' gushed a fourth, possibly one of Cameron's own PR people.[8]

During his first year in Downing Street, Cameron did take some small steps. He cut ministers' salaries by five per cent and slashed the number of ministers with a private car and driver from an astonishing seventy eight to a more modest thirteen, saving about £3 million a year. But at the same time, he created 117 new peers. That's 117 people who were not elected by the taxpaying public; most of whom were probably not even known to the taxpaying public; most of whom had never done anything of benefit for the taxpaying public; most of whom were probably already either wealthy or extremely wealthy and who had no need of taxpayers' money to support their luxury lifestyles; but all of whom could from then on claim generous and easily 'fiddleable' expenses and allowances, paid for by us, till the day they died. To get an idea of Mr Cameron's generosity with our money to people widely seen as mostly being his 'cronies', we can compare Cameron's ennobling frenzy with the 'lord creation rates' of his two predecessors. Tony Blair's motives for ennobling the good, the great and many others, who may not have been either good or great, but who apparently made generous contributions to Labour Party coffers, were often questioned by the cynical and the envious. But he only created forty three peers a year while in office – a pretty poor showing compared to David Cameron's blowout with our cash. As for the hapless Gordon Brown, he was running at a mere twelve peers a year. But that might have been because he had rather fewer friends, admirers, benefactors and acquaintances than the charismatic, gregarious Tony.

Cameron's plans to reduce the number of MPs and their costs, when fully implemented, might have saved us taxpayers around £12 million a year. However, the increase in the number of peers could cost us well over £10 million a year. So, theoretically Cameron's policies would save us about £2 million a year. But, whereas the 117 new lords could start energetically siphoning off our money immediately they were appointed, the cuts in the number of MPs would not happen till after the next election – in 2015 – if at all. So, in the period of Cameron's first and probably last five-year premiership, his cutting the cost of

politics might save less than £20 million from reduced ministerial salaries and cars, while the increased number of peers could
cost up to a staggering £50 million. The net 'benefit' to us taxpayers would thus be around minus £30 million. Not quite what
most ordinary people would call 'cutting the cost of politics'.
This was the same David Cameron who told us, 'when you have
a debt problem the one thing you mustn't do is keep adding endlessly to that debt'.[9] What is perhaps most surprising about Cameron's 'cutting the cost of politics' speech is that he managed to
keep a straight face while fooling us about his real intentions of
hugely increasing the cost of politics, mostly for the benefit of
himself and his buddies. Clearly Cameron had learnt a lot from
his reportedly admired hero, that great amateur actor Tony Blair.

George can spend too

At Number 11 Downing Street, the new Chancellor, George
Osborne, was also busy making changes which would result in
us taxpayers paying even more money for our rulers rather than
less, while at the same time banging on and on about the need for
austerity for the rest of us. One of his first actions was to set up a
new quango – the Office for Budget Responsibility (OBR) – which
would cost us long-suffering taxpayers at least £2 million a year
to do precisely what the more than one thousand five hundred
well-rewarded civil servants working for Osborne's Treasury
should already have been doing in the first place – producing
forecasts for the economy and public finances; judging progress
towards the Government's fiscal targets; and assessing the long-
term sustainability of public finances. Since its inception, the
OBR has produced loads of economic forecasts, most of which
have turned out to have been as laughably wrong as the equally
useless Bank of England's inflation forecasts. The OBR has also

graced us with piles of presumably fascinating reports such as *Alcohol Consumption Forecasts*, *Student Loans Forecasts* and umpteen *Fiscal Sustainability Forecasts*. But, judging from the ever-increasing levels of public spending in Figure 1, it seems as if the wonderful OBR has produced lots of forecasts but not much budget responsibility at all. Perhaps it should really be called the 'Office for Forecasts' (OFF) or even just the shorter and more succinct 'Forecasts Office' (F-Off)?

Osborne also set up the Office of Tax Simplification (OTS) 'to provide advice to the Chancellor on simplifying the UK tax system'. It's probably reasonable to assume that the highly-paid, highly-pensioned geniuses at the OTS played some part in the chaos caused by Osborne's 2012 budget fiasco, where supposed 'simplifications' of the UK tax system resulted in the pasty tax, the static caravan tax, the granny tax and the ceiling on charitable donations. These all led to howls of protest from various interest groups and most had to be embarrassingly repealed within weeks of the budget in a humiliating series of u-turns, backward flips, somersaults and other acrobatic contortions, which could have earned Osborne a place in the British 2012 Olympics gymnastics team. As the Government tried to undo some of the blunders contained in Osborne's hapless, hopeless budget, it deservedly earned a reputation for incompetence and its 'omnishambles'. The budget, that should never have been, also led to a stunning collapse in the Coalition's popularity in the opinion polls and a well-deserved battering in the Spring 2012 local elections.

It's rather difficult to see how creating yet another two possibly pointless and obviously poorly performing quango-type organisations quite fitted in with the Chancellor's much vaunted crusade to cut public spending. Moreover, it seems that, despite a supposed recruitment freeze, the cost of Osborne's Treasury will rise from £182 million in Osborne's first year in office to a projected £197 million in his second year – an increase of £15 million, equivalent to a rise of more than eight per cent. Not exactly a shining example of how to reduce the deficit. Perhaps Osborne, like Cameron, should be congratulated on his ability to keep a straight face when preaching to us about the need to reduce public spending when he was doing precisely the opposite in his own department? It seems as if, for both of our esteemed leaders, cutting public spending was very much a case of 'do as I say, but definitely not as I do' or 'spending cuts? Not in my back yard!'

Osborne also shifted more than five hundred staff at the Office for Government Commerce (OGC) – a Treasury department that should be helping other departments be slightly smarter when they use taxpayers' money to buy stuff – to the Cabinet Office as part of a newly created department with the impressive title of 'Efficiency and Reform Group'. Moving people from one department to another has always been a favourite civil service way of looking like you're taking action and reducing costs, when in fact you're doing precisely the opposite. We can get some idea of what the OBR and the OTS have been up to since they came into being – the OBR producing lots of usually wildly inaccurate forecasts and the OTS assisting with possibly the most calamitous budget in living memory. But it's less obvious what invaluable contribution the expensive and doubtless hardworking staff at the Efficiency and Reform Group have made to the improvement of life in the UK as, so far, not many efficiencies or reforms seem to have taken place. Perhaps one day we will find out about all the Efficiency and Reform Group's wonderful work and valuable achievements.

And what about Nick?

Before the 2010 election, Nick Clegg seemed to share big-spending, austerity-preaching David Cameron's admirable belief that the cost of politics should be cut. In a September 2009 policy document *A Better Politics for Less,* Mr Clegg made one of his many fine pre-election pledges:

> The {Labour} government employs 74 special advisers, an increase of ninety per cent since 1995, at a cost to the taxpayer of £5.9 million each year. These are political jobs and therefore should be funded by political parties. Special advisers will not be paid for by the taxpayer.[10]

But once in government, just like Mr Cameron, Mr Clegg too seems to have forgotten his 'cut the cost of politics' promise. In 2010, he had two special advisers, by 2012 this had risen to fourteen, costing us almost £1 million a year. Though, given Mr Clegg's ever-increasing unpopularity, it's not obvious that these advisers' advice has been that great. Moreover, it seems we're quite generous with the salaries we pay to Mr Clegg's many advisers. His chief of staff gets £98,000 a year and three others are on £80,000 a year. These include one who made an £88,000 donation to the Liberal Democrats. Cynics might see this donation as a pretty good investment, giving returns of almost a hundred per cent a year. One former Liberal Democrat MP who lost her seat was re-employed as a special adviser on £74,000 – more than an £8,000 pay rise from our money compared to her MP's salary. The rest averaged £64,500, plus one can assume they all will get bountiful public-sector pensions, that we'll have to pay for decades to come.

These special advisers were only the start of Mr Clegg's

generosity to himself and his mates with our money. Since taking up the post as Deputy Prime Minister, Mr Clegg has honourably/shamefully (delete as appropriate) tried to change our voting systems to either 'make Britain more democratic' or to 'make sure he got more Liberal Democrats into power' (delete as appropriate). First up was the House of Commons. Mr Clegg managed to get the Coalition to hold a referendum on introducing the alternative vote (AV) voting system. Had he succeeded, he would probably have at least doubled the number of Liberal Democrat MPs at the 2015 election. We spent about £80 million of our money on Mr Clegg's referendum. This £80 million could have paid for five hundred police officers or nurses for five years, perhaps a better use of our money than increasing the number of Liberal Democrats in Westminster. Luckily for us, this proposal got rejected by the electorate and has now hopefully sunk without trace. Had Clegg succeeded, AV would have hugely complicated our voting system and necessitated at least £100 million of our taxes being spent on a new electronic vote-counting system. Moreover, given the repeatedly-proven incompetence of government ministers and top civil servants, this new electronic vote-counting system would, like most other government computer projects, probably have cost us taxpayers several times its original budget and still wouldn't have worked properly.

Clegg clearly learnt something from this setback - that British voters are fairly conservative with a small 'c' when it comes to changing our electoral system. So, if he wanted to make other changes, the worst thing he could do would be to consult the stupid electorate again. Sure enough, when Clegg came up with new proposals to supposedly make the House of Lords more democratic by having the majority of peers elected rather than appointed - again a proposal likely to increase the number of Liberal Democrats in positions of power - he passionately argued that there was no need for a referendum. Clegg's proposal for between 300 and 450 elected peers, all in position for up to fifteen years and all receiving a full salary from our taxes, would have hugely increased the cost of the House of Lords. The total cost of the House of Commons is over £390 million a year – more than £600,000 per MP per year. The cost of the Lords now is probably around £130 million a year – about £160,000 per active peer per year. If Mr Clegg's proposed changes are adopted, the cost of the Lords will increase to anywhere between £200 million and £300 million a year. This may or may not be an example of Mr Clegg's 'better politics', but it certainly wasn't 'for less'. Moreover, Mr Clegg's arrogant disdain for proper control of spending our money was further demonstrated when there was a Tory backbench rebellion against Mr Clegg's plan. In retaliation for the Tories abandoning reform of the Lords, Clegg has threatened to block Cameron's proposal to reduce the number of MPs in the Commons to six hundred – something which would have slightly reduced the cost of politics - unless he got his way on Lords reform. Once again, Mr 'Better Politics for Less' Clegg seemed totally and selfishly unconcerned about how much of our money he would spend on his political cronies. Mr Clegg's various attempts to squander huge quantities of our tax money on his efforts to change voting systems for the Commons and Lords for the benefit of himself and his party seem to sit slightly uncomfortably with Mr Clegg's vision of *A Better Politics for Less*.

Carry on squandering?

So we are left with a bit of a conundrum. The Coalition Government claims it is cutting public spending. The Opposition harangues the Government for damaging the British economy with allegedly 'savage cuts'. The public-sector unions are outraged by what they see as a brutal campaign against their members' interests. The politically-correct BBC repeatedly and enthusiastically reports on the damaging effects of cuts to public services for the old, the vulnerable and any other victims they can either find or invent. Yet public spending rises inexorably, adding to our debts. Meanwhile, David Cameron, George Osborne and Nick Clegg are doing precisely the opposite of leading by example – they have massively and shamelessly increased the costs which were well and truly under their own personal control for the benefit of themselves and those close to them.

In fact, there have been some quite savage and worrying cuts in a few areas and a horrific squeeze on ordinary working people. But for the most part, the Coalition's modest attempts to reduce public spending have either backfired spectacularly resulting in even higher costs for us taxpayers. Or else those who have been preaching the necessity for cuts and who should have been implementing the cuts have found a variety of creative ways of avoiding taking action and in too many cases, just like Cameron, Osborne and Clegg, they have actually deliberately increased spending on themselves and their nearest and dearest.

Three of the most popular approaches to avoiding making any real spending cuts appear to be the 'NIMBY', the 'Chair Shuffle' and the 'Goodbye-Hello Game'. Many politicians and public-sector bosses adopted a NIMBY (Not In My Back Yard) attitude – agreeing that everyone else should cut, while they personally had the most excellent reasons for generously increasing their own spending of our money. This seems to be what Cameron, Osborne and Clegg did as they decided to spend even more of our money on their own favourite areas and the ruling elites, while spouting on and on about the necessity of austerity for everyone else. Other politicians and public-sector chiefs have shuffled the chairs a bit - moving people from one department to another or setting up new units with different names to hide either a failure to cut or, in most cases, real increases in people and spending. The third favourite trick – the 'Goodbye-Hello Game' – consists of giving some staff massive redundancy pay-offs (costing us taxpayers many hundreds of millions) so it looks like you're reducing your headcount and then rehiring them a couple of minutes later, often as expensive consultants.

Meanwhile, many of our top civil servants, council bosses, NHS executives, quango chiefs and others of their ilk seem to have been involved in a 'grab it while you can' to add to their own wealth at our expense. Realising that Brown was probably going to be defeated in the 2010 election, they hugely increased their own salaries just before the election. This would give them much more of our money while they carried on work-ing and much larger pensions when they retired. So for them, a big salary rise in 2009-10 could mean many tens of thousands of pounds a year more of taxpayers' money pouring abundant-ly into their bank accounts every year for thirty to forty years. Laughably, having pushed up their salaries by ten to twenty per cent in 2009-10, some of them then agreed to a three to five per cent pay cut once the Coalition's austerity programme kicked in. This allowed them to claim that they too were suffering from austerity, when the opposite was in fact true.

Cameron and Osborne and Clegg and Danny Alexan-der and many others have promised us cuts, repeatedly stressing the 'difficult decisions' and 'painful choices' they will have to make, apparently on our behalf. But it's not obvious that we're all sharing in the pain. In the wonderful world of our business, bureaucratic and political leaders, the elites have never had it so good. As spending on ordinary people is going down, spending on the comfort and security of our self-appointed masters seems to keep on rising.

Chapter 2

The Brown and Balls debacle

Lest we forget

Almost every Prime Minister's question time, Labour politicians jeer and hurl abuse at the Government for the worsening state of the economy. Likewise, in media interview after interview, Labour quite rightly lambast Coalition ministers for the extraordinary incompetence and bungling they have displayed in running Britain. But with so much mud and worse being justifiably hurled at the hapless and bumbling Coalition members, there is a risk we forget whose arrogance and ineptitude got us into the mess in the first place. Because, even though Gordon Brown may have largely withdrawn to his Scottish home to possibly sulk and write his memoirs, while still receiving his generous MP's salary, expenses and other additional eye-watering payments former prime ministers can claim, most of the rest of the guilty are still sitting on Labour's front benches itching to get the chance to finish the job they started – totally bankrupting Britain while enthusiastically filling their own pockets with our money. And none seems to be more implicated in the thirteen year long New Labour deployment of weapons of mass economic destruction than Shadow Chancellor Ed Balls.

Mr Balls had a glittering academic career, gaining a

presumably well-deserved First in Philosophy, Politics and Economics at Oxford, before going on to Harvard as a Kennedy Scholar. Then, after an impressively brief career as a journalist for the strongly pro-EU and formerly pro-euro Financial Times, he became an economic adviser to the then Shadow Chancellor Gordon Brown in 1994 and stayed close to Mr Brown till Labour's 2010 well-deserved election defeat.

We could have had it all

When Gordon Brown, ably assisted by the talented and academically gifted Ed Balls, took over as chancellor, he inherited a situation that any other chancellor would have given his or her back teeth for. Tax revenues were growing faster than public spending and the British Government's finances were moving towards a surplus – the Government was about to start taking more in taxes than it was spending. As part of New Labour's 1997 election campaign, the Party had tried to boost its economic credentials by promising to stick to the previous Tory government's public-spending plans for its first two years in office. Unable to splash out all the cash that was pouring in, Brown and his acolytes found they could use the excess money to reduce our public debt from around £350 billion to £312 billion in just a couple of years and thus reduce our annual interest payments from about £29 billion to less than £25 billion.

Brown, and one assumes Balls, seems to have always wanted to go on an unprecedented and reckless spending spree with our money. But their lust for spending our taxes need not have been a problem. Tax revenue was going up so fast that Brown and Balls could have happily shoved public spending up by a massive seventy per cent between 1997 and 2007, just under the seventy five per cent rise in tax revenues. This would have allowed them to waste hundreds of billions on whatever they wanted - unnecessary bureaucracy, huge pay rises for public-sector fatcats, hopelessly-managed grand projects like the Millenium Dome, tens of billions given to Blair's favourite management consultants, and umpteen worthless multi-billion pound computer systems - and they still would have had enough cash left over to pay off pretty much all our Government debt during their first ten years in office (see Figure 1).

Figure 1 – Brown and Balls could have had their spending spree without wrecking Britain

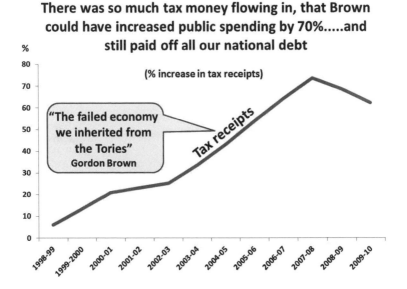

What a mess

The tragedy for all of us was that a mere seventy per cent increase in public spending over ten years didn't seem to be enough for Brown and Balls. They apparently needed more of our money to fulfil their great ambitions, whatever they were. And so they really let rip. Not satisfied with constraining themselves to slam public spending up by just a little bit less than the healthy rate at which tax revenues were increasing, Brown and Balls went for broke and more than doubled the amount of our money they spent (see Figure 2).

Figure 2 – If only Brown and Balls had kept spending going up at just below the rate of rising tax revenue, we'd be laughing and they'd still be in power

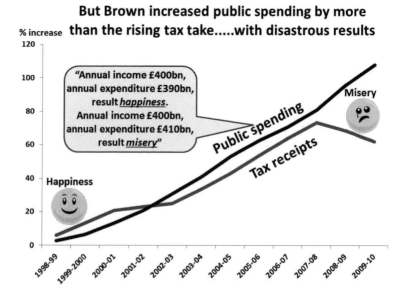

The Brown and Balls debacle

The results were as predictable as they were catastrophic. As even the rapidly rising tax take wasn't enough to satisfy New Labour's addiction to spending our money, Brown and Balls had to borrow and borrow and borrow. Rather than being comfortably paid off bit by bit with our ever-increasing tax revenues, our national debt more than doubled from a low of £312 billion to over £760 billion under Brown's and Balls's dubious stewardship of our economy. Our debt is now well on course to hitting £1.3 trillion by 2015 – about four times what it was when Brown and Balls first got their hands on our credit card and went to town. Brown, supported by Balls, could have been the greatest Chancellor in British history – instead he was probably the worst. To cheer us up, it might be worth recalling what Gordon Brown said in 1997:

> And I tell you, we have learned from past mistakes. Just as you cannot spend your way through a recession, you cannot in a global economy simply spend your way through a recovery either, in place of irresponsible Tory short-termism, there will be no risk with inflation, no irresponsible fine-tuning, no massaging of the figures, no short-term dashes for growth, but what the country wants: a long-term strategy for our public finances, the encouragement of long-term investment for our future and, in place of the boom and bust years, long-term stability for Britain (Applause).[11]

As a consequence of Brown doing the opposite of what he promised, interest payments on our national debt have now reached over £47 billion a year (more than we spend on defence) and are on course to pass £60 billion a year by 2016. If only Brown and Balls had just gone moderately wild with our money and put public spending up by an already sizeable seventy per cent, we'd have been able to laugh off the 2007 economic crash and continue to party while the debt-ridden US and the rest of Europe sank into deep economic gloom. If only Brown and Balls had just stuck to the seventy per cent, we would have had virtually no government debt and, with no interest payments to make, there would have been an extra £47 billion or so to cushion us against the effects of recession in other countries. If only Brown and Balls had even the slightest understanding of economics, we'd now all be as happy as pigs in the proverbial. But seventy per cent wasn't enough for Brown and Balls. Instead of going moderately wild with our money, they went totally crazy and so now we're actually up to our eyes in the proverbial, the proverbial will soon be up over our heads and we've no idea of how we're ever going to get out of it.

The difference between what Brown and Balls could have spent while maintaining sound finances and what they actually did spend wasn't huge. But the result of years of slightly overspending was disastrous. Never before had we seen such a perfect example of Mr Micawber's lesson in basic economics. Perhaps we could rephrase Mr Micawber's advice for our big-spending Mr Brown and Mr Balls:

> Annual income four hundred billion, annual expenditure three hundred and ninety billion, result **happiness.** Annual income four hundred billion, annual expenditure four hundred and ten billion, result **misery.**[12]

Perhaps Mr Balls should have this framed and stuck up on his office wall when he becomes our new Chancellor in 2015, if not earlier. It's a pity for British taxpayers that they don't use Dickens as part of the teaching material at Edinburgh where Mr Brown studied history or at Oxford and Harvard where Mr Balls learnt what little he seems to know about economics.

But there's worse, much worse

We now know, as I described in my book *Squandered*, that due to the stupendous incompetence of New Labour politicians and our leading civil servants and the greed of companies, many of whom generously contributed to New Labour coffers while being awarded lucrative public-sector contracts, most of Brown's and Balls's extra spending – about £1.4 trillion, give or take a few hundred billion – was wasted on things like hiring an extra million or so unnecessary bureaucrats costing us between £50 billion and £100 billion a year; giving all public-sector workers generous pay rises – at least another £60 billion a year; giving public-sector bosses totally extraordinary pay rises – billions more for their salaries and pensions; huge computer systems most of which never worked but made consultants billions richer; and hundreds of billions in benefits for a few million Brits who, even during an economic boom, couldn't be bothered to go to work and preferred to stay at home watching shows like the *X-Factor* and *Big Brother* on their large flat-screen TVs while two to three million East Europeans and others from further afield took the jobs the British couldn't be arsed to do.[13]

This massive squandering of our money meant that, in spite of splashing out all the country's rapidly increasing tax revenues and in spite of also borrowing and spending about £400 billion more, Brown and Balls still didn't have enough cash to build the schools, hospitals, roads, care homes and all the other grand projects they had set their hearts on. And that's when they created what has been called the 'shadow public sector' – even more public-sector spending which was kept off the Government's current spending accounts through long-term deals done with private-sector companies. This was mostly done through a huge programme of PFI (Private Finance Initiative) projects. With PFI, the Government signed contracts with private companies for them to build and often operate things like schools, hospitals and other public buildings. Some of these PFI contracts stretched out over twenty to thirty years, landing future taxpayers with crippling costs for decades into the future. The total capital value of more than seven hundred PFI projects is only about £56 billion. But with interest payments and running costs, we taxpayers will end up paying PFI companies over £300 billion by 2050.

Most PFI projects were so incompetently negotiated by civil servants that they became even more massively profitable for the companies involved than had originally been imagined. Profit margins of fifty to sixty per cent were not uncommon. Moreover, some PFI companies doubled or even tripled their profits by refinancing their projects, often making immediate gains of anywhere between £50 million and £100 million from just a few days' nifty financial jiggery-pokery. Others made huge gains by selling on their share of their projects to other infrastructure companies or financial speculators. But for the British taxpayer, PFI was close to a shakedown forcing us to pay significantly more than what similar projects would have cost, even if they had been directly built and run by our inefficient, wasteful public sector. However, for the big-spending New Labour government, the main advantage of PFI seems to have been that they could spend quite stupendous amounts of our money while in office, but could leave the bills for future governments to pay. Plus, of course, having landed future governments with preposterous PFI bills, the Labour politicians responsible for the PFI debacle had the enormous pleasure of being able to mockingly accuse their successors of not controlling public spending, in the full knowledge that Labour politicians were completely responsible for the country's economic chaos in the first place.

We're alright Jack

Mr Brown's and Mr Balls's performance running the British economy may have been less than stellar. And they may have condemned the rest of us to grinding austerity and possible long-term poverty as we struggle to pay the country's debts that they racked up on our credit card. But they seem to have done alright for themselves at our expense. As former government ministers, they will be entitled to inflation-protected pensions worth many millions of pounds for the rest of their and their partner's lives. Moreover, since leaving Downing Street, Mr Brown has been able to turn his period of supposed 'public service' into a fair old money spinner (see Figure 3).

It should be said that, in the *Register of Members' Interests* there are notes indicating that most of Mr Brown's payments are not personal income. The *Register* explains, 'I am not receiving money from this engagement personally. It is being held by the Office of Gordon and Sarah Brown for the employment of staff to support my ongoing involvement in public life'. Some people may see this as Gordon Brown nobly and selflessly sacrificing his opportunity for acquiring personal wealth in order to continue to make a major contribution to the rest of us through his 'ongoing involvement in public life'. But those of a more cynical disposition might believe the Office of Gordon and Sarah Brown, which is a limited company, is just a way of reducing taxes on Mr. Brown's considerable income. Moreover, Gordon Brown has also reportedly been claiming over £100,000 a year of taxpayers' money as a special allowance former prime ministers are allowed to claim each year ' to meet costs of continuing to fulfil public duties associated with the role of a former Prime Minister'.[14] No doubt, an equally glittering financial future awaits Mr. Balls after he has taken over as Chancellor and has completed the job he and Brown so effectively started - completely bankrupting Britain.

Figure 3 – In spite of possibly being Britain's worst ever Chancellor and then worst ever Prime Minister, Gordon Brown has many highly-paid engagements

Register of Members' Interests	
Just a small selection of Gordon Brown's entries	
Distinguished Global Leader in Residence (New York University)	£102,568.55
Speech in Lagos Nigeria	£62,181.32
Speech in New Delhi	£37.047.01
Book advance (profits to charity)	£78,289.61
Speech to World 50	£35,873.94
Speech to Pacific Investment Mortgage Co.	£36,174.63
Speech Economic Club Southwestern Michigan	£36,174.63
Speech to Skybridge Capital	£36,146.29
Speech to Citi Latin America (New York)	£36,292.84
Chairman World Economic Forum (Policy Co-ordination Group – Payments for staff and research)	£237,839.82

Part 2

Bad companies

Chapter 3

The executhieves cash in

Nowhere are there better examples of modern-day Britain's culture of greed, or rather outrageous rapacity, than in the boardrooms of Britain's major and once most-respected companies. In the last thirty years, the average worker income rose by a factor of four from around £6,500 to £25,900. Over the same period, pay packages for the directors of the top one hundred companies ballooned by a factor of more than sixty, from an average of £77,000 to around £4.8 million. In the mid 1980s, top executives were earning just about twelve times the average wage. By 2012 this had shot up to 185 times. This has created an ever-widening financial chasm between the majority of us and the business elites, for whom so many of us work.

How much are they really getting paid?

Many executives get paid so much money in so many different ways – salary, annual bonus, long-term incentive plans, share awards, share options, matched share awards, benefits, pensions, contractual notice periods, phantom options, golden hellos, golden handcuffs, severance payments and so on – and the terms of all these payment types are spread around pages and pages of footnotes to company accounts, that it's often extremely difficult for an outsider to work out how much a boss is actually receiving. This allows executives to claim, for example, that their £800,000 or £1 million salary is not at all excessive, when they're really pocketing many times their salary, often regardless of how brilliant or dismal their performance (see Figure 1).

Figure 1 – Most FTSE100 executives earn an awful lot more than their salaries

The astonishing upwards acceleration of executive pay might be justified if these executives were producing vast wealth for the legal owners of the companies they managed – the shareholders. Then we ordinary people might have seen some benefits, as much of our pension and other savings are invested in these companies. But sadly, the vast salaries paid to our top bosses don't seem to have given any benefits to anyone apart from themselves. In the ten years from 2000 to 2010, share prices of Britain's largest 350 companies fell by about 37 per cent (in real terms after taking account of inflation) and the total value of these 350 companies dropped by twenty four per cent. But, in

The executhieves cash in

spite of the appalling performance of the companies they managed, the pay packages handed to the bosses of these companies boomed by seventy five per cent (see Figure 2).

Figure 2 – It's difficult to see any link between often pathetic company performance and rising executive pay

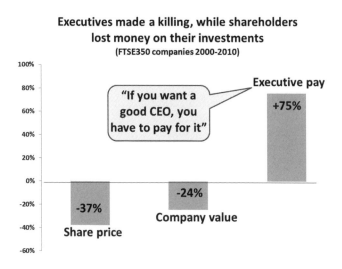

The biggest boom in executive salaries has, of course, been in our banks. While executives of the larger FTSE companies are now earning about 185 times the average salary, our bank bosses are probably on over three hundred times average salary – with some investment bankers on much more than that.

You might have expected that the enthusiasm of our corporate leaders for enriching themselves could have moderated since the 2007 financial crash, ensuing recession and increase in unemployment of over a million workers. But in fact, it was during the years of the recession that bosses' went up most, in some cases leaping up by over forty per cent between 2010 and 2012. It rather looks like our bosses got the boom and we ordinary employees got the bust. However, this extraordinary rise in executive pay, while their companies floundered and their workers lost their jobs, poses inevitable and uncomfortable questions – are our executives receiving reasonable remuneration for their talents and work or are they just looting the companies they are employed to run on behalf of shareholders? Are these people executives or executhieves?

Massive pay increases for executives, who often seem to produce little value for shareholders, is an example of what's called 'the agency problem' or 'the principal-agent problem'. The principals of any public company are the owners – the shareholders. The agents are the executives employed to run the company, supposedly on behalf of the owners. But too often there can be a conflict of interest. The principals want the agents to produce good dividends year after year and to increase the company's share price. But executives may see their positions as once-in-a-lifetime opportunities to enrich themselves as fast as possible and to hell with the shareholders.

In banking heaven

The most extreme cases of the 'agency problem' can be seen in Britain's once admired and now despised banks. It can be difficult to work out exactly how much our top bankers pay themselves. For example, depending on whether you read the *Wall Street Journal*, the *Financial Times* or other such apparently expert publications or depending on how you interpret the many footnotes in Barclays' annual accounts, you might believe that in 2011 Barclays' boss, Bob 'The Banker' Diamond earned

£13 million, or it could be £18 million or maybe £21 million. Whatever the real figure, this generous remuneration was paid in spite of Mr Diamond managing to reduce the bank's share price by about forty five per cent from around £2.93 per share, when he took over as CEO in January 2011, to close to £1.62 by the time of his departure, presumably to spend more time with his money. One apparently disgruntled shareholder, who voted against Bob Diamond's 2012 pay package, expressed his feelings, 'it's always shareholders who get shafted – why should executives have gained while returns to private investors have gone down?'[15] Moreover, even though Mr Diamond has gone, the fallout from his management or mismanagement of the bank - litigation, loss of customers and soiling of Barclays' reputation – is likely to cause further losses for shareholders for some time to come unless the bank can really pull its finger out and hire someone with some kind of credibility to sort out the mess left by Diamond.

At one of our other major banks, HSBC, the situation seems to be clearer with chief executive Stuart Gulliver taking home around £7.2 million in 2011 out of a potential maximum of £12.5 million for achieving performance that was judged to be 'satisfactory in aggregate'.[16] In general, while FTSE100 executives are earning on average around £4.8 million a year, bank CEOs are probably averaging around twice that, with some investment bankers taking tens of millions each.

Something has been going on in our banks which could make it look like the employees have hijacked the banks to run them for their own short-term financial benefit and really don't give a monkey's what the shareholders – theoretically the banks' owners – think. At almost all our banks, the amount of money paid in staff, especially executive, remuneration has been increasing, while the amount paid to shareholders in dividends has been falling. One study looked at how banks split their 'spoils'

Bad companies

(defined as net earnings plus staff costs) between employees'
pay, retained earnings (R/E - money that's kept in the bank to
fund the business) and dividends paid to shareholders.[17] It found
that there had been a huge increase in the proportion employees
(mainly executives) pocketed and an equivalent massive fall in
the proportion paid in dividends to the banks' legal owners – the
long-suffering and poorly-rewarded shareholders (see Figure 3).

**Figure 3 – Bankers have increased their own earn-
ings and the money they keep in the business while slashing
the amounts paid to shareholders**

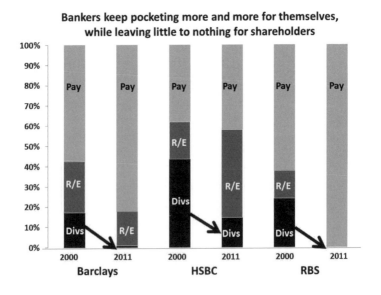

For three major UK banks – Barclays, HSBC and RBS – Figure 3 shows how staff wages have increased while dividends
have collapsed. In just the five years up to 2012, the share of the

banks' 'spoils' handed out to staff rose from fifty eight per cent to over eighty per cent, while the proportion paid in dividends shrivelled from over fourteen per cent to just over four per cent. Moreover, so appalling has been the executives' stewardship of our banks that several are to all intents and purposes bankrupt and many are facing billions in fines and compensation claims for mis-selling rubbishy financial products, rigging interest rates and commodity prices, flogging extremely dubious tax evasion schemes, laundering drug money and other questionable business practices. In all the mess, there is probably only one certainty – the billions to be paid in fines and compensation will result in even lower dividends for shareholders, while the bank executives responsible will help themselves to an even bigger share of the 'spoils'. It is astonishing or even impressive how a privileged few have received such enormous quantities of other people's money for destroying so much value.

Meanwhile, we ordinary people have been hit by a quadruple whammy thanks to the rapacity of and mismanagement by our bank executives. As customers, we've been cheated by being mis-sold largely worthless savings products and investment schemes. As savers, we've seen the value of bank shares held by our pension funds and unit trusts collapse. Also as savers, we've been hurt as the dividends paid into our pension funds and unit trusts have all but evaporated, while bankers have increased their own earnings at our expense. And as taxpayers, we've seen tens of billions of our money handed out to our banks by two (Labour and the Coalition) unbelievably useless governments. At first, these massive hand-outs were meant to save the banks from their executives' incompetence and greed. Then they were supposedly to encourage the banks to lend to businesses. But, laughing at the gullibility of politicians, regulators and ordinary people, the banks have often used our money for speculation, earning vast profits for themselves and greater bonuses for their bosses, yet depriving our businesses of the money they need to survive and preserve jobs.

You fill my pockets, I'll fill yours

The stunning rise in executive pay, in spite of generally disappointing company performance, can be largely attributed to the companies' remuneration committees (RCs). The RC is usually a sub-committee of the main board and made up of non-executive directors. Around ninety per cent of RC members come from a small, elite circle of business leaders, financiers and a few free-riding politicians and peers. About half of all RC members are either serving or former company directors. And many of them will be friends or acquaintances of the people whose pay packages they are deciding. There are few, if any, companies which have an employees' representative on the RC.

There seem to be at least four reasons why RCs keep pushing executive pay ever upwards despite the glaringly appalling results achieved by many executives. As most RC members come from the highly-paid executive and political classes, they naturally believe that they and executives merit the massive, often undeserved, rewards to which they have become accustomed. Then there is group pressure – few RC members are going to risk the unpopularity and opprobrium they would attract if they sought to restrict rises in or even reduce executive pay. There is also simple cronyism – many RC members will have no qualms about enriching their executive friends with shareholders' money. After all, there's nothing in this world as easy or as enjoyable as spending other people's cash on those in your own social circle. And there's the back-scratching principle – the more RC members raise executive salaries, the more executives will support higher pay for non-executive directors, including of course RC members. There are even quite a few cases, which for legal reasons I can't list here, where a CEO of Company A is on the RC of Company B, while the CEO of Company B is on the RC of Company A. So it's difficult not to suspect that there might be a bit of 'you fill my pockets with shareholders' cash and I'll fill yours' going on.

To this toxic situation, you have to add in the often baleful influence of remuneration consultants. Many RCs employee specialist remuneration consultants to propose how much executives should be paid and how this pay should be split between salary, bonuses, pension contributions, benefits, share options, long-term incentive plans and the rest. Remuneration consultants tend to help ratchet up executive pay as, like RC members, their own self-interest is served by ever-increasing pay awards. For a start, any remuneration consultant is unlikely to endear themselves to a company if they suggest that executives are hideously overpaid. In fact, such sacrilege is likely to result in them losing their lucrative consulting contract to a competitor. So they naturally tend to propose generous increases. As a 2012 government report stated, perhaps much more politely than it could have done, 'the interests of remuneration consultants are more closely aligned with the interests of the members of the boards who select them than the interests of shareholders'.[18] Moreover, most remuneration consultants are keen to flog further human resources and other consulting services, as consultancy directors' bonuses depend on how much they can sell each year. This too influences them to curry favour with their clients by proposing that executives pocket generously increasing quantities of shareholders' money. Furthermore, as part of their work, remuneration consultants will tend to 'benchmark' executives' pay packages against what other companies pay. These benchmarks will show the lower, average and top levels of pay in a selection of similar companies. In the same way that we all believe that we personally are above average, so most RCs will consider that their executives are also above average and consequently should be granted above-average remuneration. This naturally pushes up the average and thus pushes up executive pay.

In the few cases where remuneration committees have actually been criticised for their generosity with shareholders' cash, they have a variety of excuses to absolve themselves of any responsibility for anything. Excuse number one is usually that they have to pay their executive chums and chumesses so much money otherwise these (sometimes not terribly successful) business leaders would take their extraordinary talents some-where else. Mining giant Xstrata caused a few raised eyebrows in 2012 when it proposed giving one senior executive a £30 mil-lion golden handcuffs deal as part of a £172 million offer for the entire top tier of management if they would stay on for three years following a planned merger with Glencore. There were not even any performance targets attached to the offer. A director ex-plained the need to hand over so much of shareholders' money, 'there are plenty of other large, privately held mining groups that would make a move if they felt Mick or Trevor were avail-able'.[19] But a major investor didn't seem to be impressed, 'this is so out of touch with the current mood it's like big hair and shoulder pads. No company can hold shareholders to ransom'.

But perhaps even better is the 'we're obliged by the con-tract to pay so much' justification for their excessive largesse. Many executive pay packages will include share options that might have been agreed several years before as part of a long-term incentive plan. So the RC can claim that, as these were decided years earlier, they had a contractual obligation to pay them. Many of these plans will be worth five to six times execu-tives' basic pay. Hence we often see bosses cashing in shares worth millions or even tens of millions in years when company results might seem more than lacklustre. Then a few years later, when executives cash in further millions or tens of millions in share options, the RC can use the same excuse that it's not their fault, it's the fault of a previous RC, and therefore they are once again contractually obliged to make such generous payments to top bosses.

Politicians join the parade

By 2011, the recession was in full swing, most of us were being squeezed by austerity and public fury at massive payouts to executives, especially bankers, was reaching fever pitch. Our well-paid politicians had shown little interest in the issue of executive excess in the past. But they now saw the opportunity for increasing their popularity (or rather, decreasing their unpopularity) by getting themselves in the front of the parade of people protesting about the greed of our executhieves. Quickly, Cameron, Clegg and Miliband were all vying with each other as to who could best show their outrage by coming up with the most memorable soundbite excoriating executive greed.

Cameron, whose government reduced tax rates for the wealthy, gave us a rather patrician, 'boards have got to think when they make pay awards if it is the right and responsible thing to do...I believe in a responsible society, and that is responsibility exercised by everybody, including in the boardroom'. Nick Clegg came up with a more populist, 'I think some of them [pay awards] are incomprehensible and will strike most people as a slap in the face for millions of people who are on normal incomes and struggling to make ends meet'. And Ed Miliband, whose party when in power gained a reputation for grovelling to the rich and powerful and showering them with peerages and other honours often in return for generous donations to party funds, was now apparently Mr Angry, 'when people are struggling, when the middle is being squeezed, when people are seeing their living standards fall, it is not fair for those at the top to get runaway rewards not related to the wealth they have created'.

By 2012, following a raft of business and banking scandals where the executives involved either kept their jobs or else waltzed off into the sunset, the pain of their departure eased by being given millions more of other people's money, the public's wrath seemed to be even greater. Again, our politicians had their favourite soundbites at the ready to show how in tune they were with the popular mood. Cameron managed to appear a bit more furious and less patrician than before, 'it is this excessive growth in payment unrelated to success that is frankly ripping off the shareholder and the customer and is crony capitalism and is wrong'. Clegg started to pretend to look like he was about to do something about our corporate raptors, 'I think we now need to get tough on irresponsible and unjustifiable behaviour of top remuneration of executives in the private sector'. But he was a bit unclear about what precisely his 'getting tough' consisted of and quickly went curiously silent on the issue. And Miliband launched his great new idea - the 'responsible capitalism agenda' - 'the way we run the economy has got to change, that is the point of my responsible capitalism agenda'.

With the Tory government of millionaires forever associated with the rich and powerful and with the Liberal Democrats tainted by their participation in the Coalition, Labour's attacks on out-of-control capitalism and the predatory rich, whom Labour had so eagerly courted in the past, might well help them win the next election. But whoever does get into power, it seems rather unlikely that our politicians will take any action against the executhieves who make such generous contributions to all the parties' funds; who spend so much of shareholders' money lobbying politicians; and who offer politicians lucrative side jobs when they are in office and well-paid permanent positions when they leave Parliament.

Running or ruining?

Most corporate bosses do seem to make some attempt to
properly manage the businesses that are making them richer
than Croesus, even if they actually achieve little to nothing for
shareholders. But there are some who could be accused of being
almost indifferent to the success or failure of their businesses as
long as they can extract impressive fortunes for themselves.

There was a good deal of criticism directed at the
American Glazer family when they bought Manchester United
football club in 2006 in a leveraged buyout, largely by loading
the club with around £525 million of debt. Since the acquisition,
the club has had to pay out about £500 million in interest and
other financing charges. This is £500 million that could have been
used for building better facilities, buying new players, helping
develop sports in deprived areas of the city or keeping ticket
prices, which have doubled since the takeover, lower. Tens of
millions have also been paid in 'management and administration
fees' to companies affiliated to the Glazer family.[20] Fortunately,
the club's success on the field has generated such huge amounts
of cash that the club has managed to bear the financing charges
and even reduce its debt to about £400 million. At the time of
writing, the club was planning a share offer on the New York
stock exchange which might raise almost enough money to pay
off a decent chunk of the club's debts. Or the money might be
used for other purposes, such as further enriching the owners
who loaded the club with its large debts in the first place. Who
knows?

Many other companies have not been as fortunate as
Manchester United. Some have been pushed from making profits

Bad companies

to making losses while hugely enriching their owners. Others have been financially crippled and even destroyed, but still have made extraordinary amounts of money for their owners, even in their death throes.

In 2010, the train rolling stock leasing company Eversholt Rail Group was sold by HSBC to a group made up of 3i Infrastructure, Star Capital and US bank Morgan Stanley who own it through a Luxembourg holding company, presumably to reduce their UK tax liabilities. In 2011, Eversholt made a loss of £126.5 million on revenues of only £267 million. In fact, as far as I understand the situation, the company actually made an operating profit of £5.5 million. But this was turned into a loss because increased borrowing meant that the interest on the company's debt rose by an astonishing £132 million from £29 million in 2010 to £161 million a year later. But, in spite of massively increasing the company's debt burden, the owners set aside £92 million for repayment of shareholder loans and dividends – basically the owners were extracting a huge amount of money for themselves. Still, like Manchester United, Eversholt is still in business, generates a lot of cash and can apparently support the interest payments caused by its increased debt.

Not so lucky was Barchester – a care home group with two hundred homes and ten thousand or so residents. Shortly after paying out a £363.5 million dividend to investors, Barchester had to start talks with creditors about how it could pay back some of the £900 million in loans with which its owners had saddled it. If the company does succeed in extending the period for paying back its borrowings, it will end up paying a lot more in interest. But its owners have their £363.5 million, so they have done very nicely indeed from their investment.

Investors, often wealthy private equity companies or financial speculators, have bought up a large number of British companies, loaded them with sometimes unsustainable debt and still extracted enormous special dividend payments for themselves. Many of these companies have been turned into what have been called 'zombie companies' – they are still trading, but are pretty lifeless as they are using so much of their earnings to pay off massive debts that they can't invest or grow. These zombies are a major barrier to Britain's economic recovery as almost all the money they make goes either to their creditors – usually banks – or to their private equity owners as special dividends, leaving little cash left in the business. One news report claimed that well-known companies such as Findus, Travelodge, Thomas Cook, Punch Taverns and Fitness First had all been turned into zombies by their borrowings, yet in many cases the investors had paid themselves healthy dividends.[21] A newspaper explained this method of financial engineering when reporting on how private equity firm Permira had tried to take a £500 million dividend out of frozen foods supplier Birds Eye:

> A shortage of debt for new deals has forced investors to examine alternative ways to make money from existing investments. The most popular is a debt refinancing that enables a one-off payment like the one Permira was planning with Birds Eye. The technique is known as a 'dividend recapitalization'.[22]

This apparently ruthless extraction of money from once healthy and profitable companies has been described as the 'financialisation' of British business. It has made fortunes for the 'financialisers' but has brought many once great companies to their knees or worse. Moreover, it has harmed our economy in two ways. Firstly, by wrecking companies it has destroyed jobs and inhibited growth. And secondly, it has deprived the Government of billions in taxes and thus resulted in ordinary people having to pay more in tax to make up for the tax revenues lost when these companies went from being healthy profitable taxpaying enterprises to becoming debt-laden zombies.

One report commissioned by the private equity industry showed that about half the industry's profits came from loading companies with debt while simultaneously extracting massive dividends.[23] One of the possibly most egregious cases of taking out money while crushing a company with debt was probably the merger of the AA and Saga. Three private equity firms – Charterhouse, CVC and Permira – reportedly managed to pocket about £2 billion through doing a 'giant debt refinancing'.[24] As for AA's and Saga's customers, much of what they pay for these companies' services will disappear into the pockets of these companies' creditors or 'financialisers' leaving precious little for the employees or for future investments to build up the businesses.

Once private equity firms have feasted from their ownership of our companies, while landing them with almost unrepayable debts, this has attracted another type of financial predator – what are called 'distressed debt investors' also known as 'vulture funds'. With banks trying to improve their balance sheets by getting rid of doubtful or bad debts, they are often willing to sell their loans in zombie companies at huge discounts to these vulture funds who then turn them into controlling stakes in the zombie businesses. Freed from their crushing interest payments, some companies get a new lease of life, creating fortunes for the vultures. Others may be so far gone that they collapse and die, leaving the vultures to earn whatever they can from selling off bits of the companies' corpses. So many British companies have now been turned into zombies, that this has presented what one investor from a 'vulture fund' called 'a once-in-a-lifetime opportunity'.

Can the beast be tamed?

There have been various efforts over the years to improve what's called 'corporate governance' – the way our companies are run by their executives. Following several dramatic company failures, including the Bank of Credit and Commerce International and Polly Peck, governments started to get involved in making proposals about the role and rewards of company executives. In 1992, a report was published by Lord Cadbury detailing a Code of Best Practice including more oversight by shareholders and a greater role for non-executive directors. A few years later, after public anger over the massive salaries paid to the bosses of the newly privatised power and water companies, especially Cedric the Pig at British Gas, Sir Richard Greenbury from Marks & Spencer was asked to produce a series of proposals aimed at controlling executive pay. Two of his key recommendations were linking pay to performance and publishing details of bosses' pay deals. But, though adopted, none of these recommendations seems to have had much effect on limiting how much our top bosses were paid. In fact, the rise in executive pay has accelerated almost every year and seems to have largely ignored the 2007 financial collapse and ensuing economic recession.

Forever on the look-out for new ways to expand its powers, the EU is now considering making regulatory changes to control bankers' pay. One idea Brussels has come up with is a plan to limit the level of bankers' bonuses to a maximum of one hundred per cent of their salary. But, in anticipation of these kinds of rules, some banks quickly started giving their key employees large salary increases. Already in 2010 the *Wall Street Journal* announced:

HSBC is the latest bank to pump up base salaries in an

effort to keep employees happy amid a European-wide crackdown on bonuses, according to a person familiar with the matter. The bank will double the pay of 'several hundred' bankers.[25]

HSBC's move reportedly followed similar pay rises for investment bankers at Barclays and RBS 'to compensate for reduced bonuses'.

In 2012, we had what jubilant newspaper and TV reporters called the 'shareholder spring'. Votes by shareholders against what they saw as overly generous executive pay at several companies including Aviva, Trinity Mirror, Barclays and car retailer Pendragon even led to the departure of two chief executives and the head of one remuneration committee. But during the whole shareholder spring, only eight out of the top hundred FTSE companies were faced with these shareholder rebellions. The other ninety two per cent of companies saw their pay and bonus packages passed without significant opposition. Moreover, these votes are not legally binding - companies could just ignore them if they so wished. Thus, what the media heralded as a massive revolt against excessive executive pay needs to be put into context and our executives, both good and bad, both puritan and predatory, both wealth-creating and wealth-destroying can all sleep soundly in their plush, satin-sheeted beds, confident in the knowledge that the great unwashed are unlikely ever to rise up and deprive them of their many tens or hundreds of millions. Moreover, because of their huge lobbying power over our corrupt, expenses-fiddling politicians, our executhieves understand that, while our political elite will convincingly and enthusiastically play the part of being outraged at executhieves' greed, in fact real political action against executive excess is about as likely as a one-legged horse carrying an elephant on its back winning the Grand National. For those of you, who are unfamiliar with the ins and outs of horse racing, this is not very likely.

Chapter 4

Like candy from a baby

Ah viva Aviva!

In a book like *Greed Unlimited* there are many companies that deserve a chapter to themselves. Here I've chosen savings and insurance giant Aviva. This is partly because over nineteen million of us in the UK have savings, insurances and pensions with the company. And it's partly because of the almost miraculous way the chief executive managed to halve the share price after what could, to the untrained eye, look like a series of monumental blunders and mis-selling scandals, while increasing his own rewards and providing a certain amount of other forms of entertainment for incredulous Aviva-watchers such as myself.

The seemingly accident-prone Aviva appears to be a classic case of executives being generously gifted ever higher salaries, bonuses and perks at the same time as the company's shares headed steadily, relentlessly and worryingly in the wrong direction. At one point, towards the end of 2011, chief executive Andrew Moss admitted that 'short-term headwinds' had hit company profits. Yet according to Mr Moss, the executive team were soldiering on making the best of a tough situation, 'across the company we are right on target to meet all of our shorter-term financial targets. That is what we can control and what we

49

are focused on'.

This seems to imply that the company was at the mercy of forces outside the control of even the most talented of management teams. It can't be denied that, since the 2007 financial crash, life hasn't been easy, even for the best of companies. However, it's worth comparing the changes in Aviva's share price under the stewardship of chief executive Andrew Moss and his gang with what happened at two close competitors, in this case RSA (Royal Sun Alliance) and Prudential (see Figure 1).

Figure 1 – RSA and Prudential don't seem to have suffered as badly as Aviva from difficult business conditions

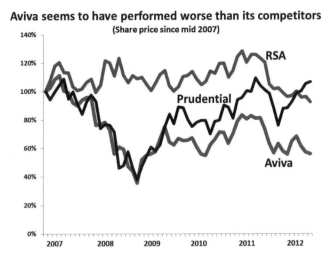

Here I've looked at the share prices of Aviva and competitors RSA and Prudential from the time that Andrew Moss took over as chief executive of Aviva in July 2007 till his slightly controversial departure in May 2012. The result suggests either

Like candy from a baby

that the headwinds encountered by Aviva were somewhat stronger than those which buffeted RSA and Prudential or else that the management teams at Aviva's main competitors were an awful lot better at dealing with the economic turmoil of the five years following 2007 than the possibly dubious bunch at Aviva.

Given Aviva's importance as a top FTSE100 share, it's likely that most of our UK unit trusts and pension funds hold considerable quantities of sad, declining Aviva's shares. So Aviva's apparent failure to perform might be slightly depressing for those of us whose unit trusts and pension funds have, as we can now see with hindsight, so foolishly put tons of our cash into the company. But it doesn't seem to have worried Aviva's remuneration committee as they considered how much of other people's money to give to the company's executives. At first sight, the remuneration committee look like they did a reasonable job - Mr Moss's salary went up quite slowly during his time as head honcho – from £913,750 in 2008 to £951,250 in 2011 – up just around a tiny one per cent a year. In fact, in one year, the annual report even proudly announced that the chief executive had declined to take a pay rise. So it seems that Mr Moss's pay was under some kind of control. But when you add in all the chief executive's bonuses and other perks, a quite different picture emerges. His whole remuneration in 2008 was a tidy £4.26 million. In 2009, this jumped 7% or £300,000 to a nice £4.56 million. In 2010, up again – from £4.56 million to £4.74 million – up another £180,000. Then in 2011, it leapt up by an impressive £410,000 to £5.15 million

So, all in all, while Aviva's share price plummeted by over forty per cent from £6 per share to just above £3 per share, reducing the company's total market value from around £20 billion to just above £10 billion, the chief executive's pay package, mainly made up of performance bonuses, went up by over twenty per cent or £890,000. To an outsider, it might seem more than incredible that someone can get bonuses for supposedly meeting their targets, pocketing over £18 million, while managing to lose almost half of the value of the company they are running. But that's the way things are in so many of our great companies in today's not so Great Britain.

Mr Moss wasn't the only person to benefit from the Aviva remuneration committee's admirable largesse when handing out shareholders' money. It was reported that another senior executive, Trevor Matthews, received a 'golden hello' of around £2.5 million when he joined Aviva from Friends Life. One commentator remarked, 'he got a £470,000 cash payment after a month at Aviva and was awarded shares worth £2.02 million, where the only performance condition was to remain with his new employer for three years'.[26] And, when he joined in January 2011, Canadian Igal Mayer, head of Aviva's continental European business, was given £449,471 to pay for such things as a £5,000-a-month London home and first-class flights between London and Toronto for him and his family in addition to the £2.8 million he was paid during his first (and last) year at Aviva. When questioned about the Aviva remuneration committee's generosity with other people's money, the committee issued the usual self-justifying statement claiming that it offered 'appropriate' compensation to Aviva executives. Perhaps, in their rush to hand Aviva bosses ever more of other people's money, the remuneration committee simply forgot to look at the plunging share price and collapse in the company's value?

The Vision thing

It's often extremely difficult to find out what is really happening inside large companies, even, or especially, if you work there. Nevertheless, there are some glimpses which suggest that Mr

Moss's time as chief executive of Aviva was not distinguished by stunning managerial genius. It has been reported that one of his first big moves on rising from financial director to CEO was to launch his 'One Aviva, Twice the Value' strategy. It seems that this was intended to build Aviva into one unified company across its many geographical locations, while doubling its market value. Mr Moss described his plan to City investors as 'accelerating transformational change to deliver a unified and more profitable company'. And Mr Igal explained, 'this is a transformation that will take place over the next two years and will provide all our employees with the products, processes and technology to give our customers and business partners excellent service, right first time, every time'.[27]

Company executives seem to have been quite pleased at the progress of their transformation programme. Mr Moss said, 'our progress in 2011 owes much to the actions we have taken over a number of years to transform Aviva'. Yet by the time Mr Moss had left, Aviva had split into two companies which together were worth just above half what Aviva had been worth when the chief executive took over in 2007. However, as usual, this remarkable apparent failure to successfully put the chosen strategy into action doesn't seem to have had any negative effect on the remuneration committee's admirable enthusiasm for giving Mr Moss and others substantial amounts of the company's money.

Taken in by the 'Transformation' trick?

I have a confession to make. In the 1990s, I worked at the management consultancy Gemini Consulting which was part of the Capgemini group – a major supplier of consultancy services and computer systems to companies and governments, especially the

British Government. A key Capgemini customer is the seemingly accident-prone HMRC, whose computer systems have become notoriously predictable for making a complete and expensive hash of millions of people's tax affairs year after depressing year.

At the time, as far as I understood the situation, Gemini Consulting was getting slaughtered in the marketplace by the big accountancies' growing consultancy businesses. The problem for us at Gemini Consulting was that the accountancies could deliver the trendy product of that time - BPR (Business Process Reengineering) - for often less than £5,000 per consultant per week. This was much cheaper than the £7,000 plus expenses per consultant per week that we at Gemini charged. The accountancies could undercut Gemini's prices because they used armies of 'billing fodder' (cheap, inexperienced consultants) while Gemini tended to have more experienced and thus more highly-paid staff.

In order to fight back against the lower-priced competition, Gemini Consulting tried to find a smart new way of dressing up its services to make them look different and more valuable than those of our competitors. After a few real turkeys, they came up with the idea of 'Business Transformation'. Gemini's big chiefs even wrote a book called *Transforming the Organization*[28] and, if I remember correctly, Gemini tried unsuccessfully to trade-mark the phrase 'Business Transformation' as a product only its consultants could deliver. Reviewing the book at the time, the respected magazine *The Economist* wrote with great prescience that a true transformation 'would employ an army of consultants for a century – and cause endless disruption'.[29]

Most organisations can be improved, but very few need to be 'transformed'. The great thing about 'transformation' was that it enabled us consultants to sell massive consulting contracts where we lucratively, and possibly sometimes unnecessarily, totally restructured our clients' organisations and also put in huge new computer systems, again lucratively but perhaps unnecessarily. So, 'transformation' could be seen by a cynic as just a consultants' trick to sell even larger projects than BPR. For a few years, transformation turned out to be a bit of a damp squib, as most commercial companies were possibly too worldly-wise to be taken in by our unlikely sales pitch and multi-million pound, euro and dollar big project prices. But luckily for us consultants, it gradually caught on till there was hardly a company that wasn't busy proudly launching its own 'transformation' programme.

Eventually, even governments caught the transformation bug. When he was PM, Tony Blair was forever using 'transform' and 'transformation'. He promised us a 'transformation' of the NHS, a 'transformation' of secondary education, 'transformations' of all our public services and even had a meeting with top civil servants where he explained the 'Seven Keys to Transformation' which would lead to a 'transformed civil service'.[30] Alistair Campbell said history would judge Blair as a 'great transforming Prime Minister'. Blair's government helpfully produced a chunky report called *The Transformational Government Annual Report* in which it detailed the many successes of its *Transformational Government* programme. The aim of the *Transformational Government* programme was: 'Delivering better, more efficient services for everyone'.[31] And the programme seemed to be central to the government's ambitions for improving public services as it explained in typical consultant gobbledegook: 'Government is committed to a range of citizen-focused activities designed to optimise service design and delivery, and is proud that the United Kingdom is held up as providing some world-class examples of Transformational Government'.[32]

So, when Aviva boss Andrew Moss and his executives

presented their 'One Aviva, Twice the Value' vision to 'accelerate transformational change' liberally using the word 'transform' plus other popular management buzzwords such as 'leverage', 'synergies', 'focus', 'hygiene factors', 'integrated' and 'agenda for change' (See Figure 2), the supposedly smart City investors in the audience should, in my humble opinion, have smelt an impending disaster and run screaming for the hills.

Figure 2 – Aviva's strategy – a sign of tough, focused management? Or an unintelligible chaotic nightmare dreamt up by expensive management consultants?[33]

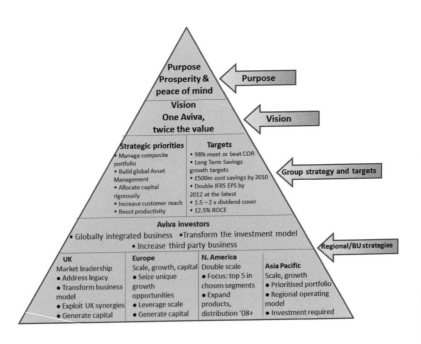

As the company's share price headed sickeningly ever downwards, a senior manager praised Aviva's consultants IBM for their assistance with the transformation, 'the work we've done in partnership with IBM has created a real win/win solution that benefits IT staff and the business. It fits very well with driving Aviva's overall transformation strategy'. Perhaps, like the apparently hopeless remuneration committee, this senior manager forgot to look at what was happening to Aviva's share price and value before opening their mouth. In fact, as far as I can see from their website, IBM even use their Aviva experience as a case study to help sell their services to other companies. Meanwhile, Aviva won three of *Communicate* magazine's Transform awards for the way they were transforming their brand and business. One might have thought that *Communicate* could also have spent a couple of minutes looking at Aviva's financial results before deciding that the company was a worthy recipient of their no doubt prestigious and but possibly not well-deserved awards.

Never a dull moment

Aviva's activities may not have been the source of much joy for the company's shareholders, but they did manage to provide some entertainment for both staff and outsiders. Here I'll just mention a few of the shenanigans going on at the company.

Perhaps most noteworthy was Andrew Moss's 2009 admission that he was having an affair with an employee. It's all a bit complicated as these things so often are, but I think the object of the chief executive's affections was the Head of HR for Aviva Investors, who also happened to be the wife of Aviva's Head of Human Resources for Europe, or something like that. Moss then left his wife of twenty five years to move in with the lady in question. Although Aviva has a policy banning long-term relationships between managers and people who work for them, the chairman announced, 'Andrew has been very open with me and I am clear that there has been no breach of company rules. I am totally satisfied that this has in no way impacted his role as chief executive and he retains my full confidence'.[34] However, even though no rules had apparently been broken, the lady in question left the company 'by mutual agreement and in order to avoid any apparent conflict'. It was reported that the lady received a pay-off with shareholders' money, agreed directly with the head of Aviva's notoriously kind-hearted and charitable remuneration committee.

In March 2010, Andrew Moss was interviewed about rival Prudential's plans to massively expand their Asian operations. But while Prudential saw south-east Asia as the 'sweet spot' for growth, Mr Moss apparently felt that Europe would deliver most of Aviva's future business success. Now, in 2012 with 20/20 hindsight, watching Europe implode while Asian economies grow exponentially, one might be forgiven for thinking that Prudential were somewhat smarter in their strategic planning than poor old declining Aviva.

In October 2011, staff at Aviva's Dublin HQ arrived at work to find large screens erected preventing waiting journalists from seeing into the company's glass-fronted offices. They then learnt that about 950 of them would be losing their jobs as Aviva relocated their work back to London. Presumably the screens were there so no photos could be taken of dumbstruck and weeping Aviva staff.

At the start of April 2012, Aviva had a bit of a problem with its computer systems and sent out hundreds of thousands of letters with customers' financial information to the wrong customers. A letter of apology followed signed by Aviva's fashionably-named 'Customer Experience Director' asking recipients to 'please confidentially destroy the previous statement we sent you, or return it unopened to the address on the back of the envelope'.[35]

On Friday 20 April 2012, more than 1,300 staff at Aviva Investors received an email informing them they had lost their jobs and should hand over company property and security passes on their way out of the building and submit any electronic passwords. Moreover, they were warned, 'I am required to remind you of your contractual obligations to the company you are leaving. You have an obligation to retain any confidential information pertaining to Aviva'. But the news was not all bad, the email ended with a cheerful, 'I would like to take this opportunity to thank you and wish you all the best for the future'.[36] A few minutes later, they all received a 'grovelling' follow-up email from HR explaining that the first email had only been intended for just one soon-to-be ex-employee and not the rest of them.

Selling to suckers

But perhaps the worst and most serious Aviva *faux pas* of the Andrew Moss years was the massive probable mis-selling of two Aviva investment funds – the Aviva Global Cautious Income fund and the Aviva Global Balanced Income fund. These two funds were launched in June 2006 by the then Norwich Union which later became Aviva. At the time, Andrew Moss was the company's finance director.

The funds seem to have been enthusiastically sold by Aviva's 'strategic partner' the highly-paid Bob Diamond's rate-fixing and recidivist mis-selling Barclays. By the end of 2008, over 12,300 Barclays customers had put around £692 million into the two Aviva funds – over £50,000 per customer on average, though many customers put several hundred thousand pounds into these two funds. This earned Barclays somewhere in the region of £30 million in upfront commission and possibly around £6.9 million a year in what's called 'trailing commission' – commission that is paid every year an investment is held.

Unfortunately, the cautious fund doesn't seem to have been sufficiently cautious and the balanced fund possibly wasn't terribly balanced as the funds' performance was less than wonderful. In the 2007-2009 financial crash, the Aviva Global Cautious Income fund lost about a third of investors' money, while the Aviva Global Balanced Income fund made around half of investors' money magically disappear. I remember being in a Barclays branch in Bournemouth at the time. I was due to meet the manager to discuss putting some of my savings into a fixed-interest deposit account, having fortunately had the good sense to reject an earlier Barclays proposal to put my money into one of the investment funds the bank was promoting. While waiting upstairs for my meeting, I heard two of Barclays' supposed financial advisers (actually just salespeople) laughing and joking about what they were going to tell a customer, a pensioner, who had just lost around half his life savings in some investment sold to him by Barclays. I imagine the poor sod had been persuaded to put his hard-earned cash into the dreadful Aviva Global Balanced Income fund. In fact, it was this experience of Barclays' apparent arrogant disregard for their customers' financial health which prompted me to investigate the financial services industry and write *Pillaged! How they are looting £413 million a day from your savings and pensions.*

But it wasn't the horrific performance of the two Aviva funds that was the main problem for Aviva and our much-loved Barclays. After all, as we are constantly warned in investment articles and adverts, the value of any investment can go up or down. Here the issue was the way these two Aviva funds were sold or, more accurately, mis-sold. It's not clear who was most to blame – Aviva who produced and managed the funds or Barclays who flogged them. In Aviva's defence, the company did classify these two funds as 'high risk' in their sales bumf. But, if Aviva knew the funds were 'high risk', one might be tempted to wonder whether it was totally honest to label one as 'cautious income' and the other as 'balanced income'. According to my dictionary, the words 'cautious' and 'balanced' suggest that the funds were far from being 'high risk'. And the word 'income' conjures up a pleasing image of a little bit of money coming in on a regular basis, rather than the horror of huge amounts of money suddenly and dramatically evaporating into thin air. Anyway, although these two funds were classed as 'high risk' by Aviva and 'adventurous' by an industry body, Barclays apparently sold them as being 'low risk' to savers who were rated by Barclays own rating system as 'cautious'. It is even possible that, given the way Aviva named the two funds, some of Barclays sales staff actually did believe they were fairly low risk in spite of Aviva's 'high risk' classification.

Many of the people advised by Barclays to put their savings into these two strangely-named funds were either approaching retirement or already retired and, with little or no income coming in, could not afford to lose their capital in what were 'high risk' long-term investment products. Some of the stories were tragic. One couple put £225,000 from the sale of their house and business into the Aviva Global Balanced Income fund and eighteen months later had lost about £120,000. A ninety-year-old couple lost somewhere in the region of £300,000 of their life savings and a ninety-one-year-old pensioner watched £200,000 of his money go up in smoke. Why, when average life expectancy is about eighty seven, people over ninety should have been persuaded to put everything they had into high-risk, longer-term stock-market investments is one question Barclays sales staff apparently failed to consider. Even when Barclays were finding instances of inappropriate selling of the two Aviva products, they reportedly did nothing.

After numerous complaints and a campaign by a national newspaper, the pusillanimous Financial Services Authority (FSA) seemed to awake from its normal well-paid slumber and take action. After an investigation, Barclays was given a record fine of £7.7 million and ordered to pay compensation of over £60 million. A FSA spokesperson explained, 'thousands of investors, many of whom were looking to invest their life savings, have suffered. To compound matters, Barclays failed to take effective action when it detected the failings at an early stage'.[37] Though, as so often happens once the dust and smoke has died down, following some wriggling by Barclays (and possibly Aviva) it's not clear how much of the lost money will actually be repaid nor how rapidly any payments will be made.

After this debacle, Barclays appears to have removed almost a thousand 'financial advisers' (actually salespeople) from its branches and decided to only offer 'financial advice' to people with several hundred thousand pounds to invest. The reason for this several hundred thousand pounds (I think it might be £500,000) minimum level is that anyone with this amount of money is considered by the financial services industry to be what they call a 'sophisticated investor'. This makes them fair game for all kinds of dodgy investment schemes as it is assumed they know enough to take full responsibility for their own investment decisions and thus cannot complain to a regulator if they get fleeced by a predatory bank or other hungry financial institution. Although Barclays bore the brunt of regulatory and media attention for this disaster, with its dreadful management of the two funds and the way it named two high-risk funds as being either 'balanced income' or 'cautious income', Aviva should perhaps also have been pilloried for its behaviour.

Anyway, there may be a new scandal about to break over the way Aviva products have been sold. Only one case has surfaced so far, but it's pretty gruesome and may just be the tip of a very nasty iceberg. A salesperson from Fred Goodwin's RBS (Royal Bank of Scotland) managed to convince a customer with terminal throat cancer to put his life savings of £500,000 into an Aviva annuity which would then pay the man an income every year for life. Given that he was seriously ill at the time of the sale, Aviva would actually only have to pay him a few thousand pounds while he was alive and then after his death could hang on to his £500,000. In fact, the man died a day before his first pension payment was due to be paid by Aviva. So the company did pretty well out of the deal – it got £500,000 and paid out £0. Not bad for a few hours' work. When the man's family complained, RBS and Aviva of course both denied any wrongdoing. Unsurprisingly, their innocence seems to have been supported by the poor excuse of a regulator responsible – the Isle of Man Financial Supervision Commission. But following a campaign by a national newspaper, the Commission reopened the case and eventually ordered RBS and Aviva to return the £500,000 to the man's family.

Goodbye, and here's lots more money

All good things must eventually come to an end, even for Aviva's possibly over-paid and underperforming bosses. At the beginning of 2012, as the share price reached a new low, chief executive Andrew Moss was reported as having 'demanded a 9.5 per cent pay rise'.[38] It was explained that the basis for his demand was that this would bring his pay into line with that of bosses at rival firms. Perhaps Mr Moss hadn't noticed that the shares of rival firms were mostly performing somewhat better than Aviva's under his possibly questionable management. This 9.5 per cent requested increase would have taken his basic pay from £960,000 to about £1,050,000. Although this may not seem excessive, you have to remember the further millions he would receive in bonuses and other perks. Surprisingly, Aviva's remuneration committee seemed to have found a little bit of backbone somewhere and the chief executive's request was rejected. Instead he was awarded a more modest 4.8 per cent salary increase.

But by this time, Aviva's shareholders were becoming a bit grumpy at the company's antics and poor results. In April 2012, the Association of British Insurers, an industry lobby group which even had Andrew Moss on its board, issued what it called an 'amber top' warning about the company's high pay levels for its executives and poor performance for its shareholders. A few days later, Pensions and Investment Research Consultants (more commonly known as Pirc) recommended that investors should reject Aviva's remuneration report at its May 3rd annual meeting. Then, at the May 3rd meeting, fifty nine per cent of shareholders voted against the company's pay report. On the day after the shareholder vote, Andrew Moss took the day off to get married in a civil ceremony to his new partner and former employee.

A few days later, the Aviva chairman announced that Mr Moss had informed him of his decision to step aside to make way for new leadership as 'he felt it was in the best interests of the company'. One journalist wrote, 'the news of his departure was greeted with joy by unions and the City'.[39]

Given that Andrew Moss appeared to be willingly walking away from his job in response to poor company performance and shareholder dissatisfaction, you might have thought that he would no longer be given any more of Aviva shareholders' cash. But you'd be quite wrong. Somehow, the remuneration committee and other Aviva bosses saw fit to hand Mr Moss a pay-off of around £1.75 million of other people's money on his way out the door. So, in defiance of all business logic, during his five years managing Aviva's decline, Mr Moss had pocketed over £20 million – nice work if you can get it.

While highly amusing, Aviva's meltdown at the same time as it so handsomely rewarded its top bosses, may be the rule, rather than the exception, for British businesses today.

Part 3

Public-sector feeding frenzy

Chapter 5

Politicians strike gold

Lots more money for us...ha, ha, ha

After the scandal over MPs' expenses, we might have expected our politicians to try to regain public trust by moderating how much money they took from us. But we would have been wrong, very wrong. Our MPs don't seem to care what the public thinks and see themselves as being 'untouchable'. In fact, our MPs have played a very clever game. On the one hand, they've accepted a pay freeze holding their salary at a quite comfortable £65,738 until at least 2013. This allows MPs to pretend that they too are making some degree of sacrifice in these tough economic times. But our MPs had a few tricks up their sleeves – if they couldn't get regular salary rises, they would just increase the amount of our money they took from us in other ways.

In the eleven months following the 2010 General Election, the amount our MPs claimed in expenses rocketed to almost £165 million from £118 million the year before – a £47 million increase, equivalent to them getting almost forty per cent more. Part of this increase would have been due to the 'golden goodbyes' that we taxpayers so generously give our politicians when they retire, resign in disgrace or are voted out of office.

These 'golden goodbyes' can be worth anywhere from £70,000 to over £100,000 per MP, depending on how long they have been in Parliament and the amount of their 'office winding up costs'. Assuming that the 220 MPs, who left Parliament following the 2010 election, pocketed somewhere between £70,000 and £100,000, say £85,000 each, then the total cost of our MPs' 'golden goodbyes' would have been around £19 million. Subtracting this £19 million from the £47 million we paid in increased expenses, that left about £28 million more in general expenses. There are 650 MPs, so on average each claimed somewhere in the region of £43,000 more in expenses than MPs did the year before. Of course, some would have claimed much more than this and some less. But given their salaries of £65,738, these extra expenses would be the equivalent of a sixty six per cent pay rise per MP. This was pretty profitable for our MPs at a time when they were preaching the need for austerity for the rest of us and pretending that they too were wearing the hair-shirts they were forcing on us, while in fact they were enthusiastically pocketing ever larger amounts of our money.

Pretty low standards

The story of how MPs managed to make such a lucrative grab for our cash while feigning restraint is probably worth telling as it shows the cynicism and chicanery the ruling elites have repeatedly used to enrich themselves at our expense, while at the same time lecturing the rest of us on how we should be tightening our belts for the good of the country.

Following the scandal of almost all MPs, not just a few rotten apples, fiddling their expenses, Sir Christopher Kelly, Chairman of the Committee on Standards in Public Life, was asked to propose reforms to the MPs' expenses system. One of the more important recommendations reportedly made by Sir Christopher Kelly to the Committee on Standards in Public Life was that scandal-hit MPs should be stripped of their resettlement grants. When leaving Parliament, MPs have been entitled to two payments. There's a resettlement grant of between six months' salary and a year's salary to help them adjust back to life outside politics. The size of the grant depends on how long an MP has served. There's also just over £40,000 each in 'office winding up costs' for closing down their offices and paying off staff. Of the many MPs caught up in the expenses scandal, only one immediately resigned thus forfeiting his right to these grants. All the others, even when some had been expelled by their parties, stayed on in Parliament right up to the election, continuing to receive salaries and expenses and presumably intending to get their hands on the resettlement grants and office winding up costs before leaving the lucrative world of what they laughingly call 'public service'.

At the time of the original recommendation, one newspaper announced to its readers the cheering news, 'Disgraced politicians to be stripped of "golden goodbyes"'.[40] However, it seems as if the Committee for Standards in Public Life, which is made up of MPs, was not too impressed by this recommendation that would deprive some of their chums, and possibly some of them, of considerable quantities of tax-free taxpayers' cash. About eighteen months later, the same newspaper informed us that, after a year long Freedom of Information battle with the House of Commons authorities, it had managed to obtain details of the 'golden goodbyes' which were paid to departing MPs. This time the headline was rather more predictably depressing for us taxpayers, 'Every single ex-MP claimed a "golden goodbye" – at a cost of millions to taxpayer'.[41] Not exactly a shining example of sharing the austerity foisted by our MPs on the rest of us.

Our honourable MPs probably hoped we'd moved on from the days of the expenses scandals and they could continue undisturbed their avid feasting in the trough of taxpayers' money. Moreover, for some MPs losing their parliamentary seat didn't even result in cutting them off from the life-enhancing flow of taxpayers' money. When she was a Liberal Democrat MP, Julia Goldsworthy was involved in a little controversy over some furniture she had bought just days before the deadline for using up that year's parliamentary expenses. When she lost her seat after only five years in Westminster, she was reported to have swiftly found another well-paid, taxpayer-funded job – as a £74,000-a-year adviser to Danny Alexander, the Chief Secretary to the Treasury.[42]

Castrating the watchdog

Perhaps the most important change made after the MPs' expenses scandals was the then Labour Government's decision to move the setting and control of MPs' expenses from MPs and the Fees Office to a new body - the Independent Parliamentary Standards Authority (IPSA). Harriet Harman, then Leader of the House, summed up the public mood, 'we recognise that it is not appropriate for this House to set our own allowances, we recognise that the public don't want us to set or administer our allowance system'.[43] IPSA was given the power to set and enforce rules on MPs' expenses and allowances. We have to be careful when judging any government body by its name. British governments tend to use and abuse the word 'independent', when they name their latest expensive and compliant quango, a bit like brutal totalitarian regimes invariably call their downtrodden, miserable countries the 'Democratic Republic' of wherever.

IPSA may well have foolishly believed its own name

and may have genuinely thought that it really would be an independent watchdog with sufficient teeth and testicles to do its job. But our MPs were having none of it. They wanted a toothless canine that was both neutered and extremely obedient to its masters' and mistresses' wishes.

It wasn't long before IPSA clashed swords with MPs. MPs had three main complaints about IPSA – that with its first-year budget of £6 million, IPSA was excessively expensive; that it was slow and bureaucratic when processing MPs' expenses claims; and that its rules were restrictive, causing MPs financial difficulties and preventing MPs having a proper family life. Possibly forgetting the public outrage against MPs' thieving of our money, MP Tom Harris said, 'IPSA was an expensive and unnecessary mistake'. Perhaps not really understanding how attractive our MPs' annual salary and expenses package of over £250,000 a year each, much of it tax-free, would look to most ordinary people, some MPs disingenuously claimed that IPSA would discourage people from becoming MPs. Adam Afriyie, MP for wealthy Windsor, asked, 'where will we be in thirty years' time if we continue down this route where only the wealthy can serve?' This worry was backed up by Speaker Bercow who expressed 'real concern' that IPSA's approach to controlling MPs' expenses would put people off standing for Parliament.[44] Having tried to become an MP myself, I can assure Mr Afriyie and Speaker Bercow (salary over £145,000 a year) that there is a long line of people, both honest and crooked, who would love to become MPs, but are prevented from pursuing their ambitions because our political parties are closed shops where only those with the right connections can hope to 'serve' as Mr Afriyie puts it. Mr Afriyie also used the austerity argument against IPSA, 'in times of austerity IPSA is burning taxpayers' money hand over fist'.[45] Some people might find this comment a bit rich considering how MPs were trying every trick in the book to avoid austerity for themselves.

Even Mr Austerity himself, PM David Cameron, weighed into the apparently well-coordinated attack on IPSA, 'it is anti-family and it is not acceptable'. In January 2011, Cameron gave IPSA an ultimatum to either improve the way it worked or else face abolition. And that's pretty much when the removal of IPSA's teeth and testicles began. Firstly, IPSA caved in on so-called 'family friendliness' and allowed MPs to claim for second homes that were large enough to accommodate themselves and their children. Previously IPSA had quite understandably assumed that MPs' children would stay in their main homes and so only allowed MPs to claim for one-bedroom second homes. Then IPSA agreed that it would pay MPs' biggest bills upfront to avoid 'financial hardship' for MPs, many of who were multimillionaires. MPs were also allowed by IPSA to use dedicated credit cards to pay for more of their expenses – credit cards that we taxpayers would, of course, be paying for. Ever generous with our money, the now obedient IPSA liberally handed MPs about a twenty per cent increase in the amount of money they could take to supposedly pay their staff. This rose from £115,000 a year to £137,200 for non-London MPs and £144,000 for those with constituencies inside the capital. This was at a time when the country was mired in recession and when those taxpayers fortunate enough to keep their jobs had to put up with their incomes rising by less than the level of inflation. IPSA Chairman Sir Ian Kennedy explained the necessity of this impressively larger wad of our money going to our MPs, 'following the review we have made a significant move to help MPs to staff their offices more effectively. This will help them in the service they provide to their constituents'.[46] Perhaps the best way MPs could serve their constituents would be to stop taking and stealing ever larger amounts of our money.

MPs seem to have been pleased by this magnanimity

with taxpayers' money as the number of MPs employing direct relatives increased from 106 to 124. In what could look like a rerun of the Tory Derek Conway scandal, Tory MP Nadine Dorries, was reported by several newspapers (in what could be either true or else be an attempt to smear her after her criticism of Tory Party leaders) to be paying her daughter over £35,000 to work as her office manager at the same time as the daughter was studying for a degree at London's BPP Law School.[47] Moreover, we don't know how many MPs are also passing on our cash to friends, live-in partners, lovers, soon-to-be lovers, ex-lovers, children of friends, friends of friends and all kinds of others who may or may not have actually been doing the jobs we taxpayers were paying them to do.

But perhaps most worryingly for us taxpayers, IPSA decided that MPs' receipts should not be made public any more. When one newspaper used the Freedom of Information Act to try to obtain three receipts, IPSA took eleven months to reply and blamed 'clerical error' for the delay. But although IPSA provided a bit more information on the three items of expenditure, it refused to release copies of the receipts even though Sir Christopher Kelly had recommended that IPSA 'should continue to publish, at least quarterly, each individual claim for reimbursement made by MPs with accompanying receipt'.[48] The newspaper warned, 'the decision means that the kind of documents which triggered the 2009 expenses scandal will in future be kept secret'.[49] A former independent MP and outspoken critic of the MPs' expenses fun and games summed up what appeared to be IPSA's grovelling obedience to protecting the interests of MPs rather than the interests of us taxpayers, 'MPs should not make expenses claims that they cannot justify in public. IPSA are in danger of becoming as much a creature of the House of Commons as the old Fees Office was'.[50] But it was too late for such warnings. By then, IPSA was completely toothless, well and truly neutered and utterly obedient to the wishes of its amoral, grasping, greedy, hypocritical masters and mistresses.

Who do our MPs work for?

There's an excellent website www.theyworkforyou.com which gives loads of details about each MP including how they vote, how much or little they actually do in terms of contributing to parliamentary debates and also all their money-making interests that so many have time for in addition to their jobs representing their constituents and making our laws. The problem is that, when you look at how much work many MPs do in addition to being an MP, you could get the impression that, though many MPs are generously paid by us, they actually spend little of their time working for us. When IPSA granted MPs a twenty per cent or so increase in the amounts they could claim for paying staff, the Unite union spokesman for parliamentary staff claimed that 'workloads have increased' and that many staff did hours of unpaid overtime. And when justifying the rise, Sir Ian Kennedy talked of helping MPs in 'the service they provide to their constituents'. But do our MPs actually have much time to work for their constituents? Here, I'll just look at the activities of three MPs, one very well known and two possibly less instantly recognisable public figures, to illustrate how busy some MPs are sometimes very lucratively doing lots of things that could seem to have little connection with the jobs for which we pay them. Though, in their defence, MPs would probably claim that having outside interests gives them a broader understanding of British life and helps them become better MPs. But if they've got so much time for second, third, fourth and even fifth jobs, why do so many of them claim that being an MP is such hard work? And if they have so much time for extra-curricular, money-making activities, why do they claim they need more of our cash for their staff due to the supposedly increasing workload of 'the service they provide to their constituents'?

The David Miliband 'money machine'

As one of Britain's leading politicians, David Miliband appears to have been able to make an impressive amount of money while also serving his constituents as an MP. He was reported as having managed to pocket over £500,000 including his MP's salary in the eighteen months after losing the battle for the leadership of the Labour Party to his brother. His financial affairs look quite complex, but as far as I can make out he has five or six jobs which earn him around £383,000 a year. He also gives speeches at anywhere from around £10,000 to £20,000 a shot and does a little teaching. The speeches and teaching appear to have earned him another £178,000 or so (see Figure 1).

Figure 1 – David Miliband seems to earn quite a lot of money

The David Miliband 'Money Machine' in action			
Sunderland AFC	Vice-Chairman	£75,000/year	12-15 days
VantagePoint Clean Tech	Senior advisor	£90,000+/year	~ 5 days
Oxford Analytica	Senior global advisor	£39,000/year	7 days
MIT	Teaching	£24,000	1 week
Stanford University	Teaching	£25,000	1 week
UAE Ministry of Foreign Affairs		£64,000+/year	~ 3 days
Indus Basin Holdings	Senior advisor	£50,000/year	
Various speeches and conferences		£129,000	
MP for South Shields		£65,000+/year	???days

Public-sector feeding frenzy

We can never know whether Mr Miliband would have got all these extra, extremely well-rewarded jobs if he had not been an MP and a former minister in Gordon Brown's catastrophically incompetent and spendthrift 'government of all the talents'. But one would at least hope that, having dedicated his life to public service, Mr Miliband would be paying a goodly amount of tax on his massive earnings to do his bit to solve the country's economic problems - problems that were mostly caused by the eye-watering financial profligacy of the government of which he was part. Unfortunately, here the Miliband 'Money Machine' has come in for a bit of criticism. If newspaper reports are to be believed, it seems that Mr Miliband has, jointly with his wife, set up a company *The Office of David Miliband Limited* into which he channels a healthy portion of his non-parliamentary earnings. The advantage of this for Mr Miliband, and disadvantage for the rest of us, is that money pushed through this company is only subject to corporation tax at between 20 per cent and 27.5 per cent. This allows Mr Miliband to avoid the top income tax rate of 50 per cent (later reduced by the Tories to 45 per cent) that was introduced by the government of which Mr Miliband was part.

Others have criticised Mr Miliband for spending too much time raking in the cash and not enough time representing the interests of his constituents. One opponent said that 'enough is enough' and called on David Miliband to resign as MP for South Shields. However, Mr Miliband defended his work for his constituents, 'my commitment to South Shields is real, proven and lasting. South Shields comes first'.[51] While it would be inappropriate to doubt anything said by a politician, it is noticeable that in terms of the number of debates in which he has spoken, the number of answers to written questions he has received and the number of times he has voted in Parliament, Mr Miliband's performance appears to be well below the average for all MPs.[52]

Politicians strike gold

Of course, this is just based on the numbers – the quantity of his actions as an MP - and does not measure the quality of Mr Miliband's parliamentary work. Given Mr Miliband's many talents, one could imagine that the quality of the limited parliamentary work he did may have been well above the average for all MPs, so his constituents would have got good value from what they pay him after all.

What busy boys you are

Another MP who seems to have an impressive amount of work in addition to being an MP is barrister and MP for Dewsbury, Simon Reevell. From what I understand from the *Register of Members' Interests,* as a barrister Mr Reevell has several major clients who appear to keep him quite busy with producing written advice, appearing in court and teaching. His clients seem to include the Royal Mail Group, the Probation Service, the Crown Prosecution Service and Northern Rail. Although, Mr Reevell doesn't appear to be earning the mouthwatering sums political superstar David Miliband can cream in for each hour of his time, Mr Reevell certainly seems to be putting in an awful lot of hours in addition to his doubtless heavy workload as an MP (see Figure 2)*

Figure 2 – Just a small extract from Simon Reevell's entries in the *Register of Members' Interests* of his work apparently for just one client[53]

Simon Reevell MP seems to be a very busy man

12 January 2012, £303.89 plus VAT in respect of one hours work and one appearance
Also £420.18 plus VAT in respect of three hours work and one court appearance
13 February 2012, £264.66 plus VAT in respect of two appearances
13 February 2012, £1,748.19 plus VAT in respect of 6 hours work and one appearance
1 March 2012, £436.85 plus VAT in respect of 3 hours work and one court appearance
1 March 2012, received £338.76 plus VAT in respect of 3 hours work and one appearance
24 February 2012, £55.80 plus VAT in respect of one appearance
7 March 2012, £198.22 plus VAT in respect of 1 hours work and one appearance
7 March 2012, £574.52 plus VAT in respect of 4 hours work and one appearance
13 March 2012, £441.79 plus VAT in respect of 3 hours work and one appearance
22 March 2012, £511.83 plus VAT in respect of two appearances and three hours work
2 April 2012, £249.96 plus VAT in respect of 3 hours work and one court appearance
5 April 2012, £46.50 plus VAT in respect of one court appearance
10 April 2012, £797.94 plus VAT in respect of 3 hours work and one court appearance
16 April 2012, £66.50 plus VAT in respect of one court appearance
23 April 2012, £1598.02 plus VAT in respect of 6 hours work and one court appearance
23 April 2012, £1193.27 plus VAT in respect of 4 hours work and one court appearance

*The entries from Simon Reevell's *Register of Members' Interests* have been slightly annotated to fit them into the diagram as the original versions are longer. I am unclear as to whether the dates are when the work was done, when payments were received or when they were entered into the *Register*.

Just to show that Messrs Miliband and Reevell are not exceptions, here (according to what I understand from the *Register of Members' Interests*) is a selection of the paid activities of Tim Yeo, Conservative MP for South Suffolk (see Figure 3).

Politicians strike gold

Figure 3 – Tory MP Tim Yeo also crams a lot into his busy schedule

1. Remunerated directorships - Tim Yeo	
ITI Energy Limited	**Eco City Vehicles plc**
- £3,750, 9 May 2011. Hours: 11	- £3,333.33, 23 May 2011. Hours: 9
- £3,750, 13 June 2011. Hours: 12	- £3,333.33, 22 June 2011. Hours: 9
- £3,750, 11 July 2011. Hours: 11	- £3,333.33, 22 July 2011. Hours: 8
- £3,750, 22 August 2011. Hours: 11	- £3,333.33, 22 August 2011. Hours: 8
- £3,750, 12 September 2011. Hours: 10	- £3,333.33, 22 September 2011. Hours: 8
- £3,750, 7 October 2011. Hours: 8	- £3,333.33, 24 October 2011. Hours: 6
- £5,000, 14 November 2011. Hours: 10	
- £5,000, 13 December 2011. Hours: 12	**Chairman of TMO Renewables Limited**
- £5,000, 10 January 2012. Hours: 9	- £1,666.73, 25 May 2011. Hours: 4
- £3,350, 8 February 2012. Hours: 8	- £4,166.66, 27 May 2011. Hours: 11
	- £1,666.73, 24 June 2011. Hours: 4
Groupe Eurotunnel SA (non-executive)	- £4,166.66, 27 June 2011. Hours: 14
- £3,622.57, 9 May 2011. Hours: 6	- £4,166.66, 22 July 2011. Hours: 13
- £3,569.33, 31 May 2011. Hours: 5	- £1,666.53, 25 July 2011. Hours: 5
- £7,238.97, 28 July 2011. Hours: 11	- £4,166.66, 22 August 2011. Hours: 14
- £6,440.62, 12 September 2011. Hours: 16	- £1,666.73, 25 August 2011. Hours: 5
- £4,245.20, 14 October 2011. Hours: 4	- £4,166.66, 22 September 2011. Hours: 14
- £3,526.97, 21 November 2011. Hours: 4	- £1,666.73, 23 September 2011. Hours: 5
- £6,885.38, 31 January 2012. Hours: 8	- £4,166, 23 October 2011. Hours: 13
- £4,649.09, 9 February 2012. Hours: 4	- £1,666.73, 25 October 2011. Hours: 5
	- £4,166, 24 November 2011. Hours: 13
	- £1,666.73, 25 November 2011. Hours: 5

It probably hasn't anything to do with his considerable range of additional responsibilities, but it is noticeable that, according to the 'theyworkforyou' website, in terms of participation in debates, written questions and votes, Tim Yeo's activity is, like David Miliband's, below the average for all MPs.

In 2009, it was reported that following the scandals about MPs' expenses, David Cameron was worried at public reaction to the huge sums earned by his shadow cabinet and the effect this would have on his party's chances in the 2010 Election. So he instructed all his shadow cabinet to give up their many well-paid outside interests by the time of the 2010 election. As his colleagues regretfully kissed goodbye to sometimes hundreds of thousands of pounds a year in extra earnings, Cameron explained, 'it does become necessary to demonstrate 100 per cent focus on Parliament, politics and setting out our credentials as an alternative government'.[54]

Are some MPs getting taxpayers to support their money-making?

Most MPs, who are doing work in addition to their parliamentary and constituency duties, employ staff paid for by the taxpayer. It is my understanding that payments of taxpayers' money made to these staff should be purely for parliamentary and constituency work. MPs can claim between £137,200 (outside London) and £144,000 (inside London) a year to pay their staff. A question that might be of interest to taxpayers is whether MPs' staff purely do work on parliamentary and constituency duties or whether they are, in fact, also getting involved in supporting MPs by helping to organise their other, often lucrative, business and professional interests. And, if some MPs are using taxpayer-funded staff for activities not directly connected with parliamentary or constituency work, are these MPs guilty of misusing taxpayer's money? Perhaps this could be something that IPSA and the Committee for Standards in Public Life should be either looking into or, more likely, covering up?

The financial joys of being a minister

MPs have often complained about their 'low' salaries of just over £65,000 a year and have enviously compared themselves to top civil servants, council bosses and hospital executives who can easily get £150,000 a year or more thanks to the Brown and Balls pay boom for bureaucrats. But, when moaning that they are hard done by, MPs possibly forget a few things - they only work for about seven months a year, if that; they can hugely increase their wealth from their expenses; they can shove £30,000 a year or more of our money into the pockets of family members, partners or friends; and, by dint of being an MP they can easily earn £50,000, £100,000 or even more from all sorts of extra jobs that so many have the time to do while also 'serving' as MPs.

Also, MPs have the most generous pension scheme in the public sector. While most public-sector employees get $1/60^{th}$ or $1/80^{th}$ of their salary as pension for every year they work, MPs can get $1/40^{th}$. So, with a salary of over £65,000 a year, an MP will receive a pension of $1/40^{th}$ - £1,625 – for every year in the Commons. With annuity rates for joint inflation-protected pensions at under 3.5 per cent, anyone in the private sector would have to save around £46,000 per year into their pension fund to get a similar pension to their MP. To get a pension at this $1/40^{th}$ level, MPs have to pay 11.9 per cent of their salary into their pension fund – about £8,000 a year. So, given that each year the equivalent of £46,000 is paid into each MP's pension fund – the MP is putting in about £8,000 and we taxpayers around £38,000. That's very generous of us, especially as many of us don't even earn £38,000 a year. Furthermore, when pleading poverty, MPs omit to mention just one other small detail – at least 150 of them actually receive considerably more from us taxpayers than the basic £65,000 or so MP salary.

Perhaps the most lucrative way for an MP to increase his or her remuneration is by becoming a minister. In the Westminster Parliament we have no fewer than 109 paid ministers, of which about ninety are from the Commons and around nineteen are from the Lords. This is extraordinary. At the time of writing, there were 362 MPs in the Coalition – 305 Conservatives and 57 Liberal Democrats. With about ninety of them being ministers of some sort, this meant that around one in four members of the Coalition was receiving considerably more than the basic MP's salary. The amounts these many ministers are paid are quite generous (see Figure 4).

Figure 4 – Britain's huge number of ministers could look like an expensive luxury in a time of austerity

Our many ministers cost us a lot of money

Position	Number	Salary	Annual Cost*
Prime Minister	1	£142,500	£142,500
Cabinet Ministers	21	£134,565	£2,825,865
Ministers of State	29	£98,740	£2,863,460
Parliamentary Secs.	33	£89,435	£2,951,355
Chief Whip	1	£145,000	£145,000**
Deputy Chief Whip	1	£107,000	£107,000**
Whips	20	£92,000	£1,840,000**
Total			**£10,875,180**

*including MPs' salary   ** full salary entitlement

There are also three MPs who are 'law officers' taking over £100,000 a year each. In the Opposition, the Leader receives £139,000, the Opposition Chief Whip £107,000, the Deputy Chief Opposition Whip £92,000 and the Assistant Opposition Whip £92,000. In the Lords there are another thirteen dignitaries all getting paid between £60,000 and £108,000 a year. And these are just the ministers in Westminster. There are loads more ministers in Scotland, Wales and Northern Ireland, all eagerly pocketing similarly enviable piles of our money.

Too much of a good thing?

Some readers might wonder why on earth we need 109 ministers in Westminster all getting paid so much of our money. Especially when, following devolution, many of the jobs Westminster ministers used to do are now done by ministers in the devolved assemblies. Moreover, as the EU now makes most of our laws in areas such as agriculture, fishing, immigration, social policy and business and as Brussels is also moving into legislating in education, financial services, transport and sport, there isn't much left for our ministers to do. The EU Commission, which runs the lives of five hundred million Europeans, only has twenty seven commissioners. There are so many because by treaty each country has to have its own commissioner. Even there, EU officials complain that it's quite difficult for them to find something for all these commissioners to do.

So how on earth can anyone explain why tiny little Britain should need 109 paid ministers at Westminster plus many more in the devolved assemblies? Part of the reason is probably to give as many members of the political elite as possible the chance to gorge themselves just a bit more generously in the trough of taxpayers' money. And partly it's due to the Prime Minister's desire to ensure support for his policies. As one former political adviser explained to the Commons Public Administration Committee, 'if the Prime Minister has his way, he would appoint every single backbencher in his party to a ministerial job to ensure their vote'.[55] So perhaps we're very lucky that the Ministerial and Other Salaries Act (1975) limits the number of paid ministers to 109, though governments often exceed this number by appointing unpaid ministers in addition to the lucky 109 who are fully paid. At the time of writing, there were ten unpaid ministers bringing the total number to 119, making about a third of Coalition MPs into ministers.

As for David Cameron's Cabinet – with twenty nine people entitled to attend Cabinet meetings, it looks a bit more like a rabble than the kind of lean, mean, low-cost governing machine we would have expected from the likes of Mr 'Cut the Cost of Politics' Cameron and Mr 'Better Politics for Less' Clegg. Even some of the world's largest companies only have an executive board of ten or so worthies. That would make Cameron's and Clegg's crowd of cabinet ministers seem quite unwieldy and excessively expensive.

Perhaps surprisingly for our money-grabbing politicians, the large number of ministers is something a committee of MPs were wondering about too. In 2011, the House of Commons Public Administration Select Committee wrote a report entitled *Smaller Government: What Do Ministers Do?* In this report, the Committee noted that Britain had many more paid ministers than most other European countries. With about one minister for every seven MPs, we taxpayers seemed to be much more generous towards our politicians than countries like Germany, Spain, Italy and France where they had less than half the number of ministers per MP than we did (see Figure 5)

Politicians strike gold

Figure 5 – Why do other countries need comparatively less ministers than we do?

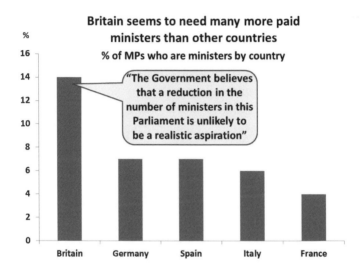

Britain seems to need many more paid ministers than other countries

% of MPs who are ministers by country

"The Government believes that a reduction in the number of ministers in this Parliament is unlikely to be a realistic aspiration"

The Committee found three main problems with there being so many ministers in Westminster. Firstly, they were hugely expensive 'placing a burden on the public purse'. Secondly, the Committee felt that having so many ministers reduced the ability of the House of Commons to hold the Government to account. As all ministers were expected to support the Government in the Commons, by making so many MPs into ministers, the Government ensured their support by creating what was called a 'payroll vote' – anyone either getting or hoping to get the benefits of a nice ministerial salary and other perks of office would be unlikely to jeopardise this by ever voting against the Government. As the Committee warned, 'the temptation to create more and more "jobs for the boys" (and girls) is not conducive either to better government or better scrutiny of legislation'. And thirdly, the Committee was concerned about the poor managerial qualities of many ministers. As one contributor to the Committee explained, 'very few ministers have ever run anything. There is no way you are going to convert them into good managers'.

Former ministers and civil servants appearing before the Committee also expressed concerns about having such a large number of ministers when there really wasn't enough work for them all. A former minister remarked, 'I think there has probably been an increase in pointless activity'. And a senior civil servant seemed to be suggesting that the large number of ministers was more linked to the Prime Minister's desire to hand out well-paid favours and ensure support rather than the number being driven by the real quantity of work to be done. The civil servant explained how officials spent far too much time trying to find things for the hordes of junior ministers to do:

> The more junior ministers you have – and we have more junior ministers than ever – the more work you have to find for them. One of the biggest single frustrations of the political process within the civil service is just the number of junior ministers you have and the work projects that have to be designed and engineered at a political level.

In 2010, a member of the Committee tabled an amendment to the House of Commons Disqualification Act requiring the Government to reduce the number of ministers in line with proposed reduction in the number of MPs from 650 to 600. Perhaps unsurprisingly, this amendment was roundly defeated in both the Commons and the Lords. It was as if, while preaching austerity for us - the ignorant, taxpaying lumpenproletariat - our honourable MPs and noble Lords were loathe to lose any of the wonderfully lucrative, taxpayer-funded jobs available to them from Britain unnecessarily but conveniently having so many government ministers.

In justifying its proposal to reduce the number of ministers, the Committee quoted David Cameron's possibly now embarrassing pledge to cut the cost of politics, 'there's something else the British public wants us to do, and that is to cut the cost of politics. Everyone is having to do more for less'. So, given, the PM's promise and the fact that under its Big Society initiative the Government was trying to devolve responsibility from central government to local communities, the Committee recommended a cut in the number of ministers to eighty. The Committee felt that if Whitehall departments were expected to cut their administrative budgets by thirty three per cent and 'do more with less' by working more efficiently, Government should be able to do something similar.

However, David Cameron's government appeared unimpressed by the suggestion that it too should adopt the austerity diet the rest of us were being put on. Francis Maude explained the Government's reason for recommending cuts everywhere else apart from in government, 'getting to the point where you have smaller government and big society requires a hell of a lot of stuff to be done'. So it seemed to be a case of 'doing more with less' for the rest of us and 'doing less with more' for government ministers. Another member of the Government told the Committee, 'it is likely at some stage in the future we will reduce the number of ministers'. Roughly translated this meant, 'there's not a snowball's chance in hell that any of us are ever going to give up our highly-paid comforts to cut public spending, so get stuffed!' And so the whole exercise ended with the predictably depressing conclusion, 'the Government believes that a reduction to eighty ministers shared between the Commons and the Lords over the course of this Parliament as suggested by the

Committee is unlikely to be a realistic aspiration'.[56]

If MPs can't become ministers, there's yet another way of earning a little extra pocket money – as chairperson of a Commons committee. There are over thirty Select Committees and General Committees providing more than thirty MPs an extra £14,582 each a year to chair them. Of course, £14,582 a year in addition to their over £65,000 salaries is peanuts for most MPs. But this is only for attending a few meetings a year and yet it's worth around twice what we pay people receiving the state pension. In 2010, the Commons 32-member Liaison Committee – made up of the chairpeople of all the Commons select committees – recommended that Parliament 'act courageously' by reducing the number of select committees. However, as with the Public Administration Committee's proposal to reduce the number of ministers, nothing happened. Our parliamentarians are quick to make tough-sounding recommendations which get good headlines because they chime with the mood of austerity and increased efficiency. But they are slower than the Continental Drift when it comes to implementing any of these when they might mean less of our money going into the bank accounts of our MPs.

Bountiful to our Lords

As for the House of Lords, austerity seemed to be a stranger there too. Firstly, as mentioned in Chapter 1 - *The NIMBY 'cuts'*, when forming his Government, David Cameron seems to have taken out his book of contacts and told one of his hirelings to call everyone in it to tell them they were being given peerages. Hence, the (expensive for us) ennobling of 117 people, many of whom were not particularly distinguished and many of whom were seen as 'Cameron's cronies'.

Politicians strike gold

It's quite difficult to know whether the costs of the House of Lords are going up and, if so, by how much. In 1997, the Lords cost us about £35 million at 2009 prices. By 2010 this had rocketed to £112 million – more than three times as much. When questioned about this massive increase, the Lords claimed that the two figures were not comparable as, in 2001 they changed the way they accounted for their costs from what they called a 'cash basis' to what they called 'resource accounting'. But if we taxpayers paid £35 million in 1997 and £112 million by 2010, however much the Lords might choose to blame accounting procedures for the differing figures, £112 million a year is an awful lot more than £35 million a year. Anyway, if we look at the Lords' expenses policies, we can see that we have been more than bountiful to our lords. Since 1997, the amount peers could claim per night more than doubled; they amount they could claim per day more than doubled; the amount they could claim for office costs per day more than doubled; and the amount they could claim for office costs when the House of Lords was not in session more than tripled. Just since the start of the recession, all the costs lords could claim increased by around ten per cent. Not many people in the private sector have seen such a rise in their incomes.

While MPs had to make some kind of attempt to pretend that their main home was their main home and their second home was their second home, the House of Lords expenses system was much more liberal. Lords only had to spend just one night a month in their supposed main home to be eligible to claim overnight costs when in London. And, of course, being peers they were trusted and never had to show receipts. You'd think that with such a generous expenses regime, it would be almost impossible to be caught cheating. But it seems that our lords are ever inventive when it comes to lining their own pockets. One by one they were exposed as what a completely ignorant outsider with no understanding of the subtleties of Westminster life might consider to be liars and thieves. Baroness Uddin, Lord Taylor, Lord Hanningfield, Lord Paul, Lord Bhatia and others, who for legal reasons must remain nameless but they know who they are, were revealed as having possibly been rather more generous to themselves with our money than even the pathetically lax Lords' expenses system allowed.

Faced with the embarrassment of being exposed by the press for being as corrupt as our expenses-fiddling MPs, the Lords authorities took decisive action. Unfortunately for us, this action had nothing to do with protecting taxpayers' money and everything to do with protecting the Lords from further embarrassment. So the Lords bosses did away with any stupid rules about main homes and second homes and about actually having to look like you'd spent some of the money you were claiming. Instead they moved to the same kind of SOSO ('sign on and sod off') system used by the European Parliament. In Brussels the SOSO system often resulted in a long line of MEPs queuing up in Brussels early on Thursday and Friday mornings to sign in quickly for their expenses before catching their flights home. With the new Lords' expenses regime, it didn't matter whether a lord lived in the South of France or next door to Westminster. All they had to do to get their £300 a day was turn up briefly and sign in. Some might then stay for a pleasant cup of tea or coffee or even a well-oiled luncheon helped down by fine wines and brandies in one of the taxpayer-subsidised House of Lords restaurants, others might head off to their real work or their game of golf or their mistresses or whatever. The Leader of the Lords, Lord Strathclyde, explained the advantages of the new system, 'we would sweep away the controversial rules on so-called second homes, which in my judgement have no logic in a House that is not elected. No more juggling of utility bills and claims forms'.[57] But others were not so convinced about the merits of the new system. The former Commissioner for Standards in Public Life commented, 'it doesn't sound like a well thought out and transparent system. I do believe that allowances should be related to costs incurred and that people should have to provide receipts'.[58] Apologists for the new expenses rules, or rather lack of rules, point out that the maximum claimable per day had dropped from £335.50 under the old rules to £300 with the new way of working. But there's only one certainty for us hard-pressed, austerity-burdened taxpayers – while we see our wealth being squeezed, our lucky lords are going to be able to claim ever more of our money, without ever having to prove they spent any of it fulfilling their duty as lords. We are truly bountiful to our lords.

Chapter 6

A bonanza for the bureaucrats

The Government's plans to reduce public spending have led to significant reductions in the number of police and quite frightening cuts in our military capabilities at a time when the world may not be becoming a safer place. But it's not clear that the same degree of pain is being felt amongst those who spend much of their lives pushing paper around, writing reports and attending important meetings – Britain's bureaucrats. Perhaps a good place to start investigating how our hardworking apparatchiks are responding to the calls to cut spending is with the people who have overall responsibility for our money and our economy – George Osborne's Treasury.

Nothing to treasure

It's always difficult to decide which government department provides the greatest entertainment to Britain's taxpayers for the many billions of taxpayers' money they spend and waste. Different people will probably have their own favourites. The hapless, hopeless Home Office no doubt features high on many Westminster watchers' Top Ten most useless bureaucracies. The Home Office has done us proud with its recidivist bungling of immigration control which has allowed several million – nobody

Public-sector feeding frenzy

has a clue how many there actually are – illegal immigrants to stay in the UK; its introduction of 'plastic bobbies' the usually fat people bulging out of their uniforms you sometimes see waddling along the high street; its tendency to let criminals out of jail while persecuting law-abiding citizens; and the billions wasted on New Labour's 'big brother' identity cards project that was scrapped by the Tories. But Gordon Brown's, Alistair Darling's and then George Osborne's Treasury has also done a pretty good job to keep us amused over the years with its often laughable attempts to do what we pay it to do.

Under Gordon Brown's slightly suspect management, spending on the Treasury shot up from around £100 million in 1998/9 to almost £170 million by the time Brown moved onwards and upwards to become possibly the worst Prime Minister Britain has ever had. Brown's largesse with our money certainly gave us lots more Treasury bureaucrats doing lots more presumably useful things to manage our economy and, in the process, all but bankrupting Britain. When Brown handed over control of the Treasury to Alistair Darling, spending by the treasury leapt up again by over £20 million from about £172 million to £194 million. Under Darling, the Treasury Group had two, what it called 'Departmental Strategic Objectives' (DSOs) – DSO1 and DSO2. DSO1 was 'to maintain sound public finances'. DSO2 was 'to ensure sustainable economic growth, well being and prosperity for all'.

Like most central government departments, each year the Treasury produces a 200 plus page annual report full of lots of pictures and graphs where it explains how hard it has been working for our benefit and how well it has achieved its ambitious plans. Yet in the year that it had 'to maintain sound public finances' as its number one goal, public sector borrowing almost tripled from just over £28 billion to close to £88 billion and was projected to rocket up to about £176 billion the year after. Moreover, our budget deficit – the difference between what the Government spends and what it takes from us in taxes – exploded from just £6 billion to over £50 billion with a forecast of about £180 billion the year after. So, it would be safe to conclude that the hardworking economic experts and advisers at the Treasury didn't exactly achieve their DSO1 – 'sound public finances'.

As for the Treasury's DSO2 – 'sustainable economic growth, well being and prosperity for all' - in the year the Treasury had that target, Britain's Gross Domestic Product (GDP) dropped by about £40 billion from £1.43 trillion to £1.39 trillion while unemployment shot up from around one and a half million to comfortably over two million. So much for DSO2. Instead of 'economic growth, well being and prosperity for all', we got economic decline, massive misery caused by a sharp rise in unemployment and the worst squeeze on people's standard of living since the Great Depression. However, as they increased their spending of our money, increased their numbers of staff and increased their own bonuses, Treasury bosses seem to have been unaware of their abject failure to come anywhere near reaching the goals that had been set for them. No doubt the new Chancellor, George 'We're all in this together' Osborne, would put an end to this sad and expensive Whitehall farce.

Osborne seems to have set two main targets for his Treasury – 'to get the public finances back on track' and, as part of the Government's 'Growth Agenda', to provide 'a new model of sustainable growth to restore Britain's competitiveness'.[59] Osborne also announced that the Treasury had agreed to 'a 33 per cent reduction' in its spending and would conduct 'a detailed strategic consideration of its own working practices to deliver better value through increased productivity and working more flexibly'.

It's quite difficult to square Osborne's ambition 'to

get the public finances back on track' with the fact that public spending would increase that year from £692 billion to £710 billion and then £720 billion a year later at the same time as tax receipts were falling. As for the 'growth agenda' – well, Britain almost immediately went into a recession following the Government's and the Treasury's complete lack of any concrete ideas about how to stimulate any growth. But at least there was some small consolation for us taxpayers – with Osborne's agreed '33 per cent reduction' in Treasury spending we could expect the Treasury to cost us less. Unfortunately, we'd have to wait a bit for that to happen. The Treasury had impressive projections of how its costs would fall by 2015. But, in Osborne's first year in charge, Treasury staff costs went up by about £2.5 million from £89.3 million to over £91.8 million and at £197 million, overall Treasury spending was slightly above what it had been under Darling, but an astonishing £27 million (or 16 per cent) higher than the highest it had been under the notoriously profligate, bureaucracy-loving Brown. It will be interesting to see whether the ever more expensive Treasury actually does meet its ambitious cost reduction targets or whether Treasury bosses will use the economic chaos, for which they have in part been responsible, to justify them employing ever more highly-paid, highly-pensioned, ludicrously underperforming bureaucrats

In spite of the Treasury's renewed failure to achieve any of the things it was meant to and in spite of the fact that it increased rather than decreased its own costs, Mr Osborne informed us that 'I have been impressed by the dedication shown by officials in the Treasury Group' and bonuses were, of course, paid. Thankfully, these were slightly smaller than under Brown and Darling, but not by much. Osborne may have been impressed by the Treasury's efforts, but it's not certain his admiration was shared by the rest of the country where fewer people in work saw their taxes significantly increased to pay for the rising cost of our government, while our economy crashed and burned around us.

Not only is the Treasury remarkably generous to its own palpably ineffectual fifteen hundred or so staff, but it also provides some handy extra pocket money for several politicians. In addition to Chancellor of the Exchequer George Osborne, there are several other MPs who benefit from the cash we pour into the Treasury. There are also a Chief Secretary to the Treasury, a Financial Secretary to the Treasury, an Exchequer Secretary to the Treasury, an Economic Secretary to the Treasury and a Commercial Secretary to the Treasury. Each of these positions pays the lucky holder anything from £30,000 to £70,000 a year over and above their MPs' salary, plus they make undoubtedly welcome contributions to the holders' pension funds. Moreover, there are in addition a few Sirs and Dames and Baronesses and suchlike well-connected members of the ruling elite who also get a few bob each year from the Treasury – in their case for being Treasury non-executive board members. It seems odd that these many worthies have apparently neither noticed nor commented on the Treasury's ever-rising costs, generous bonuses and repeated inability to achieve any of its strategic objectives. To an inexperienced outsider it could seem as if they were just a bunch of self-serving leeches, who didn't care how much taxpayers' money the bungling, over-spending, incompetent Treasury wasted, as long as they could continue to fill their own pockets with our cash.

Cuts? Us? You must be joking

Central to the whole Civil Service is the Cabinet Office. As the Minister for the Cabinet Office explained:

Public-sector feeding frenzy

> Within any great organisation is a strong and vibrant centre and at the heart of the UK Civil Service – often described as the best in the world – is the Cabinet Office. At the core of Government, the Cabinet Office is leading the way in ensuring that the Civil Service continues to be the very best by creating a modern organisation for the modern world.[60]

The Cabinet Office certainly seems to have been busy helping to drive efficiencies and reduced costs throughout the Civil Service. It claims it has renegotiated contracts with suppliers to cut costs; reduced spending on government marketing and advertising; implemented a recruitment freeze on 'non-essential back office Civil Service posts' leading to a reduction of 17,000 posts; reduced spending on consultants; improved central buying; conducted a review of over nine hundred quangos; and much more besides. It also launched the 'One-in, One-out rule' (OIOO). The OIOO rule meant that for any primary or secondary UK legislation, if any new rule ('ins') imposed a net cost on business, then that rule had to be balanced by one or more rules being changed or repealed ('outs') to produce a cost reduction for business equivalent to the costs imposed by the 'ins'. Unfortunately, the Cabinet Office slipped up when, during the first year of the OIOO rule, the Cabinet Office was responsible for two 'ins' (increasing costs for businesses) and no 'outs' (producing a corresponding reduction in costs). As is so often the case in government, it's the old 'do as I say, not as I do'.

When it comes to its own spending of our money, once again the Cabinet Office doesn't seem to be leading by example. During its first year working for the Coalition, its own staff costs went up by £1.7 million. Its overall spending did fall. There was a modest drop from £506 million under Darling to £494 million under the Coalition – about 2.4 per cent down. Moreover, further and more dramatic cuts were planned. But at £494 million, the Cabinet Office was spending over fifty four per cent more than it did during Brown's last year as Chancellor. If your weight goes up (as mine seems in the process of doing) by fifty four per cent from 80 kilos to more than 120 kilos over four years, you should be able to lose a lot of weight quite quickly if you put your mind to it. Similarly, the Cabinet Office had clearly become so bloated by the time the Coalition took over, that a drastic slimming regime should have been both necessary and not terribly difficult, rather than the pathetic 2.4 per cent we've seen so far.

There's another small, possibly worrying detail about the Cabinet Office's use of our money. It seems there was a bit of 'grab it while you can' going on in the upper echelons. In 2008-09, maybe aware the Gordon-Brownian good times were coming to an end and that government spending would soon be cut, the panjandrums at the Cabinet Office almost all got hefty increases in their pay and pensions. So, while the rest of us were being crushed by the economic crisis, Cabinet Office bosses saw their remuneration jump by between ten and seventeen per cent – quite a healthy rise considering the economic chaos all around them. When the Coalition came to power and launched its austerity programme, these same people could pretend to show a laudable sense of responsibility and admirable self-control when several of them accepted reductions in their pay of three to five per cent. But they could afford to, having whacked up their pay by around three to four times as much the year before.

Spend, spend, spend

The main government departments may or may not have started trying to control their ever-rising spending. What they claim to be doing and what they are actually doing may be quite different.

Public-sector feeding frenzy

But once you step a little bit away from central government control into the wonderful world of quangos (quasi-autonomous, non-governmental organisations) for many it seems to be a case of spend, spend, spend when it comes to their use and abuse of taxpayers' money. There are over nine hundred quangos we could look at, but many are very small advisory groups of specialists which use tiny amounts of our money and which have limited effect on our daily lives. So here I propose to look at three important quangos – the regulators of the water, energy and financial services industries. This is partly because they spend such sizeable, increasing and recession-busting amounts of our money and partly because their actions, or more often inaction, can have a huge impact on the lives of the ordinary people who pay so much for them.

Ofwat a farce

Ofwat, also known as the Water Services Regulation Authority, has a catchy slogan 'Water Today, Water Tomorrow'. Yet under Ofwat's regulatory regime we've managed to have repeated droughts in a country with the reputation of being one of the wettest in Europe. Moreover, we are an island surrounded by rather a lot of water, yet we have droughts. Perhaps Ofwat's slogan should be 'Rain Today, No Water Tomorrow'? Ofwat's mission statement shows its determination to do the right thing by users of water, 'our vision is for a water industry that delivers a world class service, representing best value to customers now and in the future'. Ofwat has not been slow to increase the amount of our money it spends on itself. This rose from £11.5 million in 2006-07 just before the economic collapse to £17.4 million by 2010-11 – a rise of over fifty per cent in five years. If Ofwat had delivered its vaunted 'world class service' and 'best value to customers', its ever-expanding use of our money at a time of economic crisis might be almost acceptable. But instead it has created a catastrophic situation where in one of the wettest countries in Europe we pay some of the highest prices for our water, while the companies which Ofwat should be regulating run off with massive profits at our expense.

On turnover of about £9 billion, the UK water industry makes gross profits of about thirty to forty per cent. Even after taxes and other charges, our water companies are making over fifteen per cent, when many companies in other industries are delighted to make just five or six per cent. Several of our water companies are owned by foreign water companies which are heavily regulated in their home markets. So for them, the UK is an incredibly lucrative market as Ofwat's pathetic efforts at regulation allow them to earn up to three times as much profit in Britain as they can in their countries of origin. It never seems to have occurred to Ofwat to look at the modest profits some French water companies can earn in France compared to the massive profits they are raking on their British operations and to wonder why there might be such a large disparity in profitability between France and the UK.

It also doesn't seem to have occurred to Ofwat to wonder why about half our water companies are owned by foreign groups, many of them based in the world's best-known tax havens. The owners of British water companies include two Chinese investment companies apparently based in the tiny British Virgin Islands; an Australian investment company operating through the small island of Jersey; a Swiss bank; an Australian pension fund; an Arab Bank; a Malaysian firm and several other equally exotic bodies. Ofwat has allowed these companies to raise the price we pay for water above the level of inflation for most of the last quarter century. Moreover, Ofwat has allowed the water companies to use the much higher Retail Prices Index (RPI) rather than the lower Consumer Price Index (CPI) when companies set the prices we pay. The companies and Ofwat claim the big price rises are needed to generate money for investment in improving water supplies. But this is patently untrue. In fact, these companies are immensely profitable cash cows that are siphoning off huge amounts of our money to put in the pockets of their owners.

Thames Water provides an excellent example of how the supine, impotent, self-serving Ofwat is allowing water companies to fleece us. In 2000, the company was bought by the German RWE for £6.8 billion. Over the six years of its ownership, RWE pocketed around £1 billion in dividends. It then sold Thames to an Australian company for £8 billion. So RWE made around £2.2 billion from its brief ownership of Thames. Yet during its ownership RWE was allowed to increase water bills well above inflation by claiming it needed the money to invest in reducing leakage. In addition to its exploitative high prices, for years Thames has further increased its profits by selling off land and facilities to people like property developers. When asked why it had closed twenty five bulk water storage facilities, Thames explained, 'all these sites were shut down when they became surplus to operational requirements following upgrades to our network'.[61] At the same time as Thames was saying this, it had imposed a hosepipe ban due to a lack of water.

But Ofwat has permitted a much worse scandal that will be disastrous for British water users for decades to come. When the water companies were privatised in 1989, they had debt levels of around twenty per cent. Now those debt levels have reached over eighty per cent. Effectively, the water companies' owners have been borrowing tens of billions, supposedly to improve infrastructure, but have actually just used much of this borrowed money to pay gigantic dividends to themselves. This has had three worrying effects. It has left the water companies needing ever more of our cash to pay off the increasing interest charges on these debts; it has allowed the water companies to offset these interest payments against tax thus reducing their contribution to Britain's finances; and it has left the water companies so indebted that however bad their service, it would be almost impossible for any government to renationalise them because no government could afford to take on the poison pill of these companies' massive debts. Although I know next to nothing about the water industry, it took me twenty minutes on Google to find out about water company bosses looting their firms and leaving them with a huge debt time bomb that we'll all have to pay for decades to come. But the two hundred plus highly-paid, highly-pensioned experts at Ofwat don't seem to have noticed any of this and certainly haven't taken any action to prevent this scam.

It's interesting to compare what Ofwat has allowed to happen in Britain with what is going on in our neighbour France. Over the years, the French Government has brilliantly used the EU to put pressure on the World Trade Organisation (WTO) to force other countries to open up their markets so that French water companies could expand their operations abroad. This French invasion has been most harmful in poorer Third World countries where privatisations of the water supply, imposed by the WTO and welcomed by corrupt local politicians and bureaucrats as opportunities to extract healthy bribes, have resulted In the French companies, which also operate in Britain, being able to take over local water companies and charge such high prices that millions of poorer people can no longer afford to pay for clean water. However, in France the government and local authorities have been doing precisely the opposite. They've been renationalising water supplies. Now over forty towns, including Paris, control their own water supply and this has given better service at a much lower cost. The city of Grenoble provides a good example of how French water customers have benefitted from this. When some former ministers and executives from French company Suez (which owns a British water firm) were imprisoned for corruption, the city took control of its water supply and went from having the highest water prices in France to having some of the lowest.

When criticised for our ever-rising water prices and re-occurring droughts, Ofwat claimed 'when we set limits on prices, we listened to customers' and 'we understand that any bill rise is unwelcome, particularly in tough economic times' and 'we will make sure customers get value for money'. But Ofwat allows a quarter of all our water to be lost in leakage; Ofwat has permitted massive profiteering by the water companies; Ofwat has failed to achieve anything like the degree of competent regulation we can see in other developed countries; and Ofwat has turned a blind eye as water companies have built up crippling levels of debt which we ordinary water users will have to pay off for the next many decades. It is almost beyond belief that successive governments have allowed the shameless Ofwat to continuously increase the amount of our money it spends on itself whilst utterly failing to do its job of ensuring a properly-managed water supply industry.

A similar farce at Ofgem?

Ogem, the regulator for the gas and electricity markets seems to have a similar strategy to the appalling Ofwat. Like Ofwat, Ofgem has massively increased the amount of our money it spends on itself; it has done little to nothing to stop rampant profiteering by the power companies; and it has allowed such a shambles to develop in Britain's power supply industry that we may start to see Third-World-style power shortages and power cuts starting around 2015.

A bonanza for the bureaucrats

Since 2006-07, the cost to us of Ofgem's staff has shot up from £18.6 million to £32.6 million – a rise of seventy five per cent – while its overall cost to us has more than doubled from £38.8 million to over £78.7 million. At the same time, although inflation has only increased prices by about twenty per cent, the price of electricity has gone up by about eighty per cent and the price of gas has more than doubled. Our power companies always blame their price rises on the increased costs they have to pay for their wholesale supplies of oil and gas. However, whenever wholesale prices go up, our power companies are admirably quick to increase the prices we pay them. But when wholesale prices fall, it often takes a worryingly long time for our bills to fall. When they do fall, it's seldom by as much as the drop in wholesale prices (see Figure 1).

Figure 1 – Power companies are quick to increase prices but rather slow to reduce them (Example – retail gas prices seldom fall when wholesale prices fall)

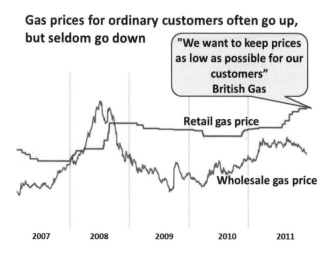

Public-sector feeding frenzy

In 2011-12, for example, when wholesale prices fell by around nine per cent, firms like EDF only reduced prices by around five per cent.

This ability to keep on increasing the prices we consumers pay has made our power companies incredibly profitable. On sales of £7.1 billion, EDF – a company 83 per cent owned by the French Government – made profits of £1.58 billion, a profit margin of an astonishing twenty two per cent. In fact, foreign companies make so much money in Britain that some of them use the money we pay them to support their operations in countries where their prices are controlled and levels of investment are properly regulated. For example, after a hefty price hike for its British customers, Iberdrola, the Spanish company that owns Scottish Power, made an £800 million loan to one of its US subsidiaries when American regulators put pressure on the subsidiary to stick to its investment commitments.

When accused of predatory pricing, the power companies and their cheerleaders have two stories to keep inquisitive journalists and the hopeless Ofgem happy. Usually they claim that they are putting up prices because of rises in wholesale prices. But when wholesale prices fall they say that they are tied into long-term contracts and so can't reduce prices by as much as the fall in wholesale prices. Of course, these oft-repeated excuses are rubbish. If the companies were tied into longer-term contracts, then they wouldn't need to put prices up so quickly when wholesale prices rose. The other story they roll out is that Britain has some of the lowest energy costs in Europe. Perhaps surprisingly, this is in fact true. But it covers up massive profiteering by the power companies. Per unit of energy, British consumer prices are lower than many other European countries. But this is mainly because tax levels on gas and electricity are much lower in Britain than on the Continent. Once you strip out the effect of higher taxes in other countries, power prices in

A bonanza for the bureaucrats

Britain are around the average level for Europe. But considering we only need to import about a third of our gas, while most other European countries import almost all their gas supplies, power prices in the UK should be lower than in most other European countries. The reason they are not is that Ofgem's laid-back, lax and ineffective regulation has allowed power companies operating in Britain to charge much more, invest much less and earn much higher profits here than they can in properly regulated countries.

High pricing and ruthless profiteering by our power companies damages British industry by making it less competitive; hurts the British economy by overcharging customers leaving them less money to spend on things like housing, clothing and food; and it can harm the vulnerable. As the charity Age UK explained:

> Each year…many thousands of people aged 65 and over die needlessly in the winter months. This is often because older people can't afford to heat their homes and they are more susceptible to illnesses caused by cold and damp….The latest figures show that last winter there were almost 22,000 additional deaths among people over the age of 65…The cost to society is enormous. For every additional winter death, there are also around 8 admissions to hospital, 32 visits to outpatient care and 30 social services calls.[62]

But the most disastrous result of Ofgem's laughable failure to do its job is the shambolic state of our power supply market. Four of our six main power companies are now foreign owned. When the power supply market was first privatised, there was a rush of American companies eager to buy our power firms because they could make much larger profits in our loosely regulated market than they could in the more effectively regulated US. These companies made so much money in Britain that they were soon able to sell the power firms they had bought for massive profits to French, Spanish and German companies. Again, these foreign firms found Britain attractive because Ofgem was much less effective at regulating the industry than the regulators in their home countries. Foreign ownership has at least three very negative effects for British energy users. Firstly, being based abroad, the companies are much less sensitive to bad PR than a British company would be and so can shrug off any negative press about overcharging and profiteering. French EDF is probably one of the best exponents of this 'we couldn't give a toss what you think' attitude. Secondly, foreign companies have no loyalty to the UK and so just use the UK as a preposterously productive cash cow while minimising any investments in modernising and improving power supply. And thirdly, their legal duty is to maximise profitability for their foreign shareholders and so they will always prioritise the interests of their French, German or Spanish owners ahead of those of British consumers.

We saw this most recently when two German companies RWE and E.ON pulled out of the bidding to build new nuclear reactors in Britain. Following German Chancellor Merkel's decision to wind down nuclear energy in Germany, these companies were landed with higher than expected costs for decommissioning German reactors. In order to maintain their profits, they decided not to make any investments in nuclear energy in Britain. Given that the only British manufacturer of nuclear plants has long since been sold, if Britain is to build the new generation of nuclear plants we need to replace those which will be taken out of service, there is probably only one company that can now build these – French Government-owned EDF. This places the British Government at EDF's mercy and the French

A bonanza for the bureaucrats

company can probably demand whatever they want to build the plants – not great for British taxpayers and energy customers, but wonderful for the big-spending French Government. Plus there is also the risk that a new French President might, like Germany's Merkel, turn his back on nuclear power. If that happens, we'll probably end up begging the Russians or Chinese or even the North Koreans to build our reactors. Let's hope that if it's the Russians, they don't use the same design they used for Chernobyl.

That's a longer-term issue. In the shorter term, if there is a harsh winter and a shortage of gas, then companies like German RWE and E.ON will ensure that German industry is well supplied even if this means supply shortages for the UK. And now that Chinese and Russian companies, strongly encouraged by our incompetent Coalition Government, are looking to buy up British power stations being sold by French EDF and North Sea gas fields, we risk handing over vital national assets to countries whose interests may be in direct opposition to our own.

In its defence, Ofgem can rightly claim that it doesn't have the statutory powers either to cap energy prices or to prevent foreign takeovers of British power companies. However, Ofgem has been spending huge quantities of our money on itself for almost twenty five years. That's really quite a long time both to look at how other countries regulate their power industries to ensure fair pricing and continuing investment and to put a case to the many governments that have been in office over this time for Ofgem to have similar powers to those given to energy regulators in other countries. Ofgem has absolutely failed to do this and has thus failed to protect the interests of British energy users. Each year Ofgem issues a thick, glossy annual report vaunting its many achievements. But actually it looks like we've got very little of any use for the more than £600 million we've paid for Ofgem's many bureaucrats over the years and it hardly seems as if the Coalition is minded to ensure that the situation improves in the years to come.

Banking bonkers

The well-paid efforts of Ofwat and Ofgem may have been laughable, farcical or tragic depending on your point of view. But nothing these two ineffectual regulators did, or rather didn't do, could match the Pythonesque absurdity of what we have seen from the Financial Services Authority (FSA). One of the FSA's primary goals is 'maintaining confidence in the financial system'. That looks a bit ridiculous now considering all that has happened since the 2007 financial crash.

When Gordon Brown, in his great wisdom, decided in 1997 to transfer policing of our banking system from the Bank of England to the FSA, we were spending just £29 million a year on the FSA. By the time of the 2007 crash, the FSA was costing us over £260 million. In the latest full year of operations, the FSA's budget had reached an astonishing £526 million. In 2007-08, the FSA employed 2,665 staff. By 2009-10 when it learned it was going to be scrapped, its staff numbers had reached 3,431. Even though it was told in 2010 that it was being closed down and replaced by two new regulators, the FSA kept on recruiting and by 2011-12 had 3,953 employees, almost fifty per cent more than it had at the start of the economic crisis.

We got a foretaste of the FSA's uselessness in 2000 when it did nothing to prevent the near collapse of Equitable Life. So appalling was the FSA's handling of the Equitable Life meltdown that the parliamentary ombudsman accused it of maladministration. The Government was then forced to introduce The Equitable Life (Payments) Bill in Parliament. This set up a compensation scheme whereby we taxpayers, rather than Equitable Life's executives and shareholders, would have to pay around £1.5 billion in compensation to people who had lost money from the Equitable Life debacle.

Things went quiet for a few years leaving the FSA to do its highly-paid ineffectual box-ticking in peace. Then 2007 arrived. First financial institution to go belly up was Northern Rock. Just a few weeks before the complete collapse of Northern Rock, the clueless FSA had done a review of the bank and declared it to be solvent. The FSA's handling of the regulation of Northern Rock was described by the chairman of the Treasury Select Committee as 'a dereliction of duty'.[63] But still the FSA kept on increasing its staff numbers and kept on spending ever more of our money.

After Northern Rock, the building society and bank collapses came thick and fast. Due to the FSA's complete and utter failure to do anything that in any way looked, sounded or smelt like regulation, we taxpayers saw around £500 billion of our money being ploughed into saving RBS, the Lloyds and HBOS Frankenstein of a bank (largely banged together by Gordon Brown) and Bradford and Bingley. It's probably little consolation that, following the nuclear explosion that was the RBS under Mr Fred 'I've got a £342,500 a year pension' Goodwin, the FSA did admit that it 'had not kept a close enough eye on the bank' and in particular its disastrous £50 billion takeover of Dutch bank ABN Amro.

In spite of several of the banks it should have been supervising imploding all around it, the FSA continued to blithely pay increasing bonuses to its staff. These went up from £13.9 million in 2007-08 to £19.7 million in 2008-09 to £22 million in 2009-10. I haven't been able to find the latest bonus figures. This may be because I am too stupid or because the FSA is too embarrassed to publish them in an easily comprehensible form. But judging from the past, we can probably assume that FSA bonuses, paid with our money, have continued to increase. Perhaps never in the field of human regulation has an organisation increased its spending and staff numbers by so much while achieving so little.

In 2010, the new Chancellor George Osborne announced that the FSA was to be abolished and its responsibilities would be split. Overall regulation of the banking system would go to the Prudential Regulation Authority back again under the control of the Bank of England. Regulation of retail financial products would pass to a new Financial Conduct Authority. So, after spending probably £3 billion on the FSA and losing who knows how many hundreds of billions more due to the FSA's abject and recidivist failures, we were pretty much back where we started before Gordon Brown 'reformed' our system of financial regulation.

Bonfire night again?

In 1995, two years before being elected, Blair promised to 'sweep away the quango state' and Brown committed to a 'bonfire of the quangos'. Sure enough, when in power, Blair and Brown did the exact opposite of what they had promised and used our money to give us probably the largest increase in the number and cost of quangos in British history. The Conservative Party 2010 election manifesto made clear that they too were planning to wage war on Britain's burgeoning quangocracy:

> Over the course of a Parliament, we will.....save a further £1 billion a year from quangos bureaucracy. The explosion of unaccountable quangos, public sector 'nonjobs' and costly bureaucracy is an indictment of Labour's reckless approach to spending other people's

money.[64]

Judging by what has happened since the Coalition took office, it does seem that there is at last some effort being made by a government to get control over the more than nine hundred quangos for which we pay tens of billions of pounds a year. The Cabinet Office conducted a review of quangos and has put in place a plan to abolish about 192 (21 per cent), merge 118 (13 per cent), retain 380 (42 per cent) and retain but reform 171 (19 per cent). Final decisions were still to be made on the remaining 40 (4 per cent). But worryingly, only nine out of 901 quangos – just one per cent – would actually be moved from the public sector to the private sector. We taxpayers would continue paying for the ninety nine per cent that remained in the public sector as, even when quangos were abolished, their activities would often just move into other government departments.

While the Tories promised significant cost reductions from quango-culling in their election manifesto, the Coalition changed its tune when in government and explained that the key aim of the review of quangos was to make them more accountable. The Coalition used four tests to decide whether a quango should be abolished, merged, reformed or kept. Value for money and performance were not included in these tests. The Government still claims that their quango reforms will save money and have included a projected saving of £500 million in their cost reduction budget – about half of what they had promised in their 2010 election manifesto. But the House of Commons Public Administration Committee did a review of the Government's reforms and concluded, 'the Government appears unsure about the extent to which the reform will result in significant savings for taxpayers'.

Meanwhile, some quango bosses are raking in enormous piles of taxpayers' cash. The head of the Nuclear Decommissioning

Bad companies

Authority was reported as having pocketed more than £675,000 in just one year because, as a spokesman explained, of the need to attract candidates with 'sufficient experience and expertise'. The head of the Olympics Delivery Authority (ODA) was given £544,000 in his last year in position, including a sizeable bonus for his 'inspirational job'. Ten staff at the ODA earn more than the Prime Minister. It was the ODA which managed to spend almost £9 billion of our money on the 2012 London Olympics when the original cost for us taxpayers should have been just £2.4 billion. Over at the Care Quality Commission, the chief executive was on a more modest salary of about £200,000, but in just one year her pension pot went up by £240,000. In many other taxpayer-funded bodies, salaries of £200,000, £300,000 or even £400,000 a year are more the rule than the exception. The Government may succeed in reducing the cost of the quango state. Or it may just reorganise the deckchairs on the Titanic, incurring massive redundancy costs while making little inroads into the amounts of our money being lavished on quangos and their fortunate employees. As we saw with Ofwat, Ofgem and the appallingly useless FSA, many quangos have been allowed by successive governments to dramatically increase their costs and their bosses' pay packages for decades while demonstrably failing to deliver anything of value to us taxpayers who pay so much for our quangos' cosseted lifestyles.

Chapter 7

EU must be joking

Austerity? What's that?

Our British bureaucrats, politicians and peers may have been highly proficient at playing the NIMBY game of 'austerity for you, but not for me'. Yet they are mere bumbling amateurs compared to the true experts over at the EU. As countries cut back on spending and as some of the PIIGS (Portugal, Italy, Ireland, Greece, Spain) are driven into deep recessions because of public spending cuts demanded by their EU masters, the amount of taxpayers' money spent by the EU on itself keeps on going ever upwards. In the few years since just before the start of the recession till 2012, the overall EU budget has jumped by almost twenty per cent from around €115 billion to €138 billion. Within this increase are some real big spenders – the cost of the European Parliament has leapt by thirty per cent, the amount spent on pensions for EU officials has rocketed up by almost fifty per cent and the pile of our money spent on EU quangos has shot up by more than sixty per cent (see Figure 1).

Public-sector feeding frenzy

Figure 1 – The word 'austerity' doesn't seem to be understood over in Brussels

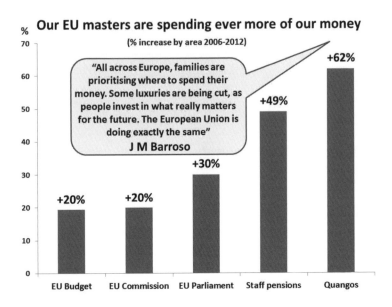

This shameless and shameful rise in EU spending is particularly harmful for us in Britain. Even as we implement cuts in police, the military and other frontline services, the net contribution we pay each year to the EU has ballooned. Our net contribution is the total of what we pay minus what we receive back in grants and payments for farmers. This has shot up since 2006 by about 120 per cent – that's six times as much as the overall increase in the EU's budget. The massive increase is thanks to a certain well-known multimillionaire Anthony Blair giving up a large part of our rebate in return for a vague suggestion that the EU would perhaps one day at some time in the future maybe consider thinking about the possibility of reforming the hugely wasteful

Common Agricultural Policy (CAP). British taxpayers' generous contributions to the EU leapt from €4 billion a year before Blair's brilliant negotiating efforts to over €9 billion a year once Blair had agreed to land the rest of us with a massive bill that he, due to his carefully organised tax affairs, would personally almost avoid having to contribute to. That's an increase of more than €14 million (£11.7 million) a day. This tidy sum could have paid for quite a few soldiers, police, libraries, care centres and whatever else is being cut by our leaders. Naturally, at the time Blair claimed he had achieved a great negotiating triumph while actually being taken for a very expensive ride by our EU friends. But it wasn't his money he was throwing away, so what did he care? Meanwhile, our continental colleagues must have been rolling around in stitches roaring with laughter at how gullible Blair and the British Government had been yet again. As for the suggestion that the EU would consider reforming the CAP – well, unsurprisingly, that sort of got forgotten.

Our costly commissars

The amount we pay for the EU Commission's twenty seven commissioners and their 33,000 or so staff has only gone up from around €1.8 billion to just over €2.2 billion – a rise of over twenty per cent since 2006. The document containing details of EU Commission employees' terms, conditions and many benefits such as pensions, expenses, relocation grants, school fees, invalidity benefits, spa holidays and much much more is 188 pages long. So I won't regurgitate all of these benefits here. But two benefits enjoyed by Commission employees are worth a little look – their tax status and their pensions.

You might feel sorry for many of the EU Commission's 33,000 employees. After all, most of them are based in Brussels and Belgium has some of the highest income taxes and social security deductions in Europe. A Belgian earning say £50,000 a year might see up to sixty per cent of their money going into the coffers of the Belgian government. But EU employees are fortunate that they don't have to pay the kinds of taxes and social costs the rest of us are compelled to. Instead they pay a special, very low EU tax rate which is around a third of what they would pay in a high tax country such as Belgium, France or Italy and about a half of what they would pay in the UK.

As for EU employees' pensions, these have become so expensive for us taxpayers, that's it's probably worth having a quick peek at what our masters in Brussels can look forward to in retirement and how much we'll be paying for this. As a lot of EU officials are beginning to retire, the cost of their pensions has shot up by almost fifty per cent just since 2006 and will probably have doubled long before 2020. While the financial future for many of us taxpayers may not look too bright, the prospects of the lucky 33,000 EU Commission employees appear decidedly rosy.

All EU Commission employees have the right to a full pension from the age of sixty three. That's quite attractive considering that the rest of us will have to work much longer to get our pensions. Should an EU employee decide to work past sixty three, they get a rather impressive hike in their pension. All EU pensions are based on final salary. Many British private- and public-sector employees are being put on 'career average' pensions if they have pensions at all. So, to have a pension based on final salary must appear quite generous – particularly when it will be people condemned to career-average pensions or worse who will be paying for these EU final-salary pensions.

Let's imagine an EU employee starting his or her career earning say €30,000 a year at thirty and ending up with €150,000 a year when they retire at sixty three. This employee would have a pension of €100,000 for the rest of their life. With annual pension contributions of 11.3 per cent a year, this official would have paid an impressive €330,000 or so into their pension scheme during their thirty three year career. However, the EU would need around €3,330,000 – ten times as much – to pay the employee's €100,000 a year pension. So, we taxpayers would be magnanimously contributing somewhere around €3,000,000 in order for this official to have the kind of retirement comforts that they would be entitled to after so many years working for the benefit of the EU's five hundred million citizens.

One of the more spendthrift of our EU rulers appears to be our very own Baroness Ashton. At the time of writing, she was the top dog (I won't use the female of this word as I might be misunderstood) at the EU's diplomatic service – the European External Action Service (EEAS). Like so many of the people who spend our money, Baroness Ashton will never have to experience the kind of financial pressures the rest of us may be subjected to. With her salary of around £230,000 a year, she is one of the highest paid politicians in the world. In fact, she earns almost as much as the US President who gets in the region of £260,000 a year and she's way ahead of her US counterpart, Hilary Clinton, on a modest £124,000 a year. Lady Ashton also has around £38,000 a year for accommodation, £10,000 for entertainment, a couple of chauffeurs and tens of thousands of pounds more in other allowances and relocation expenses. Moreover, she has the choice of paying UK taxes or much lower EU taxes. Displaying that solidarity with working people that seems to be so sadly lacking in those who have supposedly dedicated their lives to 'public service', it appears the good baroness will be saving herself around £40,000 a year by plumping for paying the less onerous EU taxes. Moreover, if she keeps her job for just five years, she will reportedly get a golden handshake of £464,000 in addition to her £64,000 pension for life.[65] This

£64,000 pension for life is equivalent to having a pension pot of about £1.8 million. It is as if we taxpayers had put £366,000 into Baroness Ashton's pension pot for every year spent in Brussels. This is, of course, in addition to the huge pension entitlements the good baroness would have accumulated from all her public-sector posts in the UK. For many years to come, British taxpayers are going to be paying an awful lot of money ensuring that Baroness Ashton has a multimillionaire lifestyle that is probably unimaginable to those whose taxes will go into Ashton's brimming bank account.

Baroness Ashton has been widely criticised for her performance as EEAS supremo. One newspaper called her 'the laughing stock of the EU'; a member of the European Parliament quipped, 'last year she was unknown in Britain. Today she is unknown all over Europe'; a fellow Labour baroness remarked, 'she is more suited to run a parish council than a major European institution'; and the head of one of the main political groupings in the European Parliament also appeared underwhelmed by Baroness Ashton's performance, 'we expect a lot for the position of High Representative. So far she has not met that level of expectation'.[66] Ashton may or may not be up to her job, but she's certainly made a good effort to increase the amount of our money she has managed to spend. Gordon Brown, who appointed her, would probably have been proud of her profligacy with taxpayers' cash. In spite of her promise that her department would be 'budget neutral' – it would not spend any more than its initial budget – the EEAS has gone on a bit of a spending spree with our money. It appears to have spent around €460 million (£383 million) in 2011, €489 million (£407 million) in 2012 and had a plan of splashing €517 million (£431 million) of our money in 2013. At a time when the British Foreign and Commonwealth Office was implementing cuts of around £40 million, our generosity to Baroness Ashton's growing diplomatic empire could appear misplaced. Some of us might even think that, when the rest of us are being squeezed, the EEAS shouldn't be regularly increasing its own spending by around €30 million (£25 million) a year. But a spokesman for the EEAS made the two usual excuses. Firstly he claimed the EEAS was actually living very frugally, 'we are making savings wherever possible'.[67] Then secondly he insisted the EEAS needed more money because it had more work to do, 'we have a mission, given by member states to build the EEAS and are responding to world events'. The rest of us may have 'to do more with less', but that doesn't seem to be the philosophy at the big-spending EEAS.

One small problem the EU has had when spending increasing amounts of our money is that its accounts have not been approved by the European Court of Auditors for the last seventeen years because of the many billions of our money that are lost each year through 'irregularities', basically fraud and corruption. But don't worry, our EU bosses have a solution. No, they're not proposing to cut down on fraud, so that our money is spent more carefully. Instead they're thinking of avoiding the embarrassment of having the European Court of Auditors look at their accounts. Their great plan is to scrap the annual audit and either replace it with a check every five years or else do away with the audit altogether. All in all, this seems to be a rather brilliant solution to a recurring problem – billions of our money being stolen by EU insiders and their friends and acquaintances.

Parliament of the privileged

One of the best jobs in recession-blighted Europe at the moment must be as a Member of the European Parliament (MEP). MEPs really struck the jackpot in 2009 while the rest of us were reeling from the impact of the financial crisis. Up till 2009, MEPs' salaries had been linked to the salaries of politicians in their home countries. But our MEPs generously decided that in 2009 they would give themselves all the same salary, regardless of country of origin. Naturally, the same salary meant the same extremely high salary. The predictable result was that well over ninety per cent of MEPs would get substantial pay rises, with some pocketing almost astronomical raises. MEPs from countries like France, Germany and Holland got about five to ten per cent more. For British and Swedish MEPs the salary rise was more than thirty per cent. And MEPs from some of the poorer, and bankrupt, countries like Portugal, Spain and Cyprus saw their remuneration double. Those, like the totally bankrupt Italians, who could have suffered a slight decrease in their pay from the harmonisation of pay rates, were allowed to choose to stay on their previous higher salary level. Overall, this extremely smart decision by our MEPs led to what we pay for their salaries and allowances going up by almost eighty per cent in just one year. MEPs now get around €95,480 a year (about £80,000) - almost £15,000 a year more than their Westminster colleagues. Plus they have very generous expenses including the SOSO ('sign on and sod off') method of getting their daily allowance of €304. This is the system which has recently been so eagerly adopted by the House of Lords as a way of avoiding peers having to show receipts to prove they ever spent any of the money they are so eagerly claiming back from us.

For more than half a century, our MEPs have wasted up to £150 million a year travelling down to their second home in Strasbourg about once a month to hold a few days of meetings, before the whole circus goes back to Brussels. The Strasbourg parliamentary buildings are unused for almost three hundred and twenty days a year. The only reason this enormous waste of our money continues is French pride and the commercial interests of Strasbourg's hoteliers, restauranteurs and prostitutes.

EU must be joking

Though, perhaps I should make clear that the majority of the prostitutes hang out on the German side of the border, where prostitution is legal, and only travel to the French side when summoned by an MEP or EU official eager to have a little boom boom in their hotel room. This Strasbourgian farcical exercise in futility has probably cost European taxpayers as much as £5 billion. But, happily for Strasbourg's hotels and whores, MEPs have consistently voted against proposals to stop wasting all this money. However in 2012, as several of Europe's largest countries' economies collapsed in smoking ruins, MEPs finally seemed to 'get it' and they voted by 429 votes to 184 to scrap the second seat in Strasbourg. This allowed our MEPs to boast self-righteously about how they too were making supposedly 'painful' cutbacks. However, our ever cynical MEPs knew well that their vote was pretty pointless as scrapping the monthly pilgrimage to Strasbourg requires a change in EU treaties to be approved unanimously by all twenty seven countries. For obvious reasons – pride, money and prostitutes - France would always oppose dropping the Strasbourg white elephant.

Great salaries, excellent expenses and the opportunity to go eating, drinking and whoring at our expense in Strasbourg once a month. Our MEPs really seem to have it all. But they also benefit from mouthwatering pensions, which are much more generous than anything on offer to our Westminster MPs or in fact anyone in the British public sector. MEPs have a non-contributory pension scheme – they don't have to pay in anything at all – and can take their pension when they reach 63 (a few years ago it was just 60). In return for contributing absolutely zilch, they get a pension of €3,341 (£2,800) for every year they serve. So, fifteen years as an MEP would give an inflation-protected pension of €50,000 (£42,000) a year for the rest of their lives. For you or I to get such a pension, we'd need somewhere in the region of £1.3 million in our pension pots. So you could say that for every year an MEP sits in the European Parliament, we taxpayers are contributing around £87,000 to their pension savings.

The CAP club for the rich

The EU's Common Agriculture Policy (CAP) costs European taxpayers around €58 billion (£48 billion) a year. That's over €300 (£240) for each European taxpayer every year. The CAP was originally introduced to make farming economically viable in Europe and to ensure European food security by encouraging farmers to increase production. Eventually it led to massive overproduction resulting in very costly lakes of unneeded milk and wine and mountains of excess beef and butter. Critics of the CAP seem to have three main grounds for attacking it. It sets trade barriers to food imports from poorer countries preventing them from trading their way out of poverty; the massive EU surpluses are dumped at low subsidised prices in Third World markets driving many local producers out of business; and it has burdened European consumers with some of the highest food prices in the world. These led one British diplomat to brand the CAP as, 'the most stupid, immoral, state-subsidised policy in human history, communism aside'.[68] But what concerns us here in *Greed Unlimited* is the way that the CAP seems to have become a means for taking money from the poor and giving it to the already rich.

Although the CAP is meant to support Europe's poorer farmers, most of the CAP's €58 billion seems to go to the least needy. Some of Europe's most prosperous countries get much more from the CAP than poorer ones. The Netherlands, for example, receive around €346 per hectare, Germany €251 per hectare, France €236 per hectare and Britain €188 per hectare, while several of Europe's poorest countries are getting less than €120 per hectare. Moreover, about eighty per cent of the CAP budget - €46 billion out of a total of €58 billion – goes to the largest EU landowners, food companies and farms. So a mere €12 billion is actually going to those who need it most. And, while several thousand recipients get more than €1 million a year, the average CAP payout is around €12,000. Some of the amounts given out to the already prosperous are impressive. In Britain, sugar company Tate and Lyle picked up more than €820 million in less than ten years and Swiss food giant Nestlé got almost €200 million in Britain alone.

While squeezing ordinary people with excessive taxes and high food prices, the CAP has done an admirable job in making Britain's rich richer. The Queen was reported as having been given around £7 million over ten years and the Duke of Westminster, with an estimated wealth of about £7 billion, received around £6 million.[69] Many other aristocratic landowners have also reportedly done quite nicely getting hundreds of thousands of pounds a year each. These include the Duke of Malborough, the Duke of Bedford, the Earl of Leicester, the 4th Baron de Ramsey, the Earl of Roseberry, and Lord Morton. Similarly, across Europe some of the wealthiest families have been made just a little bit wealthier thanks to the money we pay into the CAP. One of the most amusing cases is probably that of Hans Adam II, Crown Prince of Liechtenstein who had an estimated fortune of over €2 billion. Although neither an Austrian nor an EU citizen, the Crown Prince was revealed as one of Austria's largest recipients of CAP money. Also interesting is the fact that Romania, which has long been one of the most corrupt countries in the EU (along with Bulgaria), has around 235 beneficiaries each receiving more than €1 million each in CAP funds. This means that Romania has more 'CAP millionaires' than any other country. Whether any of these Romanian farming millionaires actually does any farming, or whether most of them are just mafia bosses, is not known.

Following lobbying by organisations pushing for transparency in government, the EU authorities instructed EU countries to publish details of the names of recipients of CAP funds and how much they were getting. That's how we know that many of Europe's great and good were making a mint out of the CAP, while the continent's poorest farmers were struggling to make ends meet. Some countries did actually reveal the information, but many fought long and hard to hide who was getting what from the CAP and when they eventually did produce the data, several did it in such a way as to make the information unusable or even meaningless. Possibly embarrassed by the revelation that the CAP had become a mechanism for taking money from hard-pressed European taxpayers and distributing much of it to the already well off, the rich and powerful fought back. In 2011 the European Court of Justice ruled that naming individuals and companies who were in receipt of our money would 'violate their right to privacy'. Following that decision, publication of CAP payments has pretty much ground to a halt and the rich and powerful can now rest easy, comfortable in the knowledge that we ordinary taxpayers can no longer find out how much of our money they are pocketing.

Jobs, jobs, jobs....for the euro-elite

The economies of the many European countries may be shrinking and unemployment may be rocketing, but if you're a lucky member of the euro-elite there are well-paid, well-pensioned jobs galore. The 33,000 or so working for the European Commission are only a small part of the euro-jobs mountain. One area that has seen massive growth in the last few years, even since the economic crash, has been EU quangos. Before the crash there were around thirty of these, by 2012 there were over fifty employing more than ten thousand people. This was an astonishing rise of over sixty per cent. The cost of each EU quango employee, including salary, office and other expenses is over €248,000 (£207,000) a year.

These many bodies deal with all sorts of things like human rights, food safety, gender equality, disease prevention, health and much more, usually duplicating, triplicating, quadruplicating and worse similar agencies that exist in many of the twenty seven EU member states. For example, we pay around £70 million a year for our own probably pointless Equality and Human Rights Commission. Yet European taxpayers have to fork out another €20 million (£17 million) a year for the equally pointless European Agency for Fundamental Rights and a further €8 million (£7 million) a year for the asinine Institute for Gender Equality.

But there's more. In addition to its own staff, the EU uses about 250 committees to help it draft new laws to keep us under control. There are so many of these committees that the EU publishes a *Register of Comitology of the European Commission* to help the uninitiated find their way around this bureaucratic maze. About 7,000 lucky folk work part time to support these committees. Then there are over a thousand 'specialist groups' with around 40,000 experts who are consulted by the EU. So, in addition to the ten thousand full-time employees of the various EU quangos, there are possibly about 47,000 part-time real and self-appointed experts who can all fly around the EU in business class, stay in the best hotels, eat at the best restaurants and claim generous expenses and other allowances for attending important meetings to assist the EU in the task of ruling its five hundred million largely obedient but increasingly distrustful citizens.

One of the demands of protesters in Greece, Spain and

Portugal is that the EU should be investing to create jobs. But the EU is already investing to create tens of thousands of jobs. Unfortunately these jobs are just for the euro-elite, their friends and family members and are just giving us more and more cripplingly expensive bureaucracy, rather than real productive economic growth.

More, more, more

EU Commission President José Manuel Barroso, a former politician from the thoroughly bankrupt Portugal, has claimed to understand the financial pressures that European countries are under, 'we know that national treasuries are facing difficult choices and, in some cases, extremely painful decisions'.[70] And in an EU press release, the Commission apparently showed its understanding of the squeeze on its citizens' finances, 'the vast majority of people across the EU feel the daily pain of the crisis as their national, regional and local governments have to make cuts'.[71] However, as so often is the case when our leaders talk of pain and austerity and cuts and so on, they automatically take the attitude not only that they personally should be exempt, but that they should get even more of our money to squander on themselves. When the EU presented its budget proposal for 2013, it decided that, while demanding many European governments cut spending, the EU should be given an extra €9 billion of our money. This would raise the amount of our money taken by the EU from €129 billion in 2012 to €138 billion in 2013, a budget increase of around 6.8 per cent. Rumour has it that EU departments were told to push up their demands for more of our money – 'to bump up' their forecasts - so that, when a final compromise figure was eventually agreed with national governments, the EU would still end up with an increased budget.[72] As Britain pays just over twelve per cent of the EU's budget, this increase would have cost us about an extra €1.1 billion (£930 million) a year. Or, to put this in terms of nurses or police, enough to pay for over thirty thousand more nurses or police officers each year.

The EU Commission tried to fend off the inevitable protests from hard-pressed governments by claiming that it too was making cuts by reducing its staff. But this seems to have just been a game of smoke and mirrors. While the EU announced that it was cutting 286 positions from its total workforce of 40,775 (a cut of less than one per cent), it was also adding 280 staff following the accession of Croatia in mid 2013. Moreover, considering that around two thousand EU staff retire or lucratively resign due to supposed ill health every year, while pretending to make cuts, the EU was actually going on a massive hiring spree.

Unfortunately for us, there are more countries in the EU that are beneficiaries of EU funding than there are countries which are net losers. These beneficiaries – countries that like to receive much more than they are prepared to give – have helpfully (for themselves) formed a group called *Friends of Cohesion Policy*. If you check the members of *Friends of Cohesion Policy* – countries like Bulgaria, Romania, Latvia, Greece – they almost read like a roll call of Europe's most corrupt and most spendthrift states. These countries naturally argue that there should not be any cuts to the EU budget. In fact, they have claimed that the requested 6.8 per cent increase was an 'absolute minimum'.[73] So, even though there are some countries who might like to oppose Barroso's grab for more of our money, they will always be outvoted by those who want ever more of our cash. This has allowed Barroso to brazenly claim that only 'a minority' of people oppose the EU's proposed budget increases. As could be expected, a compromise agreement was reached giving the wasteful, corrupt EU yet another increase in its budget. The 2.8 per cent rise would cost British taxpayers an extra £350 million a year – about £1 million a day – enough to pay for 11,000 police officers or nurses. Coincidentally, this £350 million extra from British taxpayers was the same amount that the EU was spending on a new luxury office block for EU officials. So at least our money wasn't being wasted.

As the Coalition Government forces through cuts in Britain, one might have expected our leaders to demand similar financial discipline in Brussels. Sadly this has not been the case. As a former MEP and possibly future highly-paid, highly-pensioned EU commissioner, Nick Clegg has repeatedly shown his usual complete disregard for how our tax money is squandered by often championing the EU's interests over those of the UK and has vigorously defended the blatantly wasteful and corrupt EU against its critics. As for David Cameron, the most that he has asked for is an EU budget freeze. Something more appropriate, like suggesting a five per cent a year reduction in EU spending, doesn't seem to have crossed his radar. The pusillanimity of the British and other European governments and their fear of upsetting their lords and masters in Brussels have meant that, while we get squeezed, the EU spending frenzy goes on, unaffected by the dire economic crisis engulfing the countries which have to pay for it.

Actually, our EU rulers rather dislike the constant demeaning haggling with national governments over how much money they can take from us. For years they have tried to get what they call their 'own resources' – that is the opportunity to fund their profligacy by taxing us directly rather than having to ask member governments for ever-increasing amounts of money. The EU has made at least three proposals for taxes to be paid directly into its coffers – a carbon tax, a tax on financial services and a special EU VAT. If our Brussels bosses ever get their own way and are allowed to tax us directly, then Pandora's Box will be well and truly open and there will be almost no limit to how much of our cash the eurocrats will take and waste while instructing the rest of us to live more frugally.

Chapter 8

Is the NHS clinically obese?

You're cutting. No we're not. Yes you are. No we're not. Yes...

The headlines seem to say it all. We've had 'NHS cuts will seriously damage your health', and 'Nowhere to turn for patients as cuts hit' and 'NHS cuts have affected patient care say four out of five doctors'. Moreover, healthcare professionals have not been sparing in their dire warnings about what is happening to the NHS – 'these figures are yet further evidence of the rising scale of cuts to NHS jobs and services'.[74]

Reading these, it seems clear that the Coalition must be intent on decimating our much loved National Health Service. Yet government ministers could be forgiven if they are slightly confused by the barrage of invective being so enthusiastically directed their way. After all, spending on the NHS is planned to increase every year of the Coalition's expected time in office (see Figure 1).

Figure 1 – The Coalition is not making any cuts to the NHS's budget

Year	Cash budget	Inflation adjusted
2010/11	£99.0bn	£99.0bn
2011/12	£102.8bn	£99.8bn
2012/13	£105.3bn	£99.8bn
2013/14	£108.3bn	£99.9bn
2014/15	£111.2bn	£99.9bn

So, on the one side of the great argument about NHS supposed cuts we are being told that 'NHS trusts must stop making cuts in a quick fix attempt to save money' while the Government claims 'we believe passionately in the NHS, and this is why funding will increase by £12.5 billion over the next four years, protecting the NHS for the future'.[75] This might leave some taxpayers wondering what is really happening. After all, both these opposing views cannot be right. Or can they?

Protecting the holy cow

Of all our public services, the NHS is probably the one which most frightens politicians of all parties. They know that the voting public reveres the NHS and so no party dares to suggest that

Is the NHS clinically obese?

NHS funding should ever be cut. Under Brown, the NHS was the department which was given the largest increase in taxpayers' money – from around £45 billion in 1997 when New Labour first came to power to a massive £100 billion or so by the time Brown was finally prised out of Downing Street. Moreover, this extraordinary leap in spending doesn't do justice to the real level of increase, as many new hospitals have been built using about £229 billion of Private Finance Initiative (PFI) deals. With these projects, private companies build and often run new hospitals and we taxpayers are contracted to pay for these over the next twenty to thirty years, whether we need them or not. So, the bottom line is that, by the time of the 2010 General Election, the NHS was swimming, some people might even say 'drowning', in our money. Never before in its history had the NHS had so much of our cash. Moreover, the Coalition has promised to give the NHS even more of our money because they are terrified of being branded as the party that was out to destroy the NHS.

So, given that by 2010 the NHS was getting at least twice as much of our money compared to a decade earlier, even if it was asked to make cuts of a few per cent, it should have managed these without too much trouble. However, the Coalition government didn't even dare ask the NHS to make any real cuts. Instead it gave the NHS a slight increase in its budget each year while setting the NHS a target of cutting about £4 billion a year from improving efficiency – a £4 billion saving that the NHS was allowed to keep to be reinvested in frontline services. Yet in spite of being protected from any real cuts, the NHS seems to have found it necessary to start slashing the number of medical staff to meet very generous and completely unchallenging financial targets.

More managers, fewer beds

Many millions of words have been written about the NHS by thousands of real and self-proclaimed experts. Some praise the NHS to the skies for the selfless devotion of its staff and the excellence of its service. Others accuse it of being inefficient and almost criminally wasteful with taxpayers' money. So, rather than add to the many volumes that have already been produced, it's probably better that I show just one simple picture which could be said to sum up what is actually happening in our health service. Figure 2 shows the number of hospital beds per manager since Gordon Brown first started hosing our money into the seemingly bottomless pit that is the NHS.

Figure 2 – A decade ago, we had about 8 hospital beds per manager, now there are less than 4

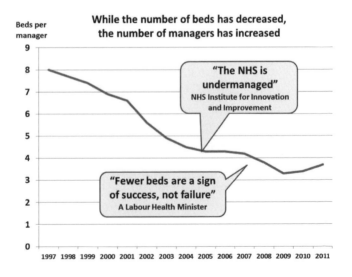

Is the NHS clinically obese?

In 1997, we had about 200,000 hospital beds and around 25,000 managers in the NHS in England. By 2011, the number of hospital beds had fallen to less than 140,000 while the number of managers apparently needed to manage ever fewer beds had shot up to around 40,000, after peaking at over 44,000 in 2009. NHS bigwigs, of course, were able to give excellent reasons how it was possible to reduce the number of hospital beds without harming patient care. A Department of Health spokesman explained, 'bed numbers have fallen because people are being treated much more quickly – spending less time in hospital – and for many conditions medical advances mean they do not need to go to hospital at all'.[76] Unfortunately, the spokesman didn't explain why, if treating patients was so much easier and quicker and simpler, the NHS absolutely had to have almost twice as many managers as it had just over a decade earlier. Nor did he explain why, if treating many conditions was cheaper, the NHS had to have ever more of our money year after year.

Moreover, while our Department of Health seemed to feel that having lots of hospital beds in a health service was something of an anachronism, health services in almost every other European country didn't appear to fully agree. By 2010, Britain was ranked as 25th out of thirty two European countries in terms of the number of beds per hundred thousand of the population. Countries like Germany, Lithuania, Austria, the Czech Republic and Hungary had twice as many hospital beds per hundred thousand people and others like France, Belgium, Finland and Latvia had almost twice as many hospital beds as us (see Figure 3).

Figure 3 – Britain has a shockingly low number of hospital beds compared to many other European countries

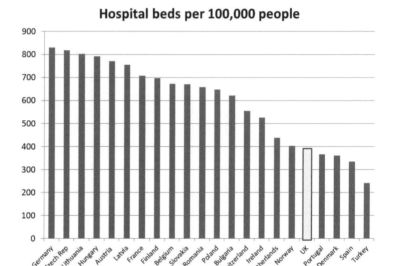

Hospital beds per 100,000 people

What has happened to our NHS is a massive 'managerialisation' of health services. While the number of nurses in England has gone from about 320,000 to around 370,000 (a rise of fifteen per cent) over a decade and the number of doctors in England has increased by a very healthy forty per cent from around 100,000 to 143,000, the number of managers and senior managers has shot up by almost eighty per cent from somewhere around 25,000 to close to 45,000 at the highest point in 2009.

More, more, more

Another change in the NHS under Gordon Brown's very unique approach to management has been an impressive increase in pay for most NHS staff. Nurses saw their pay go up by an admirable sixty eight per cent. As a result of the Department of Health's hopelessly-mismanaged negotiations on new contracts for doctors, many of them saw their take-home pay more than doubling under New Labour from an average of £36,700 to almost £75,000 with most GPs and senior hospital doctors making comfortably over £100,000 a year. But way in the lead, in terms of being paid more, were the many tens of thousands of managers whose salaries jumped by at least a hundred and twenty per cent. Those who seem to have done best from Brown's largesse with our money were hospital chief executives and other senior managers. By 2011, there were over 650 NHS managers earning more than the Prime Minister and most of these also had unfunded pension entitlements worth millions of pounds each. Paying these pensions would be a crippling drain on NHS funds for decades to come. The year 2009 to 2010 was an especially fine bumper year for NHS chiefs. Probably sensing that Labour were on the way out and that the Tories were less likely to be as generous with taxpayers' money as the apparently soft-hearted Gordon Brown, like top bureaucrats in so many other government departments, large numbers of NHS bosses did a 'grab it while you can' and managed to pocket pay rises of over ten per cent in just one year, taking the salaries of some to over £200,000 a year and also considerably increasing the generous pensions they would receive out of NHS funds for the rest of their lives.

In addition to the rising salary and managerial costs of the NHS, we taxpayers also had to pay for a more than doubling of the budget of the Department of Health, its quangos and regional authorities from about £6 billion a year to well over £12 billion a year. Over and above the many more civil servants directly employed by the Department, we also got dozens of new arms-length agencies and committees including such gems as the Cosmetic Surgery Steering Group, Advisory Board on Registration of Homeopathic Medicines, Alcohol Education and Research Council, Herbal Medicines Advisory Committee, Independent Advisory Group on Sexual Health and HIV, and the Leadership and Race Equality Action Plan Independent Panel. If you had a stroke, got pregnant, needed a new hip or were seriously injured in a car crash, it's not obvious that any of these expensive new agencies and committees would have been of much use to you.

Moreover, many billions more of our money were spent by New Labour creating even more bureaucratic bodies to assist the Department of Health in its attempts to supposedly improve the performance of the NHS. New Labour set up at least one new healthcare regulator each year it was in power, though 2004 was a bumper year with no fewer than three new regulators being imposed on us. In 2001, we got the National Patient Safety Agency – about £30 million a year and over three hundred staff. In 2002, there was the Nursing and Midwifery Council – about £24 million a year and two hundred and forty plus staff. In 2002 we also were given the NHS Confederation – £26.5 million a year. In 2003 the Health Protection Agency began work - £250 million a year and over three thousand staff. In the same year there was the Medicines and Healthcare Products Regulatory Agency - £80 million budget and eighty staff. In 2004 our healthcare bureaucrats hit the jackpot. In January, Monitor appeared on the scene – over £13 million a year. There was also the Healthcare Commission - £80 million a year and over five hundred staff. And not to forget the Commission for Social Care Inspection - £164 million and 2,335 staff. I could go on. There are still a few more to come. But you probably get the picture by now. All these new bodies were apparently Blair's and Brown's way of fulfilling the pledge given in New Labour's 1997 election manifesto, 'the key is to root out unnecessary administrative cost and to spend money on the right things – frontline care'. Looking at what had actually happened, one commentator recently remarked, 'of all the billions poured into the NHS, it is just sickening to see how much of it has been soaked up by this ever-expanding bureaucracy, particularly these quangos'. [77]

Nobody wastes it better

Awash with our money and teeming with ever increasing numbers of managers, regulators and other bureaucrats, the NHS has scored some truly remarkable own goals by wasting stomach-churning amounts of our cash. The greatest own goal of all time was probably the NHS's ludicrous computer system, the *National Programme for Information Technology* (NPfIT) which was smartly rebranded as *Connecting for Health* to make it seem like a jolly good, patient-friendly idea. For years we were told what a huge success this was and how we would all benefit from it. When I wrote my 2006 book *Plundering the Public Sector*, I was fortunate to have someone very close to the programme brief me on what was really going on behind the scenes. The person described a programme which was not necessary; which had little to no benefits for patients; which could never work either technically or organisationally; which was causing massive disruption; and which would waste billions of pounds, possibly more than £12 billion – rather more than the supposed budget of £2.4 billion. Armed with all this material, I dedicated two chapters of *Plundering* to exposing the NHS IT disaster. Shortly after the publication of my book, I was invited (or summoned) to a meeting with the then head of the National Audit Office (NAO) Sir John Bourne and a few of his obedient sidekicks. The NAO was just about to issue a report praising the *Connecting for Health* project and describing it as one of the best-run public-sector computer systems projects the NAO had ever seen. The NAO's report was later described as 'gushing' by one member of the largely impotent and easily fooled Public Accounts Committee. So, the forty pages of criticism and abuse I directed at the scheme and its management in *Plundering* were not terribly welcome by those who were making a good living running this great and costly enterprise and its various enthusiastic cheerleaders. Sir John kindly took time out of his undoubtedly busy schedule to explain to me politely but firmly why all my conclusions about the project being a ghastly, chaotic, useless and expensive catastrophe were absolutely wrong. Moreover, another Whitehall grandee and Knight of the Realm, who shall remain nameless, also called me in and took me to task for my 'irresponsible attack' on what he called an 'important and well-run government project'. And in a meeting in Westminster, I was lambasted by the £250,000 or so a year head of the project for my supposedly unfounded and inaccurate criticisms.

A couple of years later, when one of the largest firms involved in the disaster pulled, out, the authorities still maintained that all was well in the best possible of worlds and our money kept on flowing into the pockets of computer systems companies and management consultants.

But by 2011, about five years and probably more than £6 billion down the drain later, the NAO under a new boss finally realised that my source had been right all along about almost everything and, a few months after a highly critical 2011 NAO report on the project, the whole fiasco was finally abandoned. When lambasting the Coalition for its NHS cuts,

Is the NHS clinically obese?

Labour politicians, who were fully responsible for this absurd, hopelessly mismanaged, easily predictable waste of our money, seem to have forgotten that the £6 billion or more which was lost through Labour's own astounding managerial incompetence on the *Connecting For Health* fiasco could have paid the salaries of about 20,000 nurses for ten years.

Own goal number two has probably cost us about half as much as the *Connecting for Health* flop. For about ten years, the NHS has been spending over £350 million a year on management consultants. Naturally, the management consultants' trade body defended so much of taxpayers' money flowing into their members' pockets rather than being spent on apparently unimportant things like improving patient care, 'consultancies bring an invaluable external perspective, focus and discipline' and 'this spending also generates significant benefits for patients and taxpayers' and 'an organisation as complex and fast-changing as the NHS is entitled to benefit from the high quality advice and delivery that is offered by Management Consultants Association member companies'.[78] For more than a decade, the NHS has been shelling out close to £10,000 per manager per year on management consultants. Many taxpayers and patients might wonder why NHS managers needed just under £10,000 consultancy each year to help these managers do the jobs they were already handsomely paid to do or even why all these managers were ever hired in the first place if they were not capable of fulfilling their roles without consultancy help. One health service insider gave his view of this consultancy spending, 'these figures are shocking and nothing short of a scandal…. There are currently more managers within the NHS than at any point in its history, so why are Strategic Health Authorities and Primary Care Trusts buying in additional expertise?'[79] Moreover, in spite of all the hopefully excellent and expensive consultancy assistance the NHS has received over the years from members of the venerable Management Consultants Association, research for the Office for National Statistics suggests that productivity in the NHS declined every year that New Labour was pouring ever more of our money into our health service and into the bank accounts of management consultants.

The destructive effects of own goal number three are only beginning to be felt. Own goal number three was the NHS's headlong rush into building new hospitals and other medical facilities using twenty- to thirty-year PFI contracts. These have, predictably (see *Plundering the Public Sector* by Craig and Brooks and endless copies of *Private Eye*) turned out to be hugely profitable for the PFI companies and financial nightmares for the NHS. It's not yet clear how many hospitals will be driven to bankruptcy by their PFI contracts, nor how many billions of NHS money will have to be diverted from frontline care into the pockets of PFI companies to save some of these hospitals from the incompetence of their highly-paid senior managers. The true extent of own goal number three will probably not be fully known for another five or more years. But there are still many very expensive skeletons to come out of many NHS hospital cupboards.

The real NHS obesity problem

We hear a lot from the media about how Britain's obesity epidemic is imposing huge new costs on our health services. However, perhaps the real obesity problem is within the NHS itself. By 2010, we had an NHS that was getting more than twice as much money as a decade earlier; where there were many more staff than a decade earlier; where most of those staff were being paid considerably more than a decade earlier; where the biggest winners were the legions of managers; and where those who had really struck gold were senior managers with their massive salaries and eye-watering pensions. We may think that the NHS's many managers are siphoning huge amounts of money away from frontline patient care now. But the situation is going to be considerably worse when Brown's bumper-pay bureaucrats start to reach retirement age. To quote another commentator who seemed unimpressed with how the NHS was using and too often abusing our money, 'while the NHS budget has exploded over the last decade much of the cash has been spent on a big increase in management roles, meaning taxpayers' money is increasingly spent on overly generous pensions for pen pushers instead of frontline services and patient care'.[80]

It seems more than clear that our enforced generosity to the NHS has unfortunately not given us taxpayers an efficient, world-class health service. Instead, our leaders have allowed the development of an organisation that is fat, bloated, obese and lazy; that has got used to gorging itself on ever-increasing amounts of our money; where the least deserving are the most highly paid; where those who do work hard to provide real patient care are being smothered by the edicts and interference of the many thousands of bureaucrats in largely unnecessary agencies and quangos; where huge amounts of our money, many billions of pounds, are wasted without anybody raising an eyebrow; and where any suggestion that budgets could easily be cut without damaging patient care are met with howls of protest as the 'shroud-wavers' take to the barricades to defend their own privileges while hiding behind the pretence of caring only about the wellbeing of patients.

It's not obvious why hospitals now need a bunch of highly-paid, highly-pensioned directors including such posts as a chief executive, a strategy director, a director of communications, a development director, a financial director and often several other similar worthies. A letter from a retired surgeon and a nurse to a Sunday newspaper said the unsayable:

> For years it has been apparent to us that enormous sums
> can be saved by cutting bureaucracy and management
> costs in the NHS. A hospital can run its own affairs with
> a medical superintendent, matron and administrator.
> That was how it was done before modern management
> was thrust upon us.[81]

The NHS's budget increases will slow down under the
Coalition and the Government has asked the NHS to make efficiency savings of around £20 billion over four years. To its
credit, the NHS seems to have started cutting back on the number of managers. These fell from a peak of 44,600 in England in
2009 to 42,000 in 2010 and then 38,000 in 2011 a drop of fifteen
per cent over two years. But the 2011 number of managers was
still about fifty per cent higher than when New Labour first came
to power. Moreover, behind these headline figures of a reduction
in managerial headcount, there were some very lucky bunnies
indeed as NHS chiefs set off a redundancy feeding frenzy that
will cost us many millions. Moreover, in some cases executives
started playing the extremely profitable 'Goodbye-Hello Game'.
It's impossible to know how widespread this was, but some of
the figures are impressive. One NHS fatcat got £700,000 of our
money in an early retirement package from an NHS trust and
then was paid £230,000 (plus £40,000 to an agency) for twelve
months' work at another NHS trust while supposedly being retired. Another pocketed a redundancy payment of more than
£300,000 and four months later took up an interim management
job at a different hospital where he was paid £205,000 for just
six months work.

Meanwhile, other hospitals paid huge sums for interim
managers because they apparently couldn't find any capable

candidates amongst the NHS's remaining 38,000 or so managers. These interim managers probably wouldn't appear on the full-time employee headcount though they would cost us taxpayers quite a pile of money. The Imperial College Healthcare Trust in London might end up paying close to £800,000 for two years' work by its interim chief executive. NHS Croydon spent more than £625,000 on three temporary executives in 2010/11. Milton Keynes Hospital Foundation Trust forked out £213,000 for ten months of its interim chief executive while it planned to shed 280 positions. And Luton Primary Care Trust could afford to pay its interim director of commissioning £260,000 for one year's work. These situations seem to have been repeated across the NHS with hospitals in South East Essex, Dorset, Walsall, West Hertfordshire and many others feeling that their interim senior bosses all should get hundreds of thousands of pounds a year each.

However, in spite of the fact that the NHS has proved to be a recidivist squanderer of our money with plenty of fat that could be reduced, the Government's attempt to limit its budget increases without making any cuts appear to have resulted in frontline staff being culled. The NHS bureaucrats, of course, denied this, 'the fall in the NHS staff numbers is primarily in non-clinical, primarily managerial, posts'.[82] And, equally predictably, those who could be seen as protecting NHS vested interests seemed outraged 'these figures are yet further evidence of the rising scale of cuts to NHS jobs and services'.[83]

Between 2010 and 2011, the number of doctors continued to go up, from about 141,000 in England to almost 144,000. But, because of the effects of the European Working Time Directive, we were probably getting less hours work per doctor. So patients may not have benefited from the extra 3,000 doctors even though they would have cost us taxpayers at least £150 million more a year. The number of nurses, always a very sensitive political issue, did fall – from around 373,000 in England in 2010 to close to 370,000 in 2011. This was less than a one per cent drop, hardly dramatic and hardly what could be called a 'savage cut'. The fall in the number of clinical support staff - from about 356,000 to 347,000 – was perhaps more significant at around 2.5%. It's difficult to define exactly why qualified medical staff needed to be cut. Often it was because hospitals were going bankrupt because of the extortionate fees they were paying to extremely profitable PFI companies due to the incompetent way these contracts had been negotiated by highly-paid NHS bosses.

When you look at the vast amounts of money that have been hosed onto the NHS, the impressive increases in staffing levels and the more than generous pay rises given to staff, particularly managers. Then you see continuing reductions in numbers of beds and poorer outcomes than many other European countries in terms of survival rates for conditions like cancers and strokes, it's difficult to conclude that we taxpayers are really getting good value for the hundred billion or so the NHS now takes from us each year. But, the Coalition Government has a solution – yet another NHS reorganisation.

Lansley's great plan

This is probably neither the time nor the place to provide a detailed analysis of Mr Lansley's Byzantine NHS reorganisation plans. But a few small details are probably worth mentioning. Firstly, as far as I can make out, the only 'proper' job Mr Lansley has had before entering a lucrative career in politics was five years spent as a civil servant at the Department for Trade and Industry (DTI) also affectionately known by those who have dealt with it as the 'Department for Total Incompetence'. Then as

150

Is the NHS clinically obese?

Shadow Health Minister, Lansley was, in many people's opinion, curiously ineffective in exposing New Labour's uncontrolled healthcare spending and the disastrous NHS computer system.

It seems that the main driving force behind the reforms may be former PM Tony Blair's favourite management consultancy, McKinsey & Company. In fact, so great appears to be McKinsey's influence on the NHS reorganisation that one newspaper even wrote an article headlined 'The firm that hijacked the NHS'.[84] Judging from stories leaking out of the NHS, McKinsey seem to be making many millions helping the NHS implement the proposed reforms. Unfortunately, due to a broken computer hard drive, I have lost a copy of a McKinsey proposal to restructure the NHS which was prepared for New Labour about six or seven years ago. But looking at Lansley's reforms, I have a horrible feeling that McKinsey have pretty much taken the stuff they knocked out a few years ago for New Labour, changed a few diagrams and the date and expensively presented it to Mr Lansley as a great new solution for our health service. But I still have the words of a song reportedly sung by McKinsey consultants at a Christmas party (possibly to the tune of *Hark the Herald Angels Sing*). The first of five rather revealing verses goes something like this (repeat the last two lines as a chorus):

If you aim to get the best results
And maximum performance you want to see
Then you really should consult
A Management Consultancy
McKinsey management consultants are we
We take all our clients' money
We can earn many a million
Because our clients have no vision[85]

Public-sector feeding frenzy

Worryingly, Mr Lansley and others keep referring to the Government's plans for the NHS as a 'transformation' of our health service. We saw in Chapter 4 - *Like candy from a baby,* the havoc wreaked at financial services giant Aviva when its bosses, lucratively assisted by highly-paid management consultants, subjected that company to its 'transformation'. Some commentators have not been impressed by Mr Lansley's healthcare revolution:

> Those with knowledge of the health service observe that the scheme has become such an incoherent mess that it can't deliver what it originally promised. Instead of less bureaucracy, we will end up with more. Instead of saving money, it will cost more. Instead of offering patients more choice it will deliver less.[86]

The Government, which had once promised us 'no more top-down reorganisations of the NHS', claims that its top-down reorganisation will save the NHS about £5 billion by 2015. But when launching great new initiatives, governments have a tendency to over-egg the potential benefits somewhat. Moreover, against these possibly chimeric savings, we need to put the cost of the reorganisation. With consultancy fees and redundancy costs, these should be comfortably north of £1.4 billion. It seems that a fair portion of this money may go in redundancy payments to bureaucrats playing the 'Goodbye-Hello' game. The Government claims it will move around 18,000 NHS staff without paying them any redundancy money, 'this overall approach to filling posts is designed to minimise the number of redundancies required'.[87] But it remains to be seen if this will really happen or whether thousands will be given generous redundancy payments on losing their jobs when primary care trusts and strategic health authorities are scrapped and then rehired to do their old jobs working for local authorities or GP commissioning groups. Moreover, that may leave another 20,000 bureaucrats with apparently nowhere to go.

All in all, rather than producing a new, slim-line, effective health service, our government's top-down NHS reorganisation might end up being similar to the famous description of reorganisations, usually probably wrongly attributed to Gaius Petronius Arbiter, but possibly written by either a classically-trained and somewhat disgruntled British army conscript in the 1940s or by US soldier and later writer Charlton Ogburn, Jr:

> We trained hard, but it seemed that every time we were beginning to form up into teams we would be reorganised. ... I was to learn later in life that we tend to meet any new situation by reorganising; and a wonderful method it can be for creating the illusion of progress while producing confusion, inefficiency and demoralisation.

Part 4

Austerity for oiks

Chapter 9

To the bone?

Our executhieves are wallowing in money. Our politicians keep on taking more and more of our cash for themselves. Cameron has hugely increased the cost of politics while pretending he wanted to do the opposite. With his attempt to change the way we vote for MPs and his proposed reforms of the House of Lords including his ludicrous idea of having 300 or 400 or 450 or whatever number of elected highly-paid peers, Nick Clegg would have pushed up the cost of politics even more. Osborne's Treasury gets more expensive by the day. Our top bureaucrats are dodging and weaving to keep their salaries, pensions and other comforts while dutifully and hypocritically nodding obeisance to the new gods of austerity. And the EU can't see any reason why the countries it is pushing into economic collapse shouldn't pay ever more money to be wasted or stolen by our well-remunerated masters in Brussels. But in some areas, particularly the military and the police, there have been real cuts and they have been brutal.

A military massacre

Imagine what would happen if the Government was to suddenly announce that it was firing twenty per cent of NHS staff. That would include 28,800 of England's 144,000 doctors and 74,000 of England's 370,000 nurses. There would be public horror, protest marches, strikes and screaming press headlines from papers on both the Left and the Right. There would be utter chaos in the House of Commons with Opposition MPs foaming at the mouth in paroxysms of fury. In the Lords they would have had to call ambulances as both ageing, rheumy-eyed and young, ambitious peers exploded in outrage. And there would have been utter delight at the BBC as its self-righteous reporters all tried to outdo each other in a frenzy of apoplectic shroud-waving warning us how many millions would now die as a result of the Government's inhumanity and cruelty.

Yet, when the Government decided to axe about twenty per cent of our military personnel, what did we get? Virtual silence. The BBC spent a couple of minutes covering the Secretary of Defence's statement. Some papers did run a few articles worrying about the extent of the cuts. And the Shadow Defence Secretary did say, 'we are concerned about the human and military impact of these job losses. Capability is being lost, as are people's livelihoods', plus a few other things. But where was the anger? Where was the fury? Where was the outrage? Where were all the fuming, chest-beating, self-righteous, infuriated professional handwringers?

The cuts planned for our military are serious and may even be catastrophic. We should remember the old dictum 'the more you disarm, the more you make war a certainty'. Our enemies will no doubt be watching our Government's defence cuts with delight. By 2020, the navy will cut 8,500 jobs reducing its workforce from 37,500 to 29,000. The RAF will slash 11,000, slimming from 42,500 to 31,500. But the army will have to shed a shocking 20,000 taking it from 102,000 to 82,000. In all, some 39,500 military personnel will be thrown on the scrapheap along with another 18,500 civilians who worked to support the military (see Figure 1).

Figure 1 – There has been little public and media reaction to the cuts imposed on our armed forces

	Navy	Army	RAF	Civilians
The cuts to our military would provoke outrage if they were happening in any other public service				
2011	37,500	102,000	42,500	69,900
2015	30,000	90,000	33,000	57,800
2020	29,000	82,000	31,500	51,400
Cuts	-23%	-20%	-26%	-26%

Unfortunately, our military leaders were at least in part responsible for this appalling massacre. The military top brass probably made three inexcusable mistakes – they wasted billions on incompetently planned and hopelessly managed military equipment purchasing projects; they became top heavy, turning themselves into figures of ridicule when it was revealed we had more admirals than ships, more air vice marshals than squadrons and more senior army officers than regiments; and they sent their troops with inadequate equipment into Blair's seemingly endless, not always easily justifiable wars without any proper planning for an exit strategy.

Wasting away

Each year, an entertaining high point in the parliamentary calendar is when the bigwigs from the military appear before the Public Accounts Committee (PAC) to try to defend themselves against the many recurring examples of incompetence and waste revealed in the annual National Audit Office (NAO) review of the main military procurement projects. In 2006, the top twenty projects were £2.6 billion over budget and twenty two years late. Over the years the MoD has spend hundreds of millions on management consultants to teach thousands of MoD staff how to do what they call 'Smart Procurement' and how to get some proper financial controls in place. Perhaps the MoD should ask the consultants to give this money back, as by 2011 just a few of the top fifteen projects were £4.7 billion over budget and these fifteen projects were now twenty seven years late. In addition, £3.4 billion was squandered on the Nimrod project before it was cancelled altogether. In total, around £8.1 billion of our money could be said to have magically vanished.

There were two main reasons for the continuing and worsening problems with these projects. Firstly, the military were totally hopeless at proper project management and financial control. And secondly, in order to get exciting new toys to play with, military leaders would deliberately lowball the likely cost knowing well that once their favourite programme was started, it would be almost impossible to stop it, however much its costs over-ran the original budget. As the NAO concluded, much of the overspend was due to 'a weak programme management culture, which lacked transparency, neglected or overrode project control systems and disciplines, and produced forecasts that lacked "depth and reality."'[88]

Even assuming that just half of this £8.1 billion of

overspend was lost through incompetent project management, this £4 billion or so would probably have been enough to pay the salaries and equipment for at least 15,000 soldiers, sailors and airmen for five years. In other words, if this money had not been flushed down the toilet, there probably wouldn't have been any need to have made the drastic cuts in service personnel that the Government is now embarked on and the military could have reduced its numbers and spending gradually through 'natural wastage' as at least 6,000 to 8,000 retire from the military each year.

Top heavy with top brass

One critic of Britain's military elites compared the British military to the US Marine Corps and suggested that the British military had too many officers and too many hierarchical levels. In Britain we have around 490 officers of brigadier level and above for a force of 180,000, while the US Marine Corps has just 86 for their 200,000 troops. This may or may not be a totally valid comparison as the structures of the two forces are a bit different. But it does indicate that we may be paying too much for too many military bosses. Since the 1990s, as the number of other ranks has reduced, the number of officers in the British military has increased. This is an excellent example of part of Parkinson's Law that all bureaucracies grow 'irrespective of any variation in the amount of work (if any) to be done'. Parkinson derived this observation when studying how in the ten years following the First World War, the number of admiralty officials in the British navy increased by almost eighty per cent, while the number of sailors declined by around thirty per cent. In the last twenty years, the ratio of senior officers compared to other ranks in the British military has gone up by around thirty per cent – for the RAF this figure is close to sixty per cent.

Even the military realise there is a problem with over-manning at the top. In one 'Management in Confidence' report, the author stated:

> The simple truth is that the Defence senior cadre is larg-er than we can afford, is judged to be out of proportion with a reducing manpower base and also with modern working practices and societal tolerances.[89]

The report went on to explain:

> In some areas there are too many layers in our structure, which swells senior numbers and can stifle organisa-tional agility. There is evidence across Defence of over-grading of posts, excessive management layers reducing effectiveness and efficiency.

In the Navy for example, at the time of writing there were two admirals, six vice admirals and thirty three rear admirals – so forty one big cheeses in all. Plus there were eighty Commodores and three hundred Captains. That gave 421 officers for less than forty fighting ships and submarines. It's quite difficult to imag-ine how all these officers fill their working days when so few of them have ships or submarines or other such playthings to oc-cupy their time and efforts. When criticised for having so many admirals, the Navy claimed it actually had a couple more ships than were reported as the newspaper article didn't include two landing craft. In the RAF, we have twenty six Air Vice Marshals, ninety Air Commodores and 330 Group Captains for around 820 planes, included in which are only twelve fast-jet squadrons.

So, our navy didn't have nearly enough ships for all its top brass and the RAF had about two planes per senior officer.

To the bone?

This makes it look as if we have too many officers at too many different levels (see Figure 2).

Figure 2 – "The size of the senior cadre has increased as a proportion of personnel strength by approximately a third since 1990"[90]

The number of different ranks in the military could seem excessive for a modern organisation	
ROYAL AIR FORCE	**ROYAL NAVY**
Marshal of the RAF	Admiral of the Fleet
Air Chief Marshal	Admiral
Air Marshal	Vice Admiral
Air Vice Marshal	Rear Admiral
Air Commodore	Commodore
Group captain	Captain
Wing commander	Commander
Squadron Leader	Lieutenant-Commander
Flight lieutenant	Lieutenant
Flying officer	Sublieutenant
Pilot officer	Acting Sublieutenant

The current armed forces command structure might have been suitable when we were a world power with an empire to guard and when we had to fight two World Wars. But it could appear slightly top-heavy for today's much smaller and ever-shrinking military forces.

Nor has our military's reputation been helped by stories of lavish spending by the top brass on the top brass. There's £36 million a year being spent to subsidise the homes of 413 military leaders – around £87,000 per year each. Of these, thirty two receive a total of £5 million a year – over £156,000 a year each. One army general was reported to have kept a sergeant and a corporal back from going to fight in Afghanistan so they could work as servants running his home. A Tory MP and former military officer criticised the use of trained personnel as servants, 'they are being misemployed shaking out napkins and polishing cutlery when they should be with their units practising firing mortar bombs and going out on operations'.[91] Several top officers also have full-time gardeners, all paid for out of the military budget. The father of a Lance Corporal killed in Iraq didn't seem impressed by the top officers' taxpayer-subsidised lifestyles:

> My son was not given a battery for his radio or a £1.50 distress flare so he was not able to signal for help when he was attacked. Yet the MoD seems to be able to find ridiculous amounts of money so the top brass has somebody to mow their lawns and water their plants.[92]

Moreover, the military has the most expensive car pool of any government department, yet its bosses spend millions more being ferried around the UK in helicopters which perhaps could be more usefully deployed supporting our troops. In response to criticism of the amount being paid for top officers' homes and servants, an MoD spokesman said, 'senior officers filling certain posts are expected to entertain in order to enhance defence objectives'.

As part of downsizing the military, significant cuts in the number of officers are planned with the Navy going down from around 410 officers to 319 by 2020; the RAF reducing from 446 down to 330; and the army from 793 to 651. This seems to be in sharp contrast to other government departments where it looks as if the bureaucratic and managerial elites will be holding grimly on to their jobs, salaries, pensions and perks while cutting many lower-paid frontline staff. But by allowing such a build-up of excessive numbers of sometimes big-spending officers in the first place, the military's top brass have betrayed the interests and trust of the troops they command.

Not winning wars?

Perhaps the greatest betrayal of our troops was from our military leaders getting too close to New Labour politicians. This led to them embroiling British servicepeople in two decade-long wars without the proper equipment and without any clear goals or exit strategies. In spite of all the lives lost and money spent since the overthrow of Saddam Hussein in 2003, the Iraqis still seem incapable of forming a proper government and there is still a strong possibility that the country will descend into civil war or even break up. As for Afghanistan, the war there has lasted longer than the First and Second World Wars together and there is little evidence that much progress has been made in stabilising the country. In fact, as with any foreign occupying army, the longer our troops stay in the country, the more they are hated and the more ordinary Afghans are willing to rise up to force us to leave. Moreover, there are many indications that within months of foreign troops leaving, much of the Afghan military and police will desert and the country will soon be back under Taliban rule. Meanwhile, the members of the corrupt puppet Afghan government will scarper off to their luxury homes in Dubai, all probably bought with money stolen from the aid that should have gone into rebuilding Afghanistan. It seems more than incredible that our military leaders seem to have learnt absolutely nothing at all from the British debacle in Afghanistan in 1838-1842 and then the failed Soviet nine-year occupation of the country from 1979 to 1988.

Much has already been written about the inadequate equipment military bosses have provided for our troops – insufficient helicopters forcing troops to travel by road; Land Rovers and other transport vehicles which were vulnerable to roadside bombs; the expensive SA80 rifle which was inferior to the much cheaper American M16; not enough body armour and so on. And when your enemies ride around on mules, there are questions over defence chiefs spending so much on grand, possibly vanity projects like aircraft carriers, which might or might not have planes to fly off them. It costs several billion pounds to build an aircraft carrier. But it only costs a few thousand pounds to damage or even destroy one. So will our expensive new aircraft carriers turn out to be useful additions to projecting our military might? Or will they be so vulnerable to attack by relatively cheap Exocet missiles (eagerly sold to our enemies by our French friends) or even cheaper small motor boats packed with explosives, that we don't risk sending them anywhere near the action? As our German friends found during the Second World War, smaller fighting platforms like submarines were hugely effective, but large battleships were so costly and so vulnerable to small low-cost and low-tech weapons, like slow-moving biplanes with torpedoes, that they were hardly used at all.

As our troops try to survive their last year or two in the Afghan morass, their sacrifices have not gone in vain. Four out of ten former defence secretaries have gone on to take well-paid jobs working for defence companies as have many of our top army, RAF and Royal Navy chiefs. No doubt their new six-figure salaries will be a useful top-up to their already generous public-sector pensions.

Where are the police?

Policing is another area where there are real and significant cuts being made, though these don't seem to be quite as drastic as in defence. Between 2010 and 2015, the Government has planned to cut police numbers in England and Wales by around 15,000 from 143,800 to 128,800, a drop of just over ten per cent. Cuts in police civilian staff will be harsher with nineteen per cent of these to go and around ten per cent of PCSOs (Police Community Support Officers) will also be cut (see Figure 3).

Figure 3 – The police will lose 10 to 20 per cent of their workforce

We're getting ever more peers, politicians and top bureaucrats ....and ever less police

	March 2010 (actual)	March 2015 (planned)	Planned change by 2015	Change in percentage terms
Police officers	143,800	128,800	- 15,000	- 10%
Staff	83,200	67,600	- 15,600	- 19%
PCSOs	16,900	15,200	- 1,700	- 10%
Total Workforce	243,900	211,500	- 32,400	- 13%

These cuts were, of course, met with the usual howls of protest and warnings of impending Armageddon. Ed Miliband pledged to 'fight against plans to slash the number of officers on the streets'.[93] And Shadow Home Secretary Yvette Cooper called the cuts 'deeply irresponsible' and said, 'by going too far too fast the Government is putting police services at risk – putting communities at risk'. Though she did admit that Labour was apparently also considering significant cuts in police budgets, 'our view was that the police budget could sustain a reduction of about twelve per cent over the course of a Parliament'. But the most apocalyptic vision came from the Police Federation chairman who claimed the Home Secretary was 'on the precipice of destroying a police service that is admired and replicated throughout the world'.[94] As for the Government, it tried to weasel-word its way around the cuts. Given that more office-based police would lose their jobs than frontline officers, the Policing Minister was able to correctly claim, 'the proportion of the police workforce on the front line is rising'.[95] This sophistry slightly avoided the unpleasant truth that, even though the proportion of the remaining police officers who served in frontline roles would increase very slightly, the actual number on the front line would fall.

As is so often the case, the hysteria and spin displayed by those with vested interests greatly exaggerated the facts. It was true that police strength would fall by 15,000 or, in the worst case, by possibly 16,000 officers by 2015. But, as police numbers rose by 19,630 between 2000 and 2010, the drop of 15,000 or so would actually leave the police force 4,630 officers larger than it had been before New Labour went on a massive police hiring spree (see Figure 4).

Figure 4 – There will still be more police in 2015, after the cuts, than there were in 2000

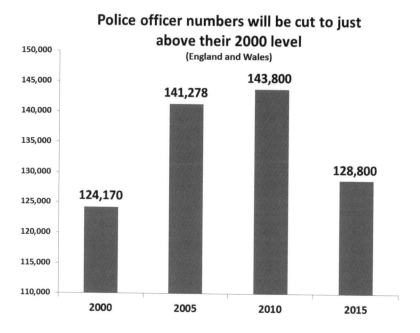

Police officer numbers will be cut to just above their 2000 level
(England and Wales)

In fact, by 2015, we will have more police officers than we had for the first five years of New Labour's thirteen years in power. Moreover, by 2015 we will still have 15,200 PCSOs to support community policing. Laughably, in January 2012 a possibly hysterical BBC journalist reported, 'police numbers fall to lowest level in decade'. I don't where he got his figures from or how or why he made them up, but taking the figures used by the House of Commons Home Affairs Committee and Her Majesty's Inspectorate of Constabulary, I can assure the either worried or else overly-ambitious and rather creative BBC reporter that there were more police in 2012 than there were in 2002 (a decade earlier) and also more than there were in 2003. But perhaps the reporter was right to do a little scaremongering. Perhaps we do need many more police than we did before New Labour came to power. Labour's policy of encouraging many of the world's thieves, rapists and murderers to move to Britain and then protecting their right to remain here by using Human Rights legislation has possibly landed us with more than our fair share of humanity's dregs. Official figures show that, although immigrants make up around eleven per cent of the population, around twenty per cent of the rapists and murderers arrested in 2011 were born abroad.

Own goals

While most ordinary police officers are probably honest, hardworking and dedicated to their jobs, like our troops they seem to have been let down by sometimes truly atrocious but highly-paid, highly-pensioned leadership. These leaders have scored some remarkable own goals combining world-class incompetence with massive squandering of public money. Much has been written in the press about the efforts of senior police officers to ram ludicrous servings of political correctness down the throats of their officers. This has created a situation where the police have alienated much of the law-abiding, taxpaying public who often feel that the police are there to protect criminals and persecute those who do no wrong. We are constantly hearing how criminals are quickly freed to rob, rape and murder again; how criminals with electronic tags keep reoffending with impunity; how some police and many PCSOs skilfully hide behind health and safety rules to avoid helping people in need; how a 'whole cohort' of inadequate police officers have been recruited to meet diversity targets; and how ordinary people are viciously persecuted and prosecuted by the police when they dare to try to protect their homes and families from thugs, vandals, drunks and criminals. But perhaps one of the worst own goals so triumphantly scored by the police's panjandrums was when they tried to set up a British equivalent of the FBI to tackle serious, organised crime.

The British FBI joke

In early 2004, several newspapers excitedly informed us 'Blair unveils plan for "British FBI"'. The New Labour Government had found out that various policing agencies wouldn't work together and tended to keep information from each other, rather than sharing it to protect the British public from increasing organised crime. So a new body, the Serious Organised Crime Agency (SOCA), was to be created. SOCA would combine the National Crime Squad, the National Criminal Intelligence Service and the investigative arms of Customs and Excise and the Immigration Service. It would employ around 4,200 police, customs and immigration experts and cost us in the region of £400 million a year. Blair promised that the new organisation would be 'ruthless', would make life 'hell' for crime's 'Mr Bigs' and that now it was time to 'stop trying to fight 21st Century crime by early 20th Century methods'.[96] Home Secretary Charles Clarke assured us that SOCA would be a 'step change' in the fight against organised crime and that it 'would be a powerful new body working across organisational boundaries and focusing resources where problems were the greatest'.[97]

At first things seemed to go reasonably smoothly. In 2006-07, its first full year of operation, SOCA claimed to have seized one fifth of Europe's cocaine supply – seventy three tonnes with a street value of £3 billion; to have secured 236 convictions; to have prevented thirty five murders; and to have drawn up a list of 1,600 crime chiefs. Home Secretary Jacqui Smith, she who apparently didn't break any rules or commit any crime when claiming for years that a bedroom in her sister's home was her main residence, lauded SOCA's success, 'we have seized record amounts of drugs, disrupting and dismantling organised drug trafficking groups'.[98] But critics wondered why SOCA's predecessors had secured 309 convictions in 2005, rather more than SOCA's 236 in 2006. Some MPs were scathing about SOCA's performance. The Shadow Home Secretary was among them:

> The Government set up SOCA with great fanfare with the pledge to sharply improve its performance in the fight against organised crime. Yet these figures show that despite drug trafficking being SOCA's number one priority – the number of people convicted has actually fallen by a quarter since it was established.[99]

In 2007-08, there were unpleasant rumblings from within the bowels of this hopefully ruthless new crime-fighting agency, Britain's FBI. Convictions went up slightly to 243, but there were rumours off excessive bureaucracy and failure to arrest any of its 130 key targets. SOCA, of course, denied this claiming it had detained thirty six of them. Moreover, SOCA had to sack around 400 officers as it had recruited too many. In its annual report, SOCA admitted that progress against crime had been 'uneven'. That's bureaucratese for 'we haven't a clue what we're doing, but we get big salaries and early retirement with generous pensions, so please don't look too closely at our bungling and ineptitude'.

By 2009, SOCA claimed that the international cocaine

market was 'in retreat' following SOCA's many successes. Though Britain's rising numbers of drug addicts suggested a different conclusion. Moreover, critics pointed out that in its first three years of operation, SOCA had cost taxpayers over £1.2 billion and only seized £78 million from crime bosses. SOCA's chairman defended his organisation by pointing out that seizing assets was not the 'be-all and end-all'.

But by 2010, the new Coalition had apparently had enough of SOCA's questionable efforts and the Home Secretary Theresa May announced as part of her *Policing In The 21st Century* proposals the creation of a new organisation, the National Crime Agency (NCA), which would replace SOCA. In words not frightfully different to those used by former Home Secretary Charles Clarke when SOCA was announced, May told us, 'we will create a powerful new body of operational crime-fighters in the shape of a National Crime Agency, which will harness and exploit the intelligence, analytical and enforcement capabilities of the current law enforcement agencies'.[100] Several newspapers informed us, 'Britain to get new FBI-style police force to tackle organised crime'. Some people, remembering the formation of the ill-fated SOCA, might have got a sense of *déjà vu* (see Figure 5).

Figure 5 – SOCA compared to the NCA – can you spot the difference?

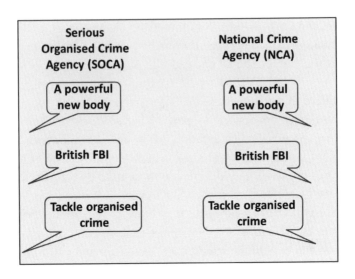

In what might have been one of the best headlines of the year, a news website summed up the situation caused by the incompetence of police bosses, 'British FBI to replace British FBI'.[101]

Chapter 10

Till the pips squeak

While the ruling elite of politicians, bureaucrats and top executhieves have done very well for themselves in spite of austerity, for many ordinary working people the last few years have been grim.

We're all in this.......blah, blah

It's probably inevitable that this chapter starts with the memorable and implausible claim made by both PM David Cameron and Chancellor George Osborne that 'we're all in this together'. Of course we're not all in this together. In fact the rich, the super rich, the mega rich and the hyper rich have never had it so good. The share of British national income taken by the top one per cent of earners was a little under twenty per cent just after the First World War. This fell to just above six per cent by the mid 1970s as the economy grew, more people became more prosperous and successive governments sought to reduce inequality by taxing the rich more and distributing more of national income to the deserving and undeserving less well-off. But over the last thirty years, the share of income taken by the top one per cent shot rapidly upwards. By the 2007 economic collapse it had reached 1918 levels. Since the crash, it has gone even higher (see Figure 1).

Figure 1 – The recession is just something the rich read about in their newspapers

Share of national income taken by Britain's richest 1%

The super rich have clearly had a very good recession indeed. Since the crash, the population as a whole have seen their real incomes fall by about six per cent, but the assets of the top one thousand people rocketed in value by about £155 billion (much more than the UK's deficit) to around £414 billion. In 1990, you needed just £50 million to make it into the top two hundred in the *Sunday Times Rich List*. By 2008, you had to have £430 million to join this august group. By 2012, in spite of the recession, the entry level into the top two hundred had crept a little higher to £450 million.[102]

Even the comfortably rich seem to have nonchalantly

shrugged off the economic chaos engulfing the rest of us. In the last ten years, take-home packages of FTSE100 executives trebled from an average of £1.5 million to around £4.8 million. Yet in the same period, the value of most of the companies they managed declined. This suggests that the 'rewards for failure' culture so prevalent in Britain's public sector has now been eagerly adopted by those in the private sector, who have often been so vocal in their justifiable criticism of widespread public-sector waste and incompetence.[103]

It's fairly clear that while the rest of us have suffered, the fortunate few have seen their share of national wealth balloon. Moreover at the same time, the few wealthy people, who deign to pay taxes, have also benefited from the top rate of tax falling from sixty per cent in the 1980s to forty per cent in the 2000s. It did then briefly go up to fifty per cent, but was reduced by the Coalition back down to forty five per cent.

Critics of the rich and super rich have called for them to pay more towards helping dig the country out of the dreadful financial quagmire into which it was dumped by the incompetence of the scandalously profligate Mr Brown and Mr Balls. However, it may be relevant to mention that the rich are generous contributors to the two main political parties. Blair was enthusiastic in cultivating relations with people with money - peerages and other honours seemed to be liberally distributed to those who stumped up large wads of cash to support the New Labour project. No fewer than twenty three bankers were given honours by New Labour. Ten of these were from banks which subsequently imploded costing British taxpayers many hundreds of billions of pounds and all but wrecking the British economy. Several of these individuals should have been prosecuted for things like false accounting, defrauding shareholders and other crimes. But predictably no action was taken against any of them. As for their honours, only one lost his knighthood, while the rest hung on to rewards which in some cases were possibly bought rather than earned.

As for the Tories, almost two hundred and fifty members of the top one thousand wealthiest people in Britain have contributed a total of over £80 million to them over the last ten years. This may help explain why, when the rest of us have seen our taxes go up, all ideas of mansion taxes, taxes on land values, closing loopholes that allow the rich to avoid stamp duty on property and other ways of making the wealthy contribute just a little more to reducing the deficit have had some difficulty getting off the ground.

Ouch!

The mega rich, the super rich and the rich may be wondering what to do with their ever-increasing piles of money. But the rest of us have been fortunate enough not to have that problem to worry about. Since 2006, the year before the crash, average incomes have increased by around thirteen per cent, while prices of many essentials have rocketed by four to five times as much. The Government and its statisticians keep telling us that inflation has only been between three per cent and five per cent a year. But that is not the reality that most of us have experienced. In five years, a basket of foods has gone up by around eight per cent a year – around twice the supposed level of inflation. Ordinary unleaded petrol has increased by slightly more than food. And, thanks to the expensive but futile efforts of Ofgem, gas and electricity prices have shot up by close to fifteen per cent a year – more than seventy five per cent in five years (see Figure 2).

Figure 2 – The squeeze on most households from rising prices has been painful

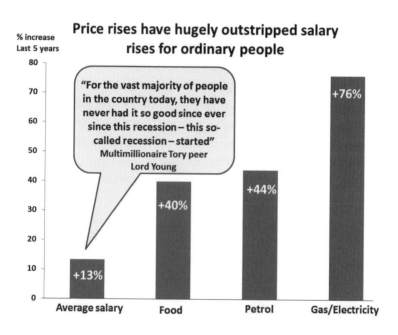

According to experts, such a prolonged squeeze on household budgets didn't even happen during the Great Depression of the 1930s. In fact, the last time ordinary families experienced such a contraction in their living standards was during the Long Depression of 1873 to 1896 when growth in the UK economy slowed from an average of three per cent a year in the decades before the Long Depression to just 1.7 per cent a year in the twenty-three-year Depression. Perhaps worryingly for ordinary families is the fact that even during the twenty three years of the Long Depression, British economic growth was higher than it was in the five years from the 2007 crash to 2012.

There has been one slightly bright spot amidst all the gloom. Because of record low interest rates, mortgage costs have fallen, so that someone on a £150,000 loan would be paying about £10 a day - £320 a month – less than five years ago. This is what prompted Tory multimillionaire peer Lord Young to give his famous Harold-Macmillian quote (see Figure 2) while eating at an exclusive London restaurant. But while the good lord was right about mortgage costs being at a record low, he seemed oblivious of the fact that many millions of people rely on their savings for some income and that the Bank of England's policy of record low interests rates meant that savers were getting so little interest that they were losing money on their savings once inflation was taken into account. Lord Young probably also forgot about the million or so who had lost their jobs in what he described as the 'so-called recession'. He presumably also forgot about the hundreds of thousands of small businesses that were struggling to survive as their takings plummeted. It may even have slipped his mind that not everyone can turn up at the House of Lords for a few minutes each day to claim generous accommodation, travel, food and other expenses and then dine in taxpayer-subsidised restaurants thanks to the enforced generosity of those who, due to stagnant earnings and rapidly rising prices, were struggling to pay their bills. But then the rich and the super rich know little of the lives of those they so lucratively rule over and so effortlessly judge in their great wisdom.

Double ouch!!

As for the record low mortgage rates, they are slowly but surely disappearing as the main banks increase their mortgage rates every few months even though the Bank of England has held base rates steady at 0.5 per cent for the past few years. In explaining away these increases, the banks play the same 'heads I win, tails you lose' game as the power companies. Whenever wholesale oil or gas prices rise, the power companies quickly pass these rises on to us. But when wholesale prices fall, the companies claim they can't reduce what they charge us as they are locked into long-term contracts with their suppliers. Similarly, whenever base rates rise, the banks are quick to pass these rises on to us. But when base rates fall, the banks claim that their funding costs have not fallen so they cannot reduce their rates on mortgages and loans. And sometimes the banks just lie about their funding costs, as they know it's almost impossible for an ordinary customer to find out the truth. In early 2012, for example, several banks increased their mortgage rates from about 3.5 per cent to close to 4 per cent, giving them a rise in profitability of fourteen per cent on each mortgage. As usual, the banks blamed a rise in their own funding costs for charging us so much more. But in fact, at the same time, the main components of banks' funding costs - the 3-month LIBOR, the 5-year swap rate and senior CDS spreads - all fell, meaning that the banks' funding costs would also have fallen.

In part the drop in banks' funding costs was due to the European Central Bank's (ECB's) 3-year Long Term Refinancing Operations (LTRO). With LTRO, the ECB lent over a trillion euros – about £830 billion – to banks for three years at just one per cent interest. The banks could then use the money borrowed at one per cent to buy increasingly dodgy Spanish and Italian government bonds paying over six per cent. By pretending that the Italian and Spanish government bonds were worth something and weren't utter junk that would never be repaid, the banks could further pretend that they had lots of assets and therefore weren't bankrupt. More cynical observers have accused LTRO of merely being a game of smoke and mirrors to make it look as if the banks were solvent, when they were actually more than bankrupt. Between them, Barclays, Lloyds and HSBC were reported to have taken more than £22 billion from LTRO funds which, thanks to the generosity of Europe's taxpayers, they could then lend at significantly more than they were paying for the money.

While the rest of us have been squeezed, the banks have managed to increase their profit margins on tracker mortgages from around 0.2 per cent before the June 2007 credit crunch to over 2.8 per cent by mid 2012 – a massive rise in bank profitability. As one expert explained, 'margins are now very generous overall. There is no doubt that the lenders have been using the Eurozone crisis as an excuse to push up prices'.[104] By July/August 2012, some banks were slightly reducing rates on some mortgages, mainly for people who could stump up deposits of thirty to forty per cent for the properties they were buying. But profit margins on mortgages were still several times what they had been just a few years earlier.

By raising the cost of mortgages, by restricting lending to families and businesses, by using government and central bank money to speculate with and by driving up our banking costs, the main banks – Barclays, HSBC, RBS, Lloyds – have significantly increased the profits they make from us. These rose from around £20 billion in 2010 to about £30 billion in 2011 and are expected to be close to £35 billion in 2012 – almost £140 million every working day. As these four banks control about seventy five per cent of all personal and small business accounts in Britain, there is limited competition and their dominance of the market allows them to extract levels of profitability that would be impossible in any truly competitive business. So, not only are ordinary working families being squeezed by rising prices at a time when their incomes are falling compared to inflation, but they have also seen the profits made from them by our banks go up by over seventy per cent in just three years since 2009. The banks' 2012 bonus pool is estimated to be around £4.2 billion. In 2012, the banks will make profits of over £1,100 for every working person in Britain and will pay bonuses to their lucky staff of about £140 for every working person in the country.

Triple ouch!!!

We working people had the double austerity whammy of stagnant incomes while prices rose and almost usurious exploitation by the main banks to increase their profits and bonuses. But there was a third austerity blow to hit us where it hurts – in our pockets. This third blow was a massive leap in the amounts we had to pay for various government services. To make up for government limits on rises in council tax, local councils have been trying to raise more revenue by pushing up charges for things like parking, burials, rat-catching and care of the elderly, while also increasing penalties for supposed offences such as putting rubbish in the wrong containers. Similarly, in order to take more of our money, many NHS hospitals have turned their parking facilities into a goldmine at our expense. These extra charges are irksome, but usually not too financially damaging for most of us.

Perhaps the most brutal attack on ordinary working families by the rich and powerful was the Brobdingnagian rise in university tuition fees. David Cameron has repeatedly said that his government wants to 'help hard-working people who want to get on and play by the rules'. Yet the gargantuan hike in university tuition fees seems to be a fairly devastating financial blow to precisely the kind of people the Coalition supposedly favours. The extraordinary leap in tuition fees – in many cases from about £3,000 to £9,000 a year – may be interesting in the context of *Greed Unlimited* as it could be seen as an almost unbelievably shameless and cynical money-grab from hard-pressed working families by the wealthy and privileged who claim to represent our interests.

In 2009, Peter Mandelson asked multimillionaire businessman and former head of BP Lord Browne to chair an *Independent Review of Higher Education Funding and Student Finance*. Until his resignation from BP under a bit of a cloud after having reportedly been found to have lied under oath in court (or something like that), Lord Browne had a highly distinguished career building BP into one of the largest and most profitable oil companies in the world.[105] During his time at the top of BP, there were some ugly rumours about BP's profits being partly funded by excessive cost-cutting and corner-cutting which were risking the safety of the company's employees and the environment of the countries where the company operated. In 2005, an explosion at a BP refinery in Texas killed fifteen workers, injured at least one hundred and seventy more and led to BP paying over £1 billion in compensation and fines. Repeated problems at an Alaskan pipeline, fifty one per cent owned by BP, led to the chairman of the US House Energy Sub-committee announcing, 'my review of the mountain of circumstantial evidence can only lead me to the conclusion that severe pressure for cost-cutting did have an impact on maintenance of pipelines'. Though it wasn't till three years after Lord Browne's slightly controversial departure from BP that the 'big one' happened – the 2010 Gulf of Mexico explosion which killed eleven workers, injured another twelve and may cost BP's shareholders up to $20 billion.

In October 2010, Lord Browne delivered his recommendations. Two of the key points for students and their families were a removal of the cap on the level of fees that universities could charge and an increase in the income level at which graduates must begin to pay back their loans from £15,000 to £21,000 a year. In 2010, the Coalition Government provoked outrage among students when it lifted the cap on tuition fees from £3,290 a year to £9,000 a year. The Government claimed that few universities would charge as much as £9,000 a year, but of course seeing the opportunity to earn much more money, most universities quickly hiked their tuition fees to close to or at the new £9,000 cap.

There were many criticisms of the Browne Review. Some people wondered why a group, who probably had their university fees and living costs paid for them by taxpayers through their student grants, should be so enthusiastic about the next generation being denied the same support for their studies. Others questioned the backgrounds of the seven members of the review. In addition to multimillionaire Lord Browne, the review group included a knighted advisor to a former Labour education minister, a former Treasury economist, two university vice chancellors, a board member of the Big Lottery Fund and the multimillionaire CEO of a major bank. Perhaps significantly, there were no students or their parents and no representatives of university lecturers. Given that the membership of the review were part of a privileged elite who were either extremely wealthy or had lived very well indeed off taxpayers' money for much of their lives and could look forward to generous five- or six-figure taxpayer-subsidised pensions, it's perhaps not surprising that they decided to drop the bombshell of £9,000 a year tuition fees onto the already burdened shoulders of those 'hard-working people who want to get on and play by the rules' whose interests PM David Cameron had repeatedly pledged to champion. After all, fees of £9,000 a year must have seemed like a mere bagatelle to most of the members of the Browne review.

Another perhaps surprising little detail about the steep rise in tuition fees was that the vastly increased fees were introduced during the time when Tory MP David Willetts was

Austerity for oiks

Universities Minister. Willetts was the author of a 2010 book *The Pinch: How the baby boomers took their children's future – and why they should give it back*. In his book, Willetts showed how the comfortable lifestyle of the baby-boomer generation was based on borrowing that would have to be paid back by future generations and he warned:

> If our political, economic and cultural leaders do not begin to discharge our obligations to the future, people entering the workforce today will be taxed more, work longer hours for less money, have lower social mobility and live in a degraded environment in order to pay for their parents' quality of life.

Given Mr Willetts' views, one might have expected him to oppose the enormous financial burden monstrously increased tuition fees would put on the younger generation and their families by the wealthy baby-boomer ruling classes.

Moreover, in his book Mr Willetts highlights the huge and rising cost of public-sector pensions and how younger people would have to pay increasing taxes to support the public-sector elites in their retirement. Perhaps it could have occurred to Mr Willetts that by doing something like setting a maximum public-sector pension of say £40,000 a year or even less and scrapping public-sector bosses getting three years' pension as a tax-free lump sum on retirement, the Government could have generated so much money that it would not have been necessary to burden the next generation with such a massive rise in tuition fees. In fact, tuition fees could possibly have been scrapped altogether. This kind of action would have been in line with Mr Willetts' argument that the older generation would have to make some economic sacrifices to help the young. Unfortunately for our students and their families, Mr Willetts' actions in banging up university fees don't quite seem to fit in with what he proposes in his book for the rest of us – restraining our standards of living for the benefit of future generations. A cynic might see Mr Willetts' decision to raise the cap on fees to £9,000 a year as being yet another case of this Government feeling that austerity was something for other people, for us oiks, while the ruling public-sector elites and their business friends and benefactors should continue to freely and enthusiastically pocket as much of our money as they felt entitled to.

Carry on squeezing

The effects of the austerity triple whammy have been depressingly predictable – widespread financial misery for millions of working families. Lower income families – those earning less than £25,000 a year - tend to spend more on essentials than the higher paid and so were more affected by the rising prices squeeze. One study estimated that around seven million people were at risk of being overwhelmed by a 'spiral of debt' as they used expensive credit cards, overdrafts and payday loans to pay off their housing costs (mortgages or rent).[106] Another survey found that about seventy per cent of families were financially 'on the edge' as they were struggling to survive, had little to no savings and would be tipped into debt if faced with a large or unexpected bill. Of these families, sixty per cent said they were short of cash each week and twenty per cent were missing meals so their children could eat.[107]

The pawn shop and payday loan industries experienced an unprecedented expansion. In 1980, there were about fifty pawn shops in Britain. By 2012 this had risen to close to two thousand, with much of the growth coming since the 2007 crash. Payday loans, whose interest rates can range between forty and four thousand per cent seemed to have become the main lifeline for many people who were finding difficulty making ends meet. In 2011, around two million people took out payday loans. In 2012 this was expected to rise to 3.5 million. While pushing many people into the welcoming embrace of payday loans companies, the Government seems to have shown little interest in regulating this industry to protect vulnerable customers. As one expert explained:

> The UK is the crock of gold at the end of the rainbow for the world's payday lenders. They've been regulated out of other countries and jump for joy at our lax supervision. That's why these 4,000 per cent lenders are exploding across British high streets.[108]

One of the UK's largest debt charities, the Consumer Credit Counselling Service (CCCS), reported that since 2009, there had been a six-fold increase in the number of people contacting it with problems linked to payday loans. In all, about 370,000 people turned to the CCCS for help in 2011. The Office for Budget Responsibility has forecast that household debt will rise by over thirty per cent from £1.62 trillion in 2010 to £2.13 trillion by the time of the next election in 2015.

Another business sector that has done particularly well out of the Coalition's austerity squeeze is the betting shop industry. Following New Labour's liberalisation of gambling in 2005, betting shops have been allowed to install up to four Fixed Odds Betting Terminals with maximum bets of £100 a time. These machines can earn tens of thousands of pounds a day for the betting shop and have become the most profitable business line for many gambling companies. On high streets in many poorer areas there used to only be one betting shop, now there are often clusters of five or six. On some high streets there's little else but pawn shops, payday loans firms and betting shops.

The increased burden of higher university tuition fees also seems to be hitting families hard. There was a surge in university applications in 2010 as people tried to get started with their studies before the introduction of the rise in 2012. But a year later, the number of UK-born applicants fell by about fifteen per cent and is expected to drop further. Probably fees will start to fall slightly, especially at the less prestigious universities, as they find many of their more pointless courses undersubscribed. But for those students who study while paying the higher fees, the future looks pretty ghastly. A study by the Chartered Institute for Taxation found:

> Most graduates will pay off their debt for the rest of their lives if they repay at the lowest possible rate due to the way the debt will increase by RPI inflation plus 3 per cent over the years that graduates repay it. Someone starting on £21,000 and seeing their salary increase by 5 per cent a year would end up paying £64,239 over thirty years, with an unpaid debt of £26,406 at the end of their working lives.[109]

If this calculation is anywhere near reality, then many graduates will be unable to buy their homes or save for their pensions due to the effects of compound interest increasing their debts faster than they can pay them off. Even if students do pay off their debts faster than they grow, it will take many graduates ten years or more to pay for their education, making their prospects of buying a home and starting a family much less attainable than they were for their parents' generation. This is precisely the kind of situation Universities Minister David Willetts warned about in his book *The Pinch* and yet he introduced a scheme which could impoverish many graduates for a large part of their working lives.

The wealthy have mostly had an excellent recession. Our politicians, peers and public-sector bosses are protected from austerity by their high salaries, lavish inflation-protected pensions and laughably lax expenses systems. And those on benefits can often take home more each week than working families. But for 'hard-working people who want to get on and play by the rules' the consequences of the Government's austerity drive have been harsh and in some cases more than they could bear.

Chapter 11

Taxed to death

The 'terrible twins'?

You could hardly have imagined two chancellors as different as Labour's Gordon Brown and the Coalition's George Osborne. They came from very different backgrounds. Brown was from a reportedly austere middle-class Scottish Presbyterian home. As he explained, 'you know I come from a Presbyterian background and the work ethic is important and being prudent is important'.[110] Clearly a fighter, Brown stormed through school to win a scholarship to Edinburgh University at the age of sixteen through his academic achievements. Osborne was born into an old Anglo-Irish aristocracy, with a whole pile of silver spoons in his mouth, heir to the Osborne baronetcy of Ballentaylor in County Tipperary and Ballylemon in County Waterford. So there was probably too not much that was Presbyterian about his family life. He cruised apparently effortlessly and wealthily from private school to Magdalen College at Oxford University where he mixed with other sons of the elites before gliding into a job with the Tory Party.

Their personal behaviour too showed they were truly chalk and cheese. Brown possibly had - how to say this politely – a number of challenges on the charm front, a questionable level of personal charisma and reportedly a tendency to throw things when angry which, again reportedly, was not an altogether rare occurrence. Osborne, on the other hand, had the laid-back charm and self-confidence that so often characterises our wealthy upper classes.

Nor could you have imagined two chancellors who had such different economic circumstances to deal with. Brown inherited a growing economy, low inflation and rising tax revenues. If he had just done nothing, or stayed in bed, or taken up Scottish country dancing full time, or gone on holiday for the rest of his life and not meddled with the economy, he would have gone down in history as one of Britain's greatest ever chancellors. Whereas Osborne took over in the depth of a recession with British public spending completely out of control (thanks to Brown), tax revenues plummeting, our major export markets collapsing and scarcely a day going by without more bad news crashing unpleasantly into his front door.

Yet there may be some disturbing similarities between these supposedly very different men facing such different situations. For a start, if you look at the kinds of statements both make in their budget speeches, there is a certain uncanny resemblance (see Figure 1).

Taxed to death

Figure 1 – After a couple of years as Brown's shadow, Osborne could seem to sound remarkably like him

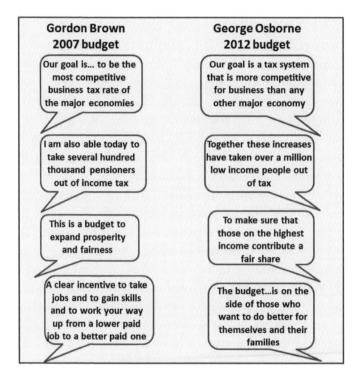

Moreover when things got tough and it turned out that their policies were demonstrably and embarrassingly failing, both were quick to claim Godlike infallibility for themselves and to blame someone else's stupidity for the mess for which they were in large part responsible.

In just one interview in 2009, Gordon Brown gave us, 'it's not just a financial problem in Britain. It started in America and it's felt round the world'. There was, 'it's a problem that started in America. A shadow banking system started to develop in America'. Also 'what happened is that unsupervised lending, mainly starting in America, allowed the banks to leverage up far more money than they were capable of sustaining once property prices started to fall'. Finally, in case we hadn't quite got the message, 'this problem that mainly started in America is something that we have got to all deal with in every country of the world'. Furthermore, Brown was absolutely adamant that the UK financial crash and ensuing recession had nothing at all to do with his own economic policies and the way his spending blowout wasted over a trillion pounds of our money while more than doubling the country's national debt, 'you see some people say it's a problem of personal debt in Britain or some people say it's the Government has borrowed too much. Actually the problem is....basically the result of a financial system that wasn't geared up to be supervised in a way that you need to have supervision'.[111]

Then when asked why during his ten years as Chancellor he didn't put in place the necessary supervision if he had always known it was necessary, he seemed to forget a few things. These included the fact that it was he who in 1997 had changed Britain's system for bank regulation, taking responsibility for regulation away from the Bank of England and giving it to the Financial Services Authority (FSA) whose supposed expertise was mostly in micro-economic matters - looking at financial products and savings schemes sold to bank customers - not more macro-economic issues like bank lending, derivatives, the shadow banking system and banks' balance sheets. Brown treated us to, 'but this is what I've been saying for ten years. If you look back on my speeches, I've been pleading with people....to have a proper system of global financial supervision' and claimed, 'I've got to say to you that the regulatory system in Britain is better than it has been in other countries'.[112] This last statement seemed to belie the fact that some of the biggest bank failures – Northern Rock, RBS and Lloyds – happened to British banks on his watch. So, once again, he placed the blame on anyone but himself.

Now over to Mr Osborne. In mid-2012, he tried to explain away Britain's disastrous double-dip recession by blaming high oil prices, Labour's overspending and problems in the Eurozone. He wrote in a newspaper article, 'our recovery – already facing powerful headwinds from high oil prices and the debt burden left behind by the boom years – is being killed off by the crisis on our doorstep'. There was also:

> Our country is bursting with entrepreneurial spirit and exciting investment plans that are being held back because of uncertainty about the future. That's why a resolution of the Eurozone crisis would do more than anything else to give our economy a boost.[113]

This narrative line overlooked the fact that Switzerland, which did a larger proportion of its trade with the EU than Britain, was growing at around a relatively healthy two per cent a year. Germany and even France were also growing, albeit slowly, while Britain's economy was shrinking like a deflating balloon. Some of Mr Osborne's Tory colleagues were less than impressed by the Chancellor's Brown-like apparent refusal to take any responsibility for anything. One said:

> It is not the Eurozone crisis we should blame for our awful economic performance, but the almost total absence of domestic economic reform coupled with the Treasury's absurd belief that monetary stimulus can engineer economic growth.[114]

Moreover, Osborne's attempt to shift blame for Britain's economic woes from himself seems to have had many of the newspaper's faithful readers spluttering over their corn flakes. Of the almost three hundred, who felt sufficiently enraged to put their comments on the newspaper website, some of the more printable included, 'I don't believe a word you say here, George'; 'he hasn't a clue what to do'; 'George, although your mind's opaque, try thinking more, if just for your own sake'; 'we have been let down by every government since Macmillan, but you are by far the most useless of them all'; and the rather direct, 'what a load of dingo's kidneys'.

The budget smoke and mirrors game

But apart from his massive spending binge and his apparent refusal to accept any responsibility for anything, perhaps what Brown will be best remembered for is the way in which, in budget after budget, he managed to claim he was not putting up tax rates, and sometimes even reducing them, when in fact he was eagerly pushing the quantity of our money he took in taxes ever upwards. During Brown's time as Chancellor, the amount we paid in taxes shot up from around £290 billion to almost £520 billion or, to put it another way, from £12,200 per household to about £20,700 per household. Part of this was due to people's incomes and house prices going up during the Brown boom. But part was also because of Brown's skill in regularly increasing how much we paid in tax, while sometimes seeming to pretend this wasn't what he was really up to.

Brown used three main ways of adding to our tax burden. One was 'fiscal drag' – not increasing tax thresholds in line with rising prices. This was most noticeable with stamp duty on property. For example, at the time of writing we pay three per cent stamp duty on properties costing between £250,000 and £500,000. Had stamp duty levels been adjusted in line with rising house prices, we would only be paying the three per cent on houses costing between £700,000 and £1,400,000. So, somebody buying a £300,000 property is now paying £9,000 in stamp duty when, if the thresholds had moved, they would only be paying £3,000, just one per cent. Yet at the same time as he failed to give us the benefits of raising tax thresholds to match rising house prices, Brown used a revaluation of properties to increase council tax revenues based on the rising value of our homes. It was very much a case of 'heads Brown wins, tails we lose'.

A second way of pocketing our money was through cutting public services while at the same time often increasing existing charges or introducing new ones. These could include hospital parking, paying more for dental services, parking fines, congestion charges, school meals and many others. One report estimated that by the time Brown became Prime Minister, each household was paying about £700 a year more on these charges than when Brown first became Chancellor.[115]

Perhaps the most impressive of Brown's techniques for taking more of our money was the camouflaged or hidden tax increase, sometimes called 'stealth taxes'. In his budgets, he would announce headline-grabbing changes which at first looked like they would let us keep more of our earnings. However, deep within the budget would be other changes which would often more than wipe out these supposed tax reductions. The most famous example of this trick was probably in Brown's last budget as Chancellor. To wild shouting and huge applause from Labour ranks, Brown finished off his budget speech with a booming, triumphant flourish which caught most Tories and journalists completely by surprise:

197

Austerity for oiks

And I have one further announcement. With the other decisions I have made today we are able to hold to our pledge made at the election not to raise the basic rate of income tax. Indeed to reward work, to ensure working families are better off, and to make the tax system fairer, I will from next April cut the basic rate of income tax from 22p to 20p. The lowest basic rate for seventy five years. And I commend this budget to the house. (Rapturous applause from Labour MPs)

However, within the speech was also the line, 'I can now return income tax to just two rates by removing the 10p band on non-savings income'. Here, what looked like a simplification of the tax system was in fact the abolition of the 10p tax rate that Brown had so proudly introduced when he first became Chancellor. This change meant that someone earning £10,000 a year would lose £223 a year from the abolition of the 10p tax rate and gain just £50 a year from the reduction in income tax from 22p to 20p in the pound, leaving the person £173 worse off. Someone on £15,000 a year would be about £70 worse off. You'd have to be earning over £19,000 a year to get any benefit from the 2p reduction in the rate of income tax. There were other measures in the budget such as changes in working tax credits and in child benefits which would protect poorer families and even leave some of them better off, in spite of the removal of the 10p income tax rate. But for many single people and for families who couldn't navigate their way through the complexities of Brown's labyrinthine benefits and tax credit systems, this was most definitely a tax reduction that was actually a tax increase. A partner at a major accountancy summed up the Chancellor's mastery of the budget game:

What the Chancellor has done here is a classic case of smoke and mirrors. The two pence reduction in income tax will seem like great news to everyone, but the much less prominently publicised increases in National Insurance and the abolition of the 10 per cent starting rate band will in many cases offset the savings.[116]

Moreover, Brown's claim that, by taking income tax down to 20p in the pound, he had reduced income tax to 'the lowest basic rate for seventy five years' sat uncomfortably beside the fact that before his budget, many lower-income workers had been paying just 10p in the pound tax.

'I can play too', said George

Gordon Brown may have been the maestro of budgetary smoke and mirrors, but George Osborne seems to have learnt a few things from the great man. In Osborne's first budget – the 2010 'Emergency Budget' – one of the many measures announced by the new Chancellor was the raising of the threshold at which we would have to start paying income tax:

> So today I can announce that we will increase this personal allowance by £1,000 in April. People will be able to earn £7,475 before they have to start paying income tax. 23 million people who are basic rate taxpayers will each gain by up to £170 a year. 880,000 of the lowest income taxpayers will be taken out of tax altogether.[117]

Moreover, the Chancellor also froze the level that the top rate of income tax kicked in, to help ensure that the wealthy paid their part towards reducing the deficit.

Austerity for oiks

On the face of it, it looks like most people should be pleased with this raising of the income tax threshold, especially as there is a table of figures in the budget document showing how the Chancellor's changes in income tax rates and National Insurance contributions would leave everybody earning less than £150,000 better off. However, once you added in all the changes the Chancellor had made in indirect taxes, like increasing VAT, and in restricting benefits, it turned out that all earners were actually left worse off after the budget, with the poorest losing a greater percentage of their income than almost any other group.

In 2011, we got a bit of a repeat performance. Once again Chancellor Osborne made much of how his raising the income tax threshold would make us all better off:

> In 14 days' time the personal income tax allowance – the amount people can earn tax free – will go up by £1,000. That's the largest rise in history. That means in real terms around £160 extra per year, or £200 in cash terms, for 23 million taxpayers….And it means, just ten months into office, this coalition Government has taken 1.1 million low paid people out of tax altogether.[118]

As in the 2010 budget, there was a table showing that everybody earning less than £150,000 would be better off as a result of the Government's income tax and National Insurance changes. But again, the reality was that, once the effects of changes in indirect taxes were taken into account, all income groups were worse off, with the poorest losing the most as a percentage of their income.[119]

Then in 2012, the Chancellor's generosity to us with our money seemed almost astonishing. With a typically Brownian triumphant flourish, Osborne proudly announced:

Taxed to death

Today, I want to go much further and much faster. I am announcing the largest ever increase in the personal allowance – the amount people can earn tax free. From next April that amount will increase by £1,100. Every working person on low or middle incomes will benefit. People will be able to earn up to £9,205 before they have to pay any tax. Millions of working people will be £220 better off every year. That's £170 better off after inflation. Because higher rate earners will also benefit, twenty four million people earning less than £100,000 a year will gain from this measure. And I can tell the country that as a result of our budgets, people working full time on the minimum wage, will have seen their income tax bill cut in half. And this coalition Government will have taken two million people on the lowest incomes out of tax altogether. (Rapturous applause from Coalition MPs)

Again, as in the 2010 and 2011 budgets, there was a table showing that everybody earning less than £150,000 would be better off as a result of the Government's income tax and National Insurance changes. The Chancellor's magnanimity was celebrated by one newspaper which produced a budget summary showing that most of us – single pensioners, professional men, married couples with children, married couples without children, married pensioners, single people with or without children, unmarried couples, you name it – would be hundreds of pounds better off each year thanks to Osborne's budget. But, as usual, deep in the details of the budget – on page 91, in case you were interested - was a chart showing that, after all the changes in direct and indirect taxes and various credits and benefits, everyone would end up worse off with the poorest losing more as a per cent of their income than almost all other groups.

One of Osborne's key pledges in the budget was, 'our purpose is not to increase taxes, but to simplify them'. But the fact that everyone ended up giving more of their money for the Chancellor to spend rather contradicted the Chancellor's claim that he wasn't intent on pocketing increasing amounts of our cash. So it seems as if with both these honourable gentlemen - Chancellors Brown and Osborne - it's not always obvious that what they say and what they actually do are one and the same thing.

Don't look now

Some of us may already be struggling to pay all the direct and indirect taxes the Government imposes on us so it can keep feeding the three permanently hungry monsters that have been greedily devouring so much of our money for so long - an inefficient public sector, the over-paid and over-pensioned bureaucratic classes and our ever-increasing, self-serving political elites. And the Government talks a great story about putting these three monsters on a strict diet. But, in spite of all the fine words, public spending is set to increase every year for the foreseeable future. And more spending means more taxes. Most people, quite understandably, don't have the time or energy to plough through Mr Osborne's 116-page budget report. But tedious though the document may be, it also contains a few hidden gems. Right near the back, we can find a rather useful table which tells us how much more of our money the Government intends to take in taxes between the time of the budget and 2016-17. It's not a sight for faint hearts or those of a nervous disposition. Overall, the budget foresees the total tax we pay jumping up by a third in the next three to four years. Within this projected increasing tax take, there are some impressive rises – revenues from income tax up by 34 per cent, from national insurance up by 36 per cent, from stamp duty on property up 85 per cent, from the climate change levy up over 300 per cent (see Figure 2).

Figure 2 – Our Government is planning to take an awful lot more of our money

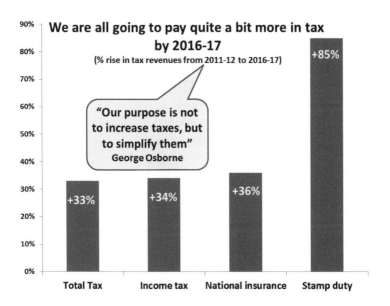

Of course, a good part of this increased tax take is based on the pleasing but possibly fanciful assumption that the British economy will suddenly leap out of recession in 2013 and start to grow by some perhaps improbable rates. One assumes these healthy but unlikely growth rates were, conveniently for the Chancellor, dreamt up by the supposedly 'independent' crystal ball gazers at the Office for Budget Responsibility (OBR). But there are more than a few rather threatening clouds on the economic horizon. The Eurozone is seemingly in a state of permanent crisis due to the indecisiveness of its incompetent leaders; the US is struggling to grow; the Arab Spring is likely to turn into a fundamentalist winter in several countries which won't be great for oil supplies or prices; the Iranians and Israelis are itching to chuck a few bombs and missiles at each other, again affecting our fuel supplies and prices; China is monopolising world supplies of critical raw materials meaning it will be impossible to manufacture many products anywhere except in China; a whole generation of young people are either jobless or crushed by debt; and, thanks to the Bank of England's failed policy of continuous pointless quantitative easing, annuity rates have fallen so low that many people with pension savings, which had once looked quite adequate, now face something close to penury in retirement.

Moreover it is strange that, while the budget was forecasting quite significant, impressive and essential economic growth year after year, at about the same time the Governor of the Bank of England was saying that he was 'pessimistic and deeply concerned' by the problems in Europe, that he didn't think we were even half way through the financial crisis and that Britons should expect 'at least another five years of pain' as he saw 'no sign of an end to global financial woes'.[120] Given the world situation and the Governor's worrying and worried comments, the folk at the OBR should probably be congratulated on maintaining their optimism about the British economy's future growth rates. Though, perhaps it's easy to be optimistic when you have a well-paid civil-service job possibly for life, a generous inflation-protected pension and the sense of self-importance and job satisfaction that comes from spending your working days at the heart of the action mixing with all the movers and shakers.

But what if the wonderfully positive OBR's growth figures turn out to be a pile of donkeys' doodoo? What if the economy doesn't grow as much as the independent OBR predicts? What if the economy doesn't really grow at all? Well that's when things get 'interesting'. In 2000, our national debt was just above £310 billion. In 2012 it's a little over one trillion pounds (£1,159,000,000,000). By 2015, even with the OBR's optimistic growth assumptions, the Government's tax increases and departmental spending cuts, our debt will hit an amazing £1.365 trillion, equal to one whole year's GDP. And by 2016 we'll owe £1.479 trillion. The ever-rising interest payments on our ever-rising debt are crushing the economy. In 2012, we'll spend about £47 billion of our taxes just paying the interest on our debt. By 2016, the annual interest payments will have reached at least £64 billion a year (see Figure 3).

**Figure 3 – Our annual interest payments
just keep on going up**

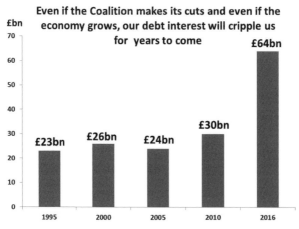

If the growth doesn't come, then the taxes aren't going to flow abundantly into Treasury coffers. This will force the Government to make one of two rather difficult choices. It could follow Labour's favourite (and only?) policy of borrow-spend-waste and let our debt go even higher than the horrific £1.479 trillion already projected for 2016/7. But this would be a disaster for the country as we'd risk getting into a vicious self-reinforcing downward spiral where lower growth leads to decreasing tax revenue leads to more borrowing leads to higher debt payments leads to the need for increasing tax levels and more cuts leads to families having less money to spend leads to even lower growth and so on and so forth. So this can't be allowed to happen. The only other alternative is that the Government continues to collect the expected amount of tax. With growth not providing rising tax revenues, the Government will be forced to put tax levels up again and again and again. As the head of the OBR explained, 'if you look at the Government's balance sheet, you might think that we're bust, but an important thing to remember, the most important asset the Government has financially, is its ability to levy taxes on us in the future'.[121]

So we can expect our taxes to go ever upwards. After all, there are bills to be paid. In addition to our spiralling interest payments, these bills include more than a hundred thousand public-sector bigwigs who expect to receive tax-free cash payments of over £200,000 each when they retire plus their inflation-protected pensions of over £70,000 a year each. The bills include at least a couple of billion a year that we pay for the 29,000 or so people in the political classes – politicians, peers, staff, advisers and hangers-on. Plus we can look forward to forking out several billion a year more in generous pensions for these lucky 29,000 who have already made a very good living at our expense. The bills also include PFI firms who want £300 billion of our money for their often ludicrously over-priced twenty- to thirty-year contracts which were so incompetently negotiated by our well-paid, well-pensioned top civil servants. These bills include hundreds of thousands of economic migrants who, after years in the UK, probably still can't believe that British taxpayers are stupid enough to give them free housing, free education, free healthcare and £20,000 or £30,000 or even £40,000 a year for producing ever more children without ever having to do a day's work. And these bills include, in addition to paying benefits to those who are genuinely unemployed through no fault of their own, also giving at least two million people, who can't be arsed to work, more in benefits each year than many people in the Third World will earn in four or five years.

Chapter 12

Siphoning off our savings

With our Government deep in the brown stuff, thanks to the massive debts built up by Messrs Brown and Balls, the amount it needs to take in taxes keeps on increasing. This leaves many ordinary people struggling to survive as prices and their taxes go ever higher. And with more tax rises in the pipeline – probably about a thirty per cent increase by 2016/7 – our battle to keep afloat financially is going to become even harder. But if we do actually manage to save a little, our fight for financial survival is far from over. There are many people who are both extremely eager to get their hands on our money and extremely skilled at convincing us to put our cash into their not always tender loving care.

There are at least three major threats to the money we have managed to save or hope to save – the massive fees we pay financial services insiders are decimating most savers' wealth; our Government's policy of forcing interest rates down is pushing people to take their money out of relatively safe bank and building society accounts and to put it into financial products that have little to no chance of ever giving the mouth-watering returns touted by those selling them; and many of the savings products we are sold are little more than scams designed to make the sellers richer and savers poorer.

How to earn a million pounds a minute

In Britain, we have about £4 trillion in savings, unit trusts, life insurance schemes and pension funds. About £500 billion of this money is in things like two- to three-year fixed-interest accounts paying anywhere from 3.2 per cent to 4.2 per cent a year. The other £3.5 trillion is in financial products where those looking after our money for us are raking off an awful lot in various fees, charges, commissions and penalties.

For example, we have around £500 billion in unit trusts. Most unit trusts will claim their 'management charges' are only around say 1.2 per cent a year. That probably seems quite modest. But their 'management charges' don't cover all that we have to pay them each year. Some may be more open and state that their 'Total Expense Ratio' (TER) is perhaps about 1.7 per cent. The TER includes management charges plus a few other bits and pieces. My pocket dictionary defines the word 'total' as 'including everything'. So, most savers could be forgiven for believing that the 'Total Expense Ratio' is all the money they will have to pay their unit trust managers. But in the wonderful world of financial services charges and commissions, 'total' doesn't really mean 'total' at all, it just means something like 'there are a few other ways we take your money that we don't really want to mention in case you realise how much you'll be paying us and decide not to give us your cash'. Because, in addition to the TER, unit trust savers also have to pay dealing costs – the costs incurred when their unit trust managers buy and sell shares and bonds. These can easily add another half to one per cent to what we have to pay for our unit trusts.

So, with the TER and the dealing costs, we're now at about 2.2 per cent to 2.7 per cent or more a year that we're losing. But we're not finished yet, not by a long way. When people put money into a unit trust, there's often an 'initial charge' of around five per cent. You can avoid this initial charge by buying your unit trust through a funds supermarket. But about three quarters of the money flowing into unit trusts comes through financial advisers and they'll usually not tell you about funds supermarkets as they get their commissions from the initial charge. If you're smart enough to avoid the initial charge, then there's no money for your financial adviser. (This might change due to new regulations coming into force in 2013). And finally, when you put money into a unit trust, you are allocated units at the 'buy' price. But when you take your money out, you can only dispose of your units at the 'sell' price. The 'buy' price is generally around five per cent higher than the 'sell' price. This means you lose around five per cent going into the unit trust and another five per cent getting out. This lost ten per cent is in addition to what you pay for the TER and the dealing costs. Paying out just a few per cent a year cent may seem pretty small beer. But if you hold your units for say five years, you're probably paying at least 2.5 per cent a year in TER and dealing costs plus the ten per cent entry and exit charges spread out over five years – another two per cent a year. In total you're forking out about 4.5 per cent a year, 22.5 per cent over the five years. Over ten years, the costs end up at a minimum of 3.5 per cent a year, 33.5 per cent over ten years. Of course, you hope that the investing genius of your fund manager will make your money grow. But when you're paying 3.5 per cent to 4.5 per cent a year, almost all the growth (if there is any) in your fund goes straight into the pockets of your unit trust company. So the unit trust can take full-page fancy colour ads in the *Money* section of your Sunday newspaper boasting about how much it has grown each year. But few savers will actually see much of this growth ever reach them.

The situation with other financial products is similar. On

many savings schemes, we've no idea how much we're paying in fees and management charges and commissions and other deductions. If we're told the charges, at first sight they may seem quite modest – usually one to one and a half per cent a year. But once you've added in all the commissions and entry costs and penalties and dealing costs and transfer costs and 'market value adjustments' and anything else the company holding your money can dream up to increase their cut, on most financial products we're paying at least three per cent a year. And paying three per cent a year for ten to twenty years gives someone else a rather impressive amount of our money. Unit trust companies pocket around £15 billion of our money each year, an almost unbelievable £59 million every single working day. Pension funds skim off well over £20 billion of our money a year, an astonishing £95 million or so every working day (see Figure 1).

Figure 1 – It's not surprising there are so many companies extremely eager to look after our money for us

The people managing our money generously take enormous quantities for themselves		
Type of savings	**£ paid in charges per year**	**£ paid in charges per working day**
Unit trusts	£15bn	£59m
Pension funds	£24bn	£95m
Insurance companies	£45bn	£177m
Others	£20bn	£80m
Total	**£104bn**	**£411m**

Each year, those who have convinced us to let them take care of our savings are creaming off something in the region of £104 billion of our cash. That's a delightful, for them, £400 million or so each working day – equivalent to almost £1 million every minute. And this stupendous amount of our money goes to a relatively small circle of people making them an awful lot richer than the people whose money they look after.

The big, big 'shares outperform cash' lie

If we're going to put our money anywhere other than a bank deposit account or under the mattress, then for most people there are just two main options – either invest directly in the stock market by buying shares or invest indirectly by getting a unit trust, exchange traded fund (ETF) or pension fund manager to buy shares for us. The repeated mantra we usually hear from those who are keen to help us shove our cash either directly into shares or into a fund is 'over the longer term, shares usually outperform cash'. What they mean is that money held just earning interest in a bank account will nine times out of ten grow less than money invested in the stock market.

There is only one small problem with this mantra – it's not true. Many people using the 'shares outperform cash' mantra are well aware that it's a lie, but it's not in their interest to admit this. Others may be so incompetent that they don't even know it's a lie. But, whether knowingly or not, every time someone uses the mantra 'shares outperform cash', they are misleading us by persuading us to put our money somewhere that usually benefits them rather more than it benefits us.

The data most journalists and financial advisers use to justify the 'shares outperform cash' claim is usually an annual report called the *Barclays Equity Gilt Study*. As we now know from repeated mis-selling scandals and the fixing of the LIBOR and possibly other rates, anything with the name 'Barclays' attached to it should be handled with the utmost caution. When calculating that shares outperform cash, Barclays, conveniently for themselves and their partners in crime in the savings and investment industry, don't look at the interest you or I would get from things like two- and three-year higher-interest bank or building society accounts. Instead, Barclays use UK Government Treasury Bills as what they call 'cash'. These Treasury Bills are not available to ordinary savers like you or I, so to use them as a proxy for 'cash', when telling us that 'shares outperform cash' is slightly questionable. Moreover, the interest paid by the kind of two- and three-year higher-interest bank and building society deposit accounts, where many of us do actually put our savings, is almost always significantly higher than the interest on Government Treasury Bills.

For example, at the time of writing you would get around 0.5% on a UK Government Treasury Bill. But a two-year fixed-interest account is paying seven times that – 3.5%. You could argue that this is not a fair comparison due to the Government's QE programme holding down interest rates on government bonds. And it's true that before the 2007 crash, Treasury Bill rates used to be higher. Though even five or ten years ago, the interest rates we could get on a two- or three-year fixed-interest account was at least one to two per cent higher than on Treasury Bills. If Barclays had used the average interest paid by two- and three-year higher-interest bank accounts in their calculation, then you would probably find that for at least eighty of the last hundred years, cash would have easily outperformed shares. But that wouldn't have been the answer wanted by those who are so keen for us to put our money in share-based savings schemes like unit trusts and pension funds. The message that cash usually outperforms shares is certainly not one that would have been welcomed by the highly-paid, highly-bonused staff at Barclays Wealth. They make a very good living indeed from investing the savings of clients with anything from a few hundred thousand to a few million pounds. The last thing they would want their gullible fee-paying clients to realise is that many of them would be better off plonking their cash in their local building society rather than have Barclays expensively investing it for them.

There was just a brief period of twenty years (the 1980s and 1990s) when shares did outperform cash. But it could be argued that this was less due to shares being a great investment from companies making healthy profits and more because a flood of baby-boomer savings into unit trusts and pension funds pushed share prices up to unsustainable levels. As the baby boomers retire and as their money gets taken out of shares and pension funds and put into annuities, we can expect stagnation or even falls in share prices. And, of course, the Barclays study doesn't take account of the effect on our share-based savings of £154 million paid every single working day in fees, commissions and many other charges to financial advisers, unit trust bosses and pension fund managers by people with money in unit trusts and pensions.

Anyway, looking to the future, our Government is drowning in debt. If interest rates on Government debt were to rise significantly, the Government could end up paying over £100 billion a year in interest costs. This would be too much. It would be game over for Britain, as that's money we simply haven't got. So for its own survival, our Government will keep the interest rates it pays as low as possible. If it is successful, the gap between the interest paid on what Barclays describes as 'cash' – less than one per cent - and what we really can get from two- or three-year bank and building society accounts – at least 3.5 per cent - will remain close to today's extreme levels and the ever-unreliable Barclays' self-serving claim that 'shares usually outperform cash' will become even more preposterous.

Stuffed by the stock market

Stock markets can only survive if people investing in them believe that they have as much chance as any other investor of making reasonable returns should the market do well. Were people to find out that markets are rigged against them, they would probably put their money elsewhere. We saw an example of this in 2002. The German small companies market, the Neuer Markt, had to close down completely when investors withdrew their money after it was revealed there had been widespread price manipulation and fraud by insiders.

A useful statistic to bear in mind when thinking about putting money into shares or a unit trust is that in the US, the average time a share was held in 2011 was about twenty two seconds, up from twenty seconds in 2010. I'm not sure if similar information is available for Britain. But even if the average time a share is held in Britain is forty seconds, or one minute or even a massive two minutes, it's pretty clear that it's not ordinary savers like you or I who are driving this incredibly fast turnover in the ownership of company shares. The main reason shares are changing hands so quickly is what's called 'high frequency trading' (HFT). Many of the large banks and other financial institutions have built powerful computer systems that identify all the 'buy' and 'sell' orders coming into the market and the prices at which these orders will be executed. The HFT systems then use this knowledge to put through millions of transactions just ahead of the buy and sell orders. In this way they can 'scalp' – make tiny profits on every order. This has nothing to do with investing in businesses – it is purely about taking a small cut whenever a share changes hands. As one expert explained, 'high frequency traders are not interested in the fundamental worth of a company. They are only interested in making a quick killing then moving on'.[122] High frequency trading companies make tens of billions every year and this is money that would otherwise have gone to ordinary savers either from their share dealing, their unit trusts or their pension funds.

Other interesting denizens of the stock-market jungle are hedge fund managers. Most investments we make can only do what is called 'going long' – they make money if the assets they buy go up in price. There are some unit trusts that can also 'short' – make money by betting on falling prices. But people like hedge fund managers can make fortunes whether shares go up or down by either going long or short. And when a hedge fund manager has tens of millions, hundreds of millions or even billions depending on whether a share or a market or a currency goes up or down, there is a strong temptation for that manager to give the market a little help in temporarily going in the right direction. This may consist of trying to push a price up by spreading false stories through the financial press that a company was about to make a major positive announcement or else working to push a price down by launching rumours that a company was hiding bad news. One hedge fund manager admitted he used the 'bozos' in the financial press to move shares the way he wanted them to move when he was ready to cash out on a trade.

Other tricks used by market insiders are quote stuffing, pumping and dumping, shorting and distorting, dividend pumping, circular trading and good old-fashioned insider knowledge. All these techniques used by insiders mean that we have three-tier stock markets. The first tier consists of high frequency traders who scalp off their billions. The second tier is made up of lucky insiders who use all kinds of techniques to make fortunes at the expense of ordinary savers. Then in the bottom tier are the rest of us who are just left a few crumbs, if we're lucky. This is what happens in supposedly well-regulated western stock markets. The kinds of things that must go on in many Wild East countries, where corruption is much more endemic than in the West, don't bear thinking about.

Can you trust your unit trust?

Most people with savings in shares will have invested their money through unit trusts. Currently, we have about £500 billion in unit trusts. Before unit trusts started, anyone wanting to put money into shares would have had to buy individual shares through a usually expensive stockbroker. Unit trusts have been described as 'a breakthrough in financial democracy' because they allowed ordinary savers to put their money cheaply into shares through pooling it with others and paying professional managers to make investment decisions for them. Twenty to thirty years ago there were just a few hundred unit trusts in Britain which could choose which shares to buy from thousands of companies. So, it could be said that unit trust managers performed a valuable service sifting through different companies to find the ones whose shares were worth buying. But unit trusts have made so much money for their managers that they have kept on launching new ones. So we are now in an absurd situation where there about 3,200 unit trusts focusing on the British market but only around 2,600 companies on the London Stock Exchange, AIM and Techmark markets. Worldwide, there are around eighteen thousand unit trusts, but only about fifteen thousand companies which attract unit trust money. As there are more unit trusts than there are companies with shares for them to buy, many of them tend to buy the same shares. If you look at the sales bumf from any UK unit trust, you'll find most of them hold shares in companies like Vodafone, the drug money laundering HSBC, Shell, our good friend Aviva, our favourite bank Barclays, GSK and Marks and Spencer. This then begs the question – why pay so much to a unit trust manager, if many of them are doing pretty much the same thing?

There are two main types of unit trust – actively-managed and index trackers. With an actively-managed fund, charges tend to be higher because you are paying for expensive fund managers and all the research they do or buy to assist them with their investment decisions. With an index tracker, the fund just buys the main shares in your chosen stock market. Trackers are much cheaper as there is no need to pay for multimillionaire investment managers and all their support staff and information requirements. However, many actively-managed unit trusts buy shares in so many companies that they automatically become what are called 'closet trackers'. They claim to be actively managing your money, but are actually just matching the performance of the overall market. Though, because of you unit trust charges, you'll get much less than the market average performance. Another problem with unit trusts is that if you follow standard investment advice and diversify by putting your money into several unit trusts, then you own so many shares that you have probably unknowingly turned your portfolio into one that just tracks the overall index, yet you are paying expensive active management fees.

As for achieving good returns, you have to be careful to ensure that your interests and those of your unit trust managers are aligned. Unit trusts tend to go through two main phases. When they are first launched, they focus on growth. They will only have small amounts under management, so it's easier for them to find a few good opportunities and achieve seemingly impressive results. Then, either from marketing their successes to financial advisers or from taking ads in the press, a unit trust can brag about its performance and attract much larger sums of money. But once a unit trust has a few hundred million or even a billion or two to play with, it's much more difficult to find those elusive opportunities. Moreover, at that point unit trust managers tend to become more risk-averse – they have a lot of money under management, they are making a fortune in charges and they don't want to make any risky investments that might turn sour and cause savers to withdraw their money. This often results in previously apparently stellar performance falling back to or below the average. Then those who jumped on the bandwagon after the initial period of above-average growth will end up pretty disappointed as they find out that past performance really is no guide to the future. In fact, past performance can often give a very misleading impression of what will actually happen in the future. One critic of the sector explained:

> You see, it doesn't really matter to the unit trusts how well they perform as long as the money keeps rolling in….As long as people can be dazzled by glittering prospectuses and cleverly reported statistics, then just how well [they perform] isn't crucially important.[123]

In a way, unit trusts may have outlived their usefulness. Many clients are now paying a lot of money and getting very little in return except excessive charges - £59 million every working day. Unit trust management charges in Britain are higher than in the US where the market is more competitive. But if you really still believe that shares usually outperform cash and you definitely want to put your money into shares through unit trusts, there's a very simple and cheap way to do this. You just go online, look at the sales material for a few unit trusts you like the look of, make a list of the main shares they hold, take out a few companies that common sense says are real turkeys and then buy the other shares directly yourself. In this way, you get the fund managers' expertise without having to pay for it. Moreover, because you're not paying unit trust managers' many fees and charges, you'll probably find your portfolio consistently outperforms the unit trusts whose share suggestions you took.

Spotting the rubbish now, not later

Our Government's attempts to save its own financial skin by keeping interest rates artificially low and encouraging inflation to inflate away its debts have created a major problem for anyone with savings in a bank deposit account. The interest they are getting paid is at or below the level of inflation, especially once they've paid tax on their interest income. But this has also created massive opportunities for the good people who work in the British financial services industry.

The British financial services industry has a long and not very glorious history of selling us products which have made billions for insiders, but have lost money for unwary savers. Time and again, these schemes are touted with exaggerated projections about their potential growth. But years later, when savers look at the results, all they see are large fees paid out but little increase in, or even the evaporation of, their savings.

Deregulation of the pensions industry in the 1980s led to millions of workers in safe, inflation-protected final-salary pension schemes being sold risky investment-based pensions by commission-hungry salespeople using fanciful examples of likely investment returns. In the late 1980s and early 1990s, around five million of us were sold endowment mortgages which would supposedly pay off our mortgages. When the investment returns were lower than expected, customers had to find about another £40 billion to clear their debts. In the mid 1990s, hundreds of thousands of savers put almost £8 billion into supposedly 'high-income' bonds. Within the industry these were called 'precipice bonds' due to the way investors would see the value of their savings plummet were stock markets to fall significantly, which they did. About £5 billion of this money may have been lost.

When savings interest rates collapsed after the 2007 financial crisis, there was a flood of money out of banks as savers searched for higher returns. Thousands of mainly elderly people, who were clearly risk averse when it came to their money, were persuaded by their banks and financial advisers to move their savings from reasonably safe deposit accounts into stock-market investments which were marketed as 'low-risk', 'cautious' and 'balanced'. Unfortunately, the most widely sold were actually high risk, not at all cautious and rather unbalanced. Billions more of savers' money went up in smoke.

Despite having been caught mis-selling risky products to the generally risk-averse by pretending they were safe, and having had to pay billions in fines and compensation, many banks have come up with a new wheeze to get more of our money. Once again they have developed products with reassuringly positive names and are enthusiastically flogging what are often called 'Growth Bonds' or 'Guaranteed Bonds' or 'Capital Protected Funds' or 'Protected Capital Accounts' or something similar. As one of my banks wrote to me in a sales leaflet:

> It's fair to say that the last few years have been a tough time for savers, with interest rates remaining low. So it's understandable that finding ways to help your money grow has never been more important. As has knowing that your savings are with someone you can trust. At Company X, we believe that we can help you with both these things. Trust us to look after your savings. Our Protected Capital Accounts are a different way to unlock

the potential of your savings.

In the financial services industry, these schemes are called 'structured products'. The actual form of these products may vary quite a bit. But they tend to be something like promising to pay around 120 per cent of stock-market index growth for a five- or six-year period yet guaranteeing to return all of an investor's capital even if the index falls by a little. Or else they commit to a minimum of about 12.75 per cent gross (2.02 per cent a year) for six years with the potential to earn up to around 48 per cent dependent on stock-market performance. One other common version is the 'kick-out bond'. Kick-out bonds guarantee to pay quite high interest – often in the range of eight to slightly over ten per cent - provided the stock-market index is higher at the end of the year than it was when you put your money in. If it's not higher, you have to leave your money in for another year. But if it is higher you get your money back plus the interest. However, that's the end of your investment with the attractive interest rate – you are kicked out and so have to find a new home for your savings.

By 2008, we had put about £37 billion into structured products. By 2012 this had leapt to £58 billion, probably generating over £1.74 billion in commissions for those who convinced us to invest our money into these products. One expert expressed concern at the flood of money going into these savings schemes:

> The surging popularity of these products is worrying. Given low interest rates and robust inflation, it's such an easy sell for sales staff and advisers because they look so attractive[124]

Austerity for oiks

What too many savers apparently don't understand is that over three quarters of the benefits of stock-market investing come from the dividends paid by the companies whose shares are bought and not from any movements in the overall market. Yet these products only pay out on increases in the market index. Most markets don't rise over the five or six year terms of these bonds, they just fluctuate around an average level. For the FTSE100 this is about 5600.

Another concern with structured products is that it's incredibly difficult for the average saver to work out if these products offer good value or not. Few people will have any idea of the statistical probability of stock markets reaching the right level on a certain date for their savings to achieve decent returns. As a couple of experts explained, 'they can be fiendishly complex with underlying levels of risk, they don't benefit from share dividends and they make it difficult to get to your money'. And, 'as a rule these products are complicated and lack transparency – and it's nearly impossible to work out the charges behind them'.

In fact, there's a simple rule of thumb with these products. If you put your money into a structured product when the FTSE100 is below 5500, you're likely to gain: if your money goes in when the FTSE100 is above 5700, you're likely to lose money compared to what a bank or building society deposit account would have paid you.

In just the first three months of 2012, more than two hundred new structured products were launched. In a few years time, when these products mature, a few lucky savers will find they have done quite well out of them. But most will probably get back less than they would have earned just leaving their money in an ordinary bank deposit account, while massive profits are being made by those selling these schemes.

Enter Mr Bean

The attitude of our rulers to the misery experienced by ordinary people reliant on interest from their savings can be seen in an interview given by the Deputy Governor of the Bank of England, the possibly appropriately named Mr Bean (Charles Richard Bean). When asked what he thought about ordinary people who were seeing their savings being eroded by low interest rates and high inflation, he suggested they should eat into their capital if they needed money to survive:

> I think it needs to be said that savers shouldn't necessarily expect to be able to live just off their income when interest rates are low. It may make sense for them to eat into their capital a bit.[125]

He also said that he 'fully sympathised' with financially-squeezed savers, though he pointed out:

> It's very much swings and roundabouts. At the current juncture, savers might be suffering as a result of bank rates being at low levels, but there will be times in the future as there have been times in the past when they will be doing very well out of the fact that interest rates are at a relatively high level and I think that's something savers should bear in mind.

While we should no doubt be grateful that the Bank's Mr Bean so clearly empathises with those who are being financially hurt by the Bank's policies, it may be relevant to mention that pensioners trying to live off their savings would never be able to replace any capital they spent now while trying to avoid starving and that he personally had a very generous, multimillion pound, inflation-protected pension (see Chapter 13 – *Pop go our pensions* for details of Mr Bean's pension) and so would never need to worry about eating into his savings in order to have lots of taxpayer-funded fun in his retirement.

You ain't seen nothing yet

Imagine you're sitting in Number 10 or Number 11 Downing Street – all your policies are failing; the British economy is in a downward tailspin; tax revenues are collapsing; public spending is spiralling upwards completely out of control; we're paying more in debt interest than we do on defence and soon will be paying more on debt interest than we do on education; all your friends in the big banks and larger companies have found ways to avoid paying anything like the tax they should; and your government's popularity is at an all-time low. So what do you do? To avoid national bankruptcy, you have to get the economy moving. To get the economy moving, you need money fast and you need an awful lot of it. Where can you get your hands on the one or two trillion pounds that would save your political skin? Conveniently, British savers have that awfully inviting £4 trillion available to be looted by our ever-hungry leaders. That's a temptation few politicians could resist. After all, just swipe a quarter of people's savings and you've solved the country's economic problems at a stroke. But you need to find some smart way to steal people's savings which makes this theft acceptable. And that's not so easy. But it's not impossible either.

Chancellor George Osborne seems to have tried to have a go at taking our money to spend on rescuing himself from the effects of his failing economic policies. In 2011, he announced a plan to start using some of our £800 billion in pension savings to pay for infrastructure projects such as roads, railways, broadband, housing and so on. Osborne himself explained his great idea:

> We are finding the resources in difficult times to build the railways, to build the roads…We have got to weather the current economic storm and we have got to lay the foundations for a stronger economic future. And we have got to make sure that British savings in things like pension funds are employed here.[126]

This should send a chill down the spine of anyone who has watched our big-spending leaders and incompetent top civil servants waste at least £1.3 trillion of our money since 2000 on supposed 'investments' in the country's future. Adapting a line used in Gordon Brown's first speech as Prime Minister to the Labour Party conference, Osborne claimed he would use 'British savings for British jobs'.[127]

The Tories appear to be mulling over various ways of taking our pension savings to spend on saving the Government from bankruptcy. They could simply put pressure on pension funds to hand over our money. Or they could issue 'Growth Bonds' and encourage/force pension funds to buy them. The chief executive of the National Association of Pension Funds has already said that the Government's plan was an 'exciting opportunity'. So it looks like the Government will get its greedy hands on our cash. At the time of writing, the Government is only talking about grabbing £20 billion to £30 billion of our £800 billion pension savings. But the problem is that, once a door has been opened and politicians have found an original new way to take and waste our money, like drug addicts they will always come back for more.

With an election due in 2015 and the likelihood that Labour will wipe the floor with the failed Coalition, we have the prospect of Gordon 'Tax and Waste' Brown's long-term adviser, Ed Balls, taking over as Chancellor. By that time, the country's finances will be in an even more parlous state than now. The new Labour Government will desperately need more money to spend on boosting the economy and, with debts of about £1.365 trillion in 2015 heading up to £1.479 trillion a year later, Britain will have trouble borrowing more. Yet there for the taking will be all our pension savings. There will also be the fortunate precedent of Osborne having already raided or having attempted to raid this money to fund a few job-creating infrastructure projects. It's not very difficult to guess what the new Labour Government will do. Under the banner of something like 'fairness' and of course 'British savings for British jobs', Labour will divert a vast amount of our pension savings into an effort to get the economy growing again. Moreover, this has already happened in less developed countries like Argentina and Hungary. Their corrupt, financially-incontinent, cash-strapped governments nationalised their private pension savings. By 2015, Britain may be well on its way to becoming the Argentina of Northern Europe – a hopelessly indebted basket case of a country - so a similar expropriation of at least some of our pension money is not unthinkable.

We already have seen something similar happen before in Britain. It was the Tories who originally came up with the idea of the Private Finance Initiative (PFI) – using private-sector money to build hospitals, schools and roads. But because most projects didn't make economic sense, very little was done by the Conservatives to put the idea into action. However, when Blair's and Brown's and Balls's New Labour took office in 1997, they saw PFI as a wonderful way of spending enormous amounts of money without immediately increasing public spending as the projects would be paid for over the next twenty to thirty years. So, even though many projects were almost criminally over-priced, the New Labour Government went on a massive PFI spending spree which has saddled us with decades of payments which will eventually reach over £300 billion. We can expect the next Labour Government to do something similar with Osborne's 'British savings for British jobs' wheeze – a Tory idea will be turned by Labour into a massive tax-and-spend blow-out that will waste hundreds of billions of pounds of ordinary people's money while achieving less than nothing.

To use the wise words of Bachman-Turner Overdrive, 'B-b-b-baby, you ain't seen nothing yet, here's something you'll never forget'.

Chapter 13

Pop go our pensions

The ugly truth

In his 2011 budget speech, Chancellor George Osborne explained the need to make public-sector workers pay an average of three per cent more into their pension schemes 'to make sure that our public service pensions are both fair to those who give their working lives to help others, and fair to the taxpayers who have to fund them'.[128] He then went on to propose, 'I believe this House should also recommend similar changes to the pensions of MPs'. That sacrilegious suggestion probably went down like the proverbial lead balloon. So perhaps we shouldn't hold our breath. But while MPs and top civil servants and council bosses and NHS executives and military bigwigs and all the other members of the 'The 100,000 Club' – the more than one hundred thousand public-sector employees who each pocket more than £100,000 of our money every year – grimly hang on to their extraordinarily generous pensions, for many of the rest of us, financially our twilight years could look pretty bleak.

Of the thirty million or so private-sector workers in Britain, only just over two million – a mere seven per cent – are in final-salary pension schemes. When Gordon Brown first moved into the Treasury there were over five million private-sector members of final-salary schemes. But despite Labour's pledge of 'encouraging and rewarding saving, and enabling people to meet their income aspirations in retirement', this number has more than halved. In the lucky public sector about ninety per cent of employees are in final-salary schemes. Moreover, the number in private-sector final-salary schemes will fall further and faster in coming years as the few companies still offering them close their schemes or buy out their employees' final-salary pension rights. Some companies have been quite brutal as they tried to avoid their final-salary pension responsibilities. For example, when it closed its final-salary scheme, Britain's possibly favourite bank Barclays claimed that taking away employees' pension rights was 'in the best interests of employees'. One might be forgiven for suspecting that Barclays' highly-paid, highly-bonused bosses kept some kind of magnificently magnanimous final-salary scheme for themselves while downgrading their employees' pension rights.

As for the other twenty eight million private-sector workers, around eight million of these pay into pension schemes that are highly risky because they are dependent on the investment performance of their pension fund managers and the level of fees these managers decide to charge. The remaining twenty million have no pension savings at all and are relying entirely on the state pension to fund a life of fun and frivolity in their old age.

Danger - heffalump traps ahead!

For those of us who do decide to save for a pension, there are quite a few both obvious and well-camouflaged traps to avoid, as falling into them tends to make our financial masters just a little bit richer at our expense.

Give us your money, young man (woman)

The advice we're frequently given by those who are enthusiastic about us letting them look after our money is that the earlier we start saving for a pension, the more we'll have in our 'pension pot' by the time we retire. Various retirement experts are continuously warning us that it's in our own best interests to give them our money, 'you're never too young to start saving'; 'it is imperative for anyone looking to secure a sufficient income when they retire to begin saving as much as they can as early as they can'; 'for those who are still working, it has never been a more important time to save into a pension'; and 'if you don't start saving for retirement till you're middle-aged, you have left it too late'. But, as with so much advice we get from possibly interested parties, these exhortations to save for our retirement should be taken with a healthy dose of scepticism.

There are two groups of people who should be energetically putting money into a pension fund. These are people whose employers match their own contributions and higher-rate taxpayers. If you have a scheme where your employer's contribution is dependent on how much you save, then you get the benefits of both the employer's payments and the income tax benefits. If you're a higher-rate taxpayer, then you receive tax relief at the higher rate but are then likely to be a lower-rate taxpayer when you eventually take your pension. However, if you're a basic-rate taxpayer with no employer contribution, then all you're doing when saving for a pension is making your pension fund manager richer at your expense. Yes, you'll get twenty per cent tax relief on your pension savings. But, over a longer period, the fees taken by your fund manager will more than wipe out any tax benefits. For example, on any pension savings you make between the ages of thirty and forty, you'll have ended up paying between forty and fifty per cent of your money in fees by the time you retire. As for any money put in a pension in your twenties, this will incur fees of around sixty per cent by the time you retire – rather more than the paltry standard-rate tax benefits of twenty per cent. As one adviser explained, 'for a basic rate taxpayer with no employer contribution, there isn't much difference between a pension and an ISA'.[129]

In fact, if you're a basic-rate taxpayer, the best thing you can do with your money is to stay debt-free and pay off your mortgage as early as possible, rather than putting your money into the welcoming hands of a pension fund manager. On a twenty-five-year mortgage of £150,000, a borrower is going to end up paying in the region of £300,000. Just £2,000 a year extra paid for the first five years would knock about £20,000 and three years off that mortgage. Then there is also the fact that, as you get past the first five or ten years of your mortgage, you're more likely to move towards becoming a higher-rate taxpayer and that's when you should start slamming money into a pension. So, beware the 'start early' cheerleaders. Starting early may be right for some groups of people, but for others it's a terrible decision that will make financial services insiders much wealthier at the savers' expense.

Falling for the 'switch and get rich' trick

Many older pensions have higher charges than newer schemes and have often delivered dreadful performance for years. This makes it quite easy for financial advisers, insurance companies and others, who may or may not have our best interests at heart, to persuade us to move our savings from an expensive or poorly performing older pension fund to a newer, cheaper and hopefully more dynamic one. Often when switching our money, we'll have to pay some kind of penalties called 'Market Value Adjustments' or 'Market Value Reductions'. These can easily be as much as ten per cent or more of our money. In these cases, whoever is advising us to switch will probably use exaggerated growth projections for the fund to which they want us to move our money in order to prove to us that it's worth paying the penalties. Those who convince us to switch to another pension fund can immediately pocket anywhere from three per cent to over seven per cent of our savings in commission from the move – we switch, they get rich. One expert warned:

> Some financial advisers are still telling their customers to move their pension from one company to another just to earn commission – and some pension providers are even encouraging advisers to switch their clients' plans with the promise of a financial kickback, which comes out of the investor's pension fund.[130]

Another hidden danger with 'switch and get rich' is that older pensions might have guaranteed bonuses or annuity rate guarantees hidden away in the small print. Many of these will date from the 1980s and 1990s when interest rates were higher and stock-market performance was much better than it is today and will be for at least the next five to ten years. Most savers probably don't know about these guarantees and may be lured into switching from older, better funds and thus losing valuable benefits.

Making your cheap SIPP expensive

One of the most popular pension schemes people are turning to are Self-Invested Personal Pensions (SIPPS). These are usually much cheaper than traditional pension funds – typically charging about half a per cent a year – and they allow the saver to choose which shares, funds, bonds or whatever to buy with their pension money. But a classic mistake many savers make out of ignorance or else are persuaded to make due to the self-interest of people marketing various financial products is to inadvertently make their supposedly cheap SIPP even more expensive than a traditional pension.

If we imagine someone moving money from an older pension scheme, charging an extortionate 2.5 per cent a year, to a SIPP charging just half a per cent. This person is probably saving two per cent a year in charges from the move. So far, so good. But then this person is convinced by some advert or financial adviser that it's a really smart idea to put their SIPP money into a few unit trusts. Unfortunately, this leaves the saver paying half a per cent to the SIPP provider and maybe another two and a half per cent to the unit trust manager – three per cent in all. Plus you've got all the charges for buying into and later leaving unit trusts. Suddenly a SIPP invested in things like unit trusts has become more expensive than a high-cost older pension scheme and much more expensive than a newer scheme with one to one and a half per cent charges. However, it seems that a large number of SIPP savers are doing precisely this.

Believing the growth projections

Every year pension savers should get a statement showing the current value of their pension savings and giving projections about what their savings could be worth by the time they retire. The former financial services regulator, the Financial Services Authority (FSA), allowed pension companies to make these projections using three possible growth rates – Low 5%: Medium 7%: High 9%. These make great reading for pension savers as they allow the companies to project our savings turning into deeply satisfying, impressively large piles of money when we hit sixty five. The only problem is, of course, that for the last ten to twenty years virtually no pension fund has ever consistently achieved anything within shouting distance of these three commonly-used projected growth rates. And, when preparing our annual statements, our multimillionaire pension fund managers are well aware that these are just works of fiction, journeys into a fantasy world of happy, financially-healthy pensioners that doesn't exist and never will exist.

The average growth rate achieved by pension funds over the last fifteen years was just 3.4 per cent a year. That's significantly lower than even the lowest growth rate – around five per cent – typically used by the pensions industry. Even companies that have posted growth of less than one per cent a year for decades still have the gall to use the five, seven and nine per cent projected growth rates when fooling us about how much our pension fund will be worth when we retire. The medium rate of seven per cent is more than double what most pension funds have been able to make. Even the very best-performing fund only managed 6.7 per cent, below the medium growth rate used for projections. As for the top rate of nine per cent, well, as one newspaper put it, 'an annual return of nine per cent seems as likely as bankers voluntarily opting to forgo their bonuses'.[131] Moreover, given the vast amounts of debt to be paid off by most Western countries, economic growth is likely to be more than sluggish for the next five to ten years, making it extremely unlikely that pension funds will even be able to match the 3.4 per cent they have averaged in the past.

A study by the Organisation for Economic Cooperation and Development (OECD) found that 'British savers have suffered bigger losses from their workplace pensions in the last decade than virtually every other nation in the developed world'.[132] The only worse performing countries were the US and Spain. In contrast, countries like Germany, Poland, Chile and Australia achieved growth of between three and five per cent a year in spite of the last five years' economic turmoil.

The laughably hopeless FSA seems to have been dimly aware that there was a problem with pension projections. By mid 2012, it finally got around to consulting with the pensions industry about lowering the growth rates used, from five, seven and nine per cent to two, five and eight per cent.[133] While obviously a step in the right direction, these rates are still a country mile above what most funds will actually achieve over the next decade or two. So, on their retirement date, any savers foolish enough to have taken their pension managers' projections seriously and to be expecting a large river of cash to come sloshing their way are going to be more than sorely disappointed when they see the piteous actual value of their pension savings.

The destructive effect of even small charges

As with unit trusts, the charges of just one and a half to two and a half per cent that we pay to pension fund managers can look quite trivial at first glance. But over the longer term, these charges can have a disastrous effect on our retirement income and a correspondingly wonderful effect on the retirement income of our pension fund managers. Just to give an idea of the destructive effect even apparently small charges can have on our retirement savings, I've taken an example of someone who believes that saving for a pension is a great use of their money. As soon as the saver starts work at twenty five, they begin saving for their pension. Between twenty five and thirty five, the saver puts in £2,000 a year made up of own contributions, money from an employer and tax relief. From thirty five to forty five this goes up to £5,000 a year and from forty five to sixty five it rises to £7,000 a year, mainly thanks to the fact that the saver now gets higher-rate tax relief. By the time the person is sixty five, they will have put £210,000 into their pension fund. Of this, the saver and their employer will have contributed £140,000 and there will be tax relief of £70,000.

We'll assume that the saver's savings grow by the pension fund industry average of 3.4 per cent. If the money is in a low-cost pension scheme with just 1.5 per cent in fees, the £210,000 will have grown by £76,000 to £286,000. But the fund manager will have taken a healthy £65,500 for his or her efforts. If, as is more likely, the total charges including high first- and second-year commissions, annual fees and dealing costs are actually around 2.5 per cent, then the £210,000 will have only crept up by a very modest £28,500 to £238,500. But the fund manager won't be too worried as they'll pocket £96,600 (see Figure 1).

Figure 1 – Savers may be disappointed by the final value of their pension pots, but fund managers should be delighted

Someone paying in £210,000 over 40 years pays a lot in management charges.... (growth 3.4% a year)		
Pension charges	Growth for saver	Pension fund manager takes
1.5%	£76,000	£65,500
2.5%	£28,500	£96,600
...but there's not too much left for the saver		

What this example hopefully shows is that 2.5 per cent fees on a pension are almost equivalent to extortion, with fund managers pocketing more than three times as much as the saver gets in growth. Even fees of 1.5 per cent are unjustifiably generous to pension fund managers. Like savers in countries like Denmark and the Netherlands, we should actually be paying fund charges of no more than 0.3 per cent to 0.5 per cent a year.

Only half way there

Assuming you've managed to save a bit in your pension fund and you've avoided the various traps such as excessive charges, deliberately fanciful growth projections, the 'switch and get rich' scam, paying two lots of charges on your SIPP and so on, you might feel that you've successfully navigated your way through to pension paradise – a financially comfortable retirement. Unfortunately, you may be disappointed. Because ahead lies another almost insurmountable obstacle to your future happiness – the great annuity disaster.

Most people will use their pension savings to buy an annuity which guarantees them an income for the rest of their, and if they wish their partner's, lives. But there's some bad news – annuity rates have been going down for more than twenty years and there's no sign of them recovering any time soon. In 1990, pension savings of £100,000 would have bought you a flat-rate annuity (not inflation-linked) of over £15,600. By 2012, this had fallen almost two thirds to around £5,800. And if you wanted your annuity inflation-protected, by 2012 you'd only get about £3,500 a year for every £100,000 you had saved up.

There are several reasons for plummeting annuity rates. The most significant is that we're living longer. Since 1990, both men's and women's life expectancy has increased by about seven years. More recently, annuity rates have been further depressed by new solvency rules for insurance companies forcing them to hold more government bonds and by the EU gender directive which prevents men getting higher annuities than women even though men tend to die younger. But perhaps the two biggest dangers to your retirement bliss are the British Government's quantitative easing (QE) programme and widespread mis-selling in the annuities market.

The quantitative ease squeeze

Annuity rates are based on the yields paid on British Government bonds. Since 2009-10, as part of its QE policy, the Bank of England (BoE) has spent around £375 billion buying British government bonds. The BoE would probably claim that this QE programme helped keep the economy afloat by stimulating demand and reducing financing costs for companies. A cynic might liken QE to someone using one credit card to pay off the debts on another card. Moreover, critics of QE have claimed that the main reason the BoE did QE had little to do with boosting the economy and was really an attempt to use British taxpayers' money to lower the interest rates the British Government was paying on its massive £1 trillion of debt. We've already seen that the policy of low interest rates and QE has had a pretty disastrous effect on people with savings (Chapter 12 – *Siphoning off our Savings*). But it has probably been even more catastrophic for people moving into retirement.

QE damages our pensions in two main ways. Firstly, it pushes down the rates we receive from annuity companies. The chief executive of the National Association of Pension Funds (NAPF) warned:

> People who are retiring now are finding that annuity
> rates have been squashed by QE, and that they will get
> a smaller pension than they expected. Retirees who get
> locked into a weak annuity will find that the Bank's
> money printing leaves them out of pocket for the rest of
> their lives.[134]

Secondly, QE reduces the returns companies with final-salary
pension schemes can get on their funds and so leaves many
schemes with too little money to meet their liabilities. One es-
timate suggested that QE had increased company pension fund
deficits from about £260 billion to over £310 billion. To quote
the NAPF chief executive again:

> For companies that run final-salary pensions, QE is a
> headache which pushes their pension funds further into
> the red. This means businesses have to put more money
> into their pension schemes, instead of spending it on
> jobs and investment. Our fear is that firms struggling
> with a weak economy will simply choose to close their
> pension schemes.[135]

Enter, Mr Bean - again

When asked about the deleterious impact of QE on pension annuity rates, the BoE's Mr Bean did admit that there had been a
'downward impact on annuity rates which have fallen about a
percentage point over the past three years since we started our
purchases'. However, he also claimed that the impact of QE on
pension funds is 'often exaggerated' as QE would have helped
push up the value of assets like shares and bonds held by pension funds:

Those pension funds will typically have been invested in a mixture of bonds and equities, with perhaps a bit of cash too. The rise in asset prices as a result of quantitative easing consequently also raises the value of the pension pot, providing an offset to the fall in annuity rates.[136]

But several experts did not seem convinced by Mr Bean's explanation. One wrote:

The Bank of England argues that because the value of gilt investments increase as prices increase, this will compensate for falling yields and lower annuity rates. The vital flaw in this argument is that many individuals do not invest their pension funds in gilt or corporate funds as they approach retirement. In fact many are suffering from the so-called double whammy as both equity based pension funds and annuity rates head south.[137]

Another commented, 'QE is a key ingredient in a recipe that is destroying the value of the UK's retirement savings. It's a torture for pension funds because it artificially suppresses long-term interest rates'.[138]

It's difficult to know who to believe in this argument. One BoE executive explained that QE could cause suffering to some people:

It is inevitable that there are some people who have been made worse off by the direct impact of the Bank's asset purchases on gilt yields, and that have not benefited much from the effects on prices of other assets. These people are amongst the losers from very low gilt yields…But if monetary policy actions could be vetoed so long as someone was made worse off then there could be no monetary policy.[139]

But if you work for the BoE and have a generous inflation-protected public-sector pension for yourself, then you don't have to worry about things like retirement savings and annuity rates. After all, they don't affect you. In fact, as BoE bosses' pension money is invested in government gilts, QE has caused the value of these to rise sharply, giving massive increases in the value of these pensions (see Figure 2).

Figure 2 – Leading lights at the Bank of England have done very well indeed out of QE

Key Bank of England bosses saw huge increases in their pension funds

	Cash equivalent as at 28/2/11 £	Cash equivalent as at 29/2/12 £	Increase in %
Mr C R Bean	2,520,400	3,555,600	+41%
Mr P Tucker	3,656,600	5,006,600	+37%

Just in the twelve months from end February 2011 to end February 2012, Mr Bean's pension pot rose by over £1 million - a jump of an incredible 41 per cent. Paul Tucker's leapt up even more, by £1.35 million. By the time they retire, both these fine gentlemen can expect annual pensions of somewhere between £150,000 and £200,000 a year each, depending on how long they work. And we're the ones paying for these remarkably generous pensions. It must be very easy for BoE executives to preach pain, sacrifice and austerity for others, while they themselves are drowning in taxpayers' cash. As one commentator wrote, 'isn't that just a wonderful side benefit of being a central banker? Your actions can impact the ultimate value of your pension! How cool is that?'[140]

Annuity agony

Annuities are pretty complex financial products with an enormous number of different variations. You can have one that is level, increasing or inflation-protected. Your annuity can be guaranteed (it pays out for an agreed number of years even if you pop your clogs) or not guaranteed (if you go to a better place, the annuity provider keeps all your money). There are investment-backed annuities and with-profits annuities. And there are normal annuities and enhanced or impaired annuities. This complexity creates the space for massive mis-selling and people already receiving annuities are probably losing up to £1 billion a year – around £20 million a week – because they have been sold an annuity which doesn't suit their particular circumstances. Our annuity companies are probably quite content to receive this £1 billion a year in extra but unmerited profits.

The most common problem seems to be that people are not using what's called the 'open market option' (OMO). Before

1988, most people bought their annuities from the companies which held their pension funds. Following the 1988 Income and Corporation Taxes Act, companies were under an obligation to let savers know that they could buy their annuity from any company and so get the best rates on the market. Most people could increase their pension income by fifteen to twenty per cent by buying the best annuities available rather than automatically taking the product being sold by their pension company. But often, the OMO is hidden so deep in the annuity contract, that people aren't aware of it and so don't shop around.

Another major issue is that too many retirees are not taking what are called 'impaired' or 'enhanced' annuities. If you have been a smoker or have any condition like high cholesterol, the annuity company will expect that you depart this earth a few years earlier than a healthier person. So they can offer you a higher pension while you're still around as they believe they'll have to pay it for fewer years. Smokers, for example, can get about five per cent more; high cholesterol and blood pressure can push your annuity up by twenty five per cent. Only about six per cent of retirees get enhanced annuities even though over twelve per cent of them have been smokers. Many more retirees will also have other conditions – diabetes, a dodgy ticker, high blood pressure, first signs of dementia - or be overweight. Experts have estimated that between thirty and forty per cent of annuitants should be receiving these higher annuity payments, rather more than the six per cent or so who actually receive them.

As soon as you hit sixty five, your pension company or financial adviser will probably encourage you to hand over your money in return for the tempting 'security of an income for the rest of your life'. But buying an annuity immediately on hitting sixty five may be a terrible decision for you, though not for them. Say you retire at sixty five and expect to hang around annoying everybody for another thirty years till you finally check out at ninety five. At sixty five, apart from an abundance of wrinkles, the odd twinge and occasional problems in the waterworks department, you'll hopefully be reasonably healthy. By seventy, a few parts of your body may be creaking and groaning or worse. By seventy five, various bits and pieces may have stopped working altogether or may even have dropped off. If you had bought an annuity when healthy at sixty five, you'd get the lowest payment level for the rest of your life. But if you hang on till seventy or even seventy five, you're much more likely to qualify for an enhanced annuity. Plus, as you've less time left on this earthly paradise, you'll get higher payments anyway. So, while it's clearly in the interests of your pension provider and financial adviser to get hold of your money as soon as they can, it's probably in your interest to buy your annuity as late as possible or at least to wait until your failing health qualifies you for an enhanced annuity.

Moreover, you may rush off to meet your maker slightly earlier than you expected. If you drop dead soon after buying an annuity, then your pension savings stay with your annuity provider and make them very happy indeed to have got so much of your money while having to pay out so little for so few years. But if you'd waited before buying an annuity and suddenly go to that great spaceship in the sky before handing over your cash, then your family or friends or your dog will get your money - rather them than some greedy financial adviser and insurance company.

Welcome to the 'banana skin and grave brigade'

Our friends in the financial services industry have many nice and not so nice names for their older, slightly mature customers. One of the more polite is the 'banana skin and grave brigade' because they have one foot on a financial banana skin as they don't know much about finance, savings and investments and the other in the grave as they'll presumably soon be going on to a better place where they won't be needing their money any more, so there's no real harm done relieving them of their cash before they depart. Financial services salespeople, usually claiming to be advisers, really like banana skin and gravers as they tend to have lots of accumulated savings and investments – certainly much more than young people who might be trying to pay off student loans or saving up to buy their first home.

There have been hideous examples of banks convincing older people to put almost all or all their life savings in just one savings product or fund. When the product turned out to be a dud or the fund crashed and burned, these customers were ruined and, being retired or close to retirement, they had no way of rebuilding their lost savings. But the banks pocketed generous commissions from fleecing their older customers.

In another scandal concerning banana skin and gravers, a subsidiary of HSBC was found to have been sending its salespeople into retirement homes and care homes persuading the elderly, some of whom were chronically ill, to put their life savings into longer-term (five or six years) investments. When quite a few customers died before their supposed 'investments' matured, their heirs found they had to pay usurious early withdrawal penalties to get hold of granny's or grandad's cash.

Even if banana skin and gravers don't have much ready cash, they'll often own their own homes making them 'asset-rich but cash-poor'. The asset-rich, cash-poor make excellent targets for sellers of products like equity release schemes. With these, customers can get a lump sum or an income in return for handing over some of the value of their home. The money is paid back when the home is sold. Interest rates and charges tend to be quite high on equity release products – interest rates were about six to seven per cent at the time of writing, considerably higher than a traditional mortgage.

We can use the example of someone taking out the average equity release sum of a quite modest £50,000 at sixty five against a home worth £200,000. Perhaps they want the money to do up the house, pay for grandchildren's education, a round-the-world trip or whatever. But by the time they were eighty five, thanks to the wonders of compound interest, they would owe the whole value of their £200,000 home, leaving not too much to pay for nursing home fees or to hand on to their survivors. As one critic of these schemes wrote, 'the only winners in equity release are the companies and elderly people who die just a few years after taking out the policy.'

Part 5

Fightback

Chapter 14

Missed opportunities

The situation inherited by the Coalition was a horror story of truly epic proportions. The country was to all intents and purposes bankrupt, with public spending spinning out of control while tax revenues were collapsing. Moreover, with the Eurozone in crisis and the US in recession, there was no possibility of growing our way out of the mess. So it wasn't exactly 'business as usual' for the incoming government. What were needed were honesty, courage, economic competence and imagination. Sadly, in spite of significantly increasing the number of special advisers that we had to pay for, so their cost rose from £4.8 million in 2010 to £6.2 million by 2012, the Coalition has showed itself to be dishonest, cowardly, economically incompetent and totally lacking in imagination. As one Tory MP, perhaps ruefully, remarked:

> The more advisers this Government recruits, the bigger mess it seems to make of things. What is the point of them? If they were experts in policy, the cost might just be acceptable. But they are not. Most of them look no more than fifteen years old and seem more suited to making the tea than advising senior Cabinet ministers.[141]

The economy will always go through cycles of growth

and contraction – the booms and busts that the great historian Gordon Brown, ably assisted by the economic genius of Ed Balls, claimed he had abolished. Governments therefore need to pursue counter-cyclical policies to try to mitigate the effects of the booms and busts. In periods of rapid growth, they should dampen property and share-price bubbles and use increasing tax revenues to pay down national debt. In times of economic contraction, they should use public money to stimulate investment and create jobs. Unfortunately for us, Brown and Balls pursued pro-cyclical policies and managed to hugely increase spending and borrowing during the boom. So when the bust came, there was, as former Accenture consultant and then Chief Secretary to the Treasury Liam Byrne so accurately pointed out 'no money left'.

With our national debt heading towards the stars, the Coalition has correctly maintained that it would be disastrous to follow Labour's proposals to borrow even more to try to boost the economy. So the Coalition has grimly stuck to its failing austerity policies. Labour has repeatedly claimed that we have 'a recession made in Downing Street'. While this is somewhat of an exaggeration, it is true that the recession has been made much worse by Downing Street since the Coalition took office. But what was actually needed was not Labour's cherished solution to every problem - more borrowing and spending that we couldn't afford. Instead there should have been a rapid transfer of money from unproductive areas, like pointless bureaucracy, into job-creating activities such as house and road building. Sadly, the Coalition has hypocritically preached to us about the need to cut public spending, while dishonestly increasing the spending which was under leading politicians' direct control. Moreover, the Coalition lacked the courage to take on the vested interests of the public-sector bureaucracy; lacked the economic competence to understand the need to stimulate growth and jobs

Missed opportunities

while squeezing public spending; and lacked the imagination to find ways of transferring unproductive public spending into productive spending.

Moreover, the Coalition's one, and seemingly only, 'big policy' to promote growth – quantitative easing (QE) - turned out to be a totally predictable and avoidable farcical failure. The main point of QE was supposedly to provide cheap money for businesses and homeowners to borrow and this should have theoretically increased private-sector spending and investment. But Osborne had previously made an agreement with the banks, called Project Merlin, that they would increase lending to businesses. Project Merlin was a flop because, with the economy in recession, there was little demand for new loans. Why would companies want to take on more debt, if their turnover was shrinking by the day? The problem in the economy was not a lack of lending, but rather a lack of demand for this lending. Many of our companies were actually sitting on historically high levels of cash, but didn't have the confidence to invest any of this. So what did the Government and the Bank of England do? They gave even more of our money to the banks. Much of this will end up in bankers' bonuses as they will either use the cheap money to speculate on things like oil, grain and other commodities or else they will increase their profit margins on the rare occasions they do actually lend out some of our cash. All that QE actually succeeded in doing was hugely impoverishing anyone with savings or buying a pension. Though QE did significantly decrease the Government's cost of borrowing, which is perhaps the real reason we have had repeated doses of QE, even though it has done less than nothing to boost economic growth.

So, what could and should the Government have done? There are at least five major actions that could have cut unproductive public spending, dramatically reduced tax evasion, eased the financial squeeze on households, boosted economic growth and shown that we had a government that was acting in the interests of the majority, not just the wealthy political, business, banking and bureaucratic elites:

1. Slay the bureaucracy monstrosity

Under Gordon Brown's and Ed Balls's massive spending splurge, our bureaucracies got used to wasting massive amounts of our money on themselves. As the Coalition Government tries to cut public spending, we're hearing worrying stories about the numbers of police, nurses, soldiers and other frontline workers losing their jobs. But we're not going bankrupt because we have too many nurses, doctors, carers, police officers, ambulance drivers, binpersons or teachers. In fact, while public spending more than doubled under the financially incontinent Gordon Brown and Ed Balls from £322bn to over £700bn, the number of frontline workers in the NHS, policing, local government and education only went up by a modest ten to fifteen per cent.

But in the wonderful world of public-sector management, it was quite a different story, with the number of managers doubling, and sometimes more than doubling in the NHS, education, the probation service, councils and policing. Productivity in the public sector fell every year under New Labour with ever less being achieved by ever more managers. Not only do we now have many more managers, but they're also getting paid much more. Jobs which once had salaries of £50,000 a year now get £150,000 a year or more. In central government and quangos, there are probably over 100,000 people being paid more than £100,000 each. In local government, the number of people pocketing over £50,000 a year shot up since 1997 by a factor of eleven from 3,300 to 38,000, while in the economy as a whole it only went up by a factor of three. Some councils now have an astonishing twenty to thirty times as many staff earning £50,000 a year or more than they did just over ten years ago.

Once any organisation has built up layer upon layer of unnecessary and wasteful bureaucracy, it's difficult to cut costs without severely reducing vital services. The many levels of management cannot see that it is actually they who are overpaid and superfluous. So the only way they can think of reducing costs is by cutting usually lower-paid, frontline staff – the people who do the real work. Unless we attack the underlying problem with public spending, the relentless rise of self-serving bureaucrats, the politicians' cuts are going to devastate our essential services while preserving all the costly and wasteful bureaucratic empires that have caused the massive and unproductive explosion in public spending in the first place.

Just a quick look at the *Guardian's* public-sector *Jobs* section suggests that our bureaucrats have learnt nothing and are still looking to expand their own empires with pointless bureaucratic 'non-job' appointments, while cutting frontline staff (see Figure 1).

Figure 1 – The *Guardian* still has hundreds of well-paid public-sector jobs, which could seem to be 'non-jobs'

Are Britain's bureaucracies are still wasting our money on 'non-jobs'?
(from Guardian jobs section 23 July 2012)

Online Community Manager
London   £36,238
Are you passionate about giving Londoners a say in the decisions that affect their lives? Can you inspire conversation and debate? If the answer is 'yes' then this could be the job for you

Democratic Services and Governance Manager
Scale 8 – 9 (up to £42,671)
At Blaby District Council we are proud to serve a community where people want to live and work, where we provide valued services that respond to the needs and aspirations of all our communities

Head of Market Management and Governance
Newham   Up to £92,500
You will need a strong commercial focus to develop provider frameworks, ensuring we manage risk whilst also developing a flexible and responsive market.

Many of these jobs look decidedly unnecessary and the descriptions of some of them just seem to be collections of meaningless verbiage taken at random from a dictionary of fashionable management gobbledegook.

In Britain, the balance of power has shifted so that our bureaucracies feel that ordinary taxpayers are there to serve them, rather than them being employed to serve those who pay their generous salaries and pensions. Given the appalling state of the country's finances, we don't have five or ten years to try to wean our bureaucrats off their addiction to wasting our money on themselves, while they desperately cut frontline jobs to preserve their own positions, salaries and pensions. Our Government needs to deliver a short, sharp shock to the bureaucrats to remind them that they work for the people and not the other way round.

A few of us might remember Edward Heath's 3-day week, brought in at a time of national emergency – a lack of power. Now we have a new national emergency – a lack of money. Instead of firing frontline workers, the government should immediately implement a 4-day week for all public-sector managerial and administrative staff who are not directly delivering services to the public. This would include all council executives and managers; all executives and managers in the NHS; all executives, managers and most administrative staff in the main government departments like Health, Education, Environment, Business Enterprise and Regulatory Reform (or whatever it's called this week) and many others; and almost all staff working for regulators and quangos like the absurd and unaffordable Equalities and Human Rights Commission. Administrative staff processing things like driving licences, passports, benefits, pensions and so on could be exempted, but their managers should also be put on the 4-day week. Probably the least disruptive solution would be to make them take every Friday off. Plenty of manufacturers cut shifts when they were hit by the recession, so why can't the public sector do something similar?

Moving managers and bureaucrats to a 4-day week should immediately bring real cash savings of well over £100 million a week - worth more than £5 billion a year - without any redundancy packages or any early retirement payments. Moreover, we will probably find that frontline workers actually deliver the same if not better services without the army of policy advisors, executives, managers, communications professionals, diversity officers, community relations specialists, involvement officers and others of their ilk. After three months, at least half these people should be put on a 3-day week saving us another £50 million a week. After all, how many of us would notice if the Department of Health or the Equality and Human Rights Commission or the Carbon Trust only worked Monday to Wednesday? Investing this £100 million to £150 million a week in say building new houses and other infrastructure projects could create more than 100,000 jobs. That's 100,000 less people claiming benefits and 100,000 more paying tax.

It's not a tough decision. As the politicians survey the disastrous state of our public finances, we're constantly hearing the expressions 'tough decisions' and 'difficult choices'. Yet bringing in a 4-day week and then a 3-day week for executives, managers, administrators, diversity officers and suchlike wouldn't be tough at all. Unfortunately our Government is incapable of implementing such a simple solution as most ministers have never had a proper job and so haven't got a cutting clue what they're doing.

2. **Scrap corporation tax**

Revelations of how little tax our major banks and multinational companies pay may have got many ordinary taxpayers fuming in impotent rage. Yet we should remember that many taxes only have a limited useful life. For a time they will raise revenue. But some taxes will outlive their usefulness because they cause changes in behaviour and people find ways of avoiding paying them.

In Britain, we've had several taxes that have come and gone. There was Henry VIII's beard tax introduced in 1535. Avoidance was easy – you just shaved off your beard. In 1662 Charles II brought in an early type of poll tax, the hearth tax. It was considered too difficult to count how many people lived in each home, so instead the tax was based on the number of chimneys. The result was that enterprising citizens started combining several fireplaces into a single chimney. A few hundred people are thought to have died from the ensuing house fires, but at least they paid less tax. In 1696 William III brought in a window tax leading to many homes bricking up some windows. 1795 saw the introduction of a tax on wigs and wig powder. Result – wigs became less fashionable. And around 1800 the government started a hat tax. Each hat had to have a stamp sewed into it showing that it was legal. The penalty for forging these stamps was death, which might give some people odd ideas about how to deal with our tax-avoiding elites.

Corporation tax came in with the 1965 Finance Act. Prior to that, companies and individuals paid the same income tax with an additional profits tax levied on companies. But perhaps like so many taxes before it, corporation tax is getting past its sell-by date. As companies become increasingly international and as more of them are taken over by financial speculators rather than

Missed opportunities

businesspeople, they find ever more ways of avoiding paying corporation tax. During the Gordon Brown boom of 1997 to 2007, the amount paid by small companies in corporation tax shot up by over 130 per cent. But at the same time, even as their profits and bonuses soared into the stratosphere, financial services firms only paid a modest 27 per cent more. Our largest, often international, companies handed over just five per cent more. Corporation tax is on the way to becoming a hugely onerous tax on small and medium-sized businesses (SMEs) and a tax that larger companies can more or less ignore.

Banks and larger companies have a bewildering variety of ways to pay as little tax as possible. And when they do pay tax, it's usually in a country where tax rates are minimal. The world's largest computer systems and management consultancy, for example, has over a hundred thousand employees worldwide. Yet for tax purposes it's based in Bermuda where it employs around a dozen staff. So, one might be tempted to think that the Bermuda incorporation had more to do with tax avoidance than the island being a critical centre for the company's major customers.

Given that about fourteen million people – around half of private-sector employees – work for Britain's 4.5 million SMEs, we only need one in four SMEs to hire just one person each for unemployment to drop by over one million and for the economic recovery to be in full swing. That's why we have to get rid of a tax that penalizes SMEs, while letting larger companies off paying their fair share.

Chancellor George Osborne has proposed to cut corporation very slightly over the next two to three years. But perhaps he's missing a trick. Maybe corporation tax should go the same way as the taxes on beards, hearths, wigs, windows and hats. As it currently works, corporation tax has an immensely destructive effect on our economy. It places an unfair burden on smaller companies; it encourages financial firms and larger companies to move their profits and sometimes even their people out of Britain and it makes it advantageous for financial manipulators to borrow huge sums of money to buy productive, tax-paying companies as they can extract massive payments for themselves while using the interest payments on their borrowings to minimize the amount of taxable profits. The takeovers at firms like BAA and Cadbury's have made their acquirers wealthy while slashing our government's tax receipts.

If we are to deal with the deficit and create growth, we need to scrap corporation tax completely. Instead, we should have a transaction tax on all business activities carried out in Britain, regardless of whether a company claims to be based in Switzerland, Bermuda, Ireland, the Cayman Islands or on the Moon. In fact, we already have that tax – it's called VAT. Instead of fully refunding VAT to businesses, the government should get rid of corporation tax and replace it by retaining the necessary amount of VAT. For financial firms, there should be a tax on their assets.

Binning corporation tax would have quite a few almost miraculous benefits for our economy. Firstly, it would make tax avoidance virtually impossible as the government would already have collected the money in VAT payments. Also, there would be no need for companies to play all sorts of games to hide their profits or shift them offshore. Moreover there would be a huge incentive for our companies to stay in Britain and for many thousands of foreign companies to move their bases to Britain, creating hundreds of thousands of well-paid jobs. And, of course, the practice of buying companies while loading them with massive debts would no longer make sense for financial predators.

As a meerkat might say, 'it's simples'. Scrapping corporation tax would be the most imaginative and beneficial act

George Osborne could ever do. It's a pity that today's politicians and their many expensive and ambitious advisers are lacking the necessary imagination.

3. Bring in a False Claims Act

In mid-2012, several newspapers reported that four former GlaxoSmithKline (GSK) employees could be in line for a $250 million (£159 million) payout from the US Government under the Federal False Claims Act. The four had been key to the US Government securing a $3 billion (£1.9 billion) fine against drugs giant GSK for mispromoting several drugs and for failing to submit required safety data to regulators on a diabetes drug. Three years ago, in my book *Fleeced* I explained why we needed a False Claims Act in Britain.

Since the American Civil War the USA has had a law rejuvenated by Congress in 1986 called the False Claims Act. This allows ordinary citizens with evidence of fraud or corruption against government contracts or programmes to sue, on the government's behalf, in order to recover any money taken illegally. As a reward for their efforts, whistleblowers are given somewhere between fifteen and twenty five per cent of the money recovered or saved. Just one partner in a US consultancy, which also works extensively throughout Britain's public sector, stood to gain $10 million for revealing how his employer had been cheating various US government departments over travel expenses. It's quite likely that the same company has been using exactly the same travel expenses scam in Britain to steal many millions of pounds of our money. But the company has a lot of influence with both Labour and Conservative politicians and so no action has been taken against it here.

The False Claims Act protects taxpayers' money in

two ways. Firstly, it encourages whistleblowers to take action. Secondly, and perhaps much more importantly, it has an incredibly strong deterrent effect – it discourages individuals and companies from overcharging or defrauding government departments because they will always know that they run a serious and real risk of being sued by any concerned or even disgruntled employee who knows what they are up to.

If any British government really was serious about ensuring value for taxpayers' money, it would introduce a version of the False Claims Act whereby whistleblowers supported by no-win-no-fee lawyers would be able to launch prosecutions on behalf of the taxpayer and take a share of the money that was saved. While the Act only leads to the recovery of a few billion a year from suppliers in America, it is generally accepted that it dissuades companies from trying to overcharge and defraud the US Government of many hundreds of billions more.

At the moment, if a company employee in Britain wants to expose his or her bosses for ripping off the taxpayer, it's likely they will lose their job, never work again and even be sued by their employer. If we had a False Claims Act, then employees would know they could score millions by reporting any company taking advantage of the incompetence of our civil servants to fleece us taxpayers. That would make companies more circumspect when planning to plunder the public sector. Just a three per cent reduction in purchasing costs from a False Claims Act would save taxpayers over £5 billion a year.

4. Turn key business sectors into national assets

When the French yoghurt-maker Danone was targeted by a German company in an attempted takeover, the French Government acted quickly to protect French interests. It declared Danone a 'strategic national asset'. Under European Union rules, businesses which are 'strategic national assets' are exempt from the open competition regulations which apply to normal firms. In a disastrous policy of Britain being 'open for businesses', successive governments have allowed key industries like electricity, gas and water supply and airports to be sold off to new foreign owners. These owners have either loaded our companies with massive debts while extracting huge management fees for themselves as BAA's (British Airports Authority) Spanish bosses did or else they have used their ownership to transfer tens of billions from British customers, frequently through tax havens, into their own pockets. EDF with its 5.5 million British customers, for example, is little more than a mechanism for the company's majority owners, the French Government, to fill its own coffers with our money.

These companies don't care if they get bad press by ripping off British companies as they have no loyalty to this country and anyway this country represents only a small part of their international business interests. If our politicians had any cojones, they would declare all our gas, water and electricity companies and our airports to be 'strategic national assets' which can only be owned by British companies based for tax purposes in the United Kingdom. The Government could then give foreign owners a period of say five years to dispose of their UK operations. This would give two major benefits. Firstly, British-based companies would be more sensitive to negative publicity and thus would be less likely to squeeze their customers by charging punitive prices. And secondly, the profits made by these companies would be taxed in Britain and so would benefit this country.

5. Cut the cost of politics

Oliver Cromwell is credited with having given the following speech when he dissolved Parliament on 20th April 1653:

> It is high time for me to put an end to your sitting in this place, which you have dishonored by your contempt of all virtue, and defiled by your practice of every vice; ye are a factious crew, and enemies to all good government; ye are a pack of mercenary wretches, and would like Esau sell your country for a mess of pottage, and like Judas betray your God for a few pieces of money.
>
> Is there a single virtue now remaining amongst you? Is there one vice you do not possess? Ye have no more religion than my horse; gold is your God; which of you have not barter'd your conscience for bribes? Is there a man amongst you that has the least care for the good of the Commonwealth?
>
> Ye sordid prostitutes have you not defil'd this sacred place, and turn'd the Lord's temple into a den of thieves, by your immoral principles and wicked practices? Ye are grown intolerably odious to the whole nation; you were deputed here by the people to get grievances redress'd, are yourselves gone! So! Take away that shining bauble there, and lock up the doors. In the name of God, go!

Most people observing how shallow, self-serving, corrupt and greedy today's politicians have become would probably feel Cromwell's words were just as relevant now as they were over 350 years ago, if not more so. Cameron and Clegg both pledged to cut the cost of politics, but both actually increased it. With modern communications, with the EU making most of our laws, and with many responsibilities devolved to the hundreds more politicians in the Scottish, Welsh and Northern Ireland administrations, we obviously don't need so many MPs at Westminster any more. We don't even need Cameron's proposed 600, or for that matter 500 or 400. In the US, there are just 435 members of the House of Representatives and 100 in the Senate for almost three hundred million people. In Britain we have an extraordinary 650 MPs in the Commons and around 800 peers in the Lords for just over sixty million people. Any politician serious about cutting the cost of politics would reduce the House of Commons to somewhere between 200 and 300 MPs at most and replace the House of Lords with fifty to sixty elected senators. That would cut the cost of politics.

Of course, this can never and will never happen – turkeys, Christmas, don't vote and so on. But as our politicians demand more money, a shorter working week, more holidays, higher expenses and even more elected politicians, it's perhaps worth us ordinary taxpayers remembering that the most we need are two to three hundred in the Commons and say sixty in the Lords. This will better help us see through all the lies and misinformation spread by our greedy, self-serving politicians as they try to justify increasing their own numbers and pocketing ever more of our cash.

In no particular order

There are many other smaller measures the Government could enact to show that it represents voters rather than the vested interests of the ruling business, bureaucratic and political elites. So here, in no particular order, are just a few.

Prosecute any bankers found to have broken the law.
There's a wonderful book called *Ship of Fools* which describes
the corruption, cronyism and incompetence of the Republic
of Ireland's mafia-like ruling elite. In the book the author
reveals how Ireland's top bankers made hundreds of millions
in loans to themselves and their close friends. Now even the
thoroughly corrupt Irish establishment is tentatively starting
police investigations and prosecutions. But in Britain, bankers'
criminality is still rewarded by massive payoffs and pensions.

The problem for Britain is that our politicians of all
parties are doing everything they can to protect their banking
paymasters. After all, one in eight lords is already on the banks'
payroll and think how many MPs are hoping to get nice, highly-
paid sinecures with a bank or two when they leave Parliament.
Yet there seem to be strong grounds for bringing prosecutions
for things like obtaining money by deception, conspiracy to
defraud, issuing false prospectuses and knowingly trading
while insolvent. In case our useless Serious Fraud Office and
pointless, politically-correct police don't know where to look,
here are a few people they could start with – Fred Goodwin,
Sir Tom McKillop, Andy Hornby, Adam Applegarth, Lord
Stevenson, Lord Green from the money-laundering HSBC,
Peter Cummings, Sir James Crosby and of course Bob Diamond
and Jerry del Missier from the rate-rigging Barclays.

Make our multimillionaire sports stars fund grassroots sports.
Maybe it's also time for those who make so many millions out
of sport to put something back? The Government could impose
a thirty per cent tax on football transfer fees. That would raise
many millions that could be put into grassroots sport. Moreover,
the FA could introduce a rule whereby each time a footballer
gets a yellow card, they have to pay one week's wages as a fine.
Each red card could cost a month's wages. This would reduce

the number of fouls in football and also raise considerable sums to be donated to encouraging sport in deprived communities.

Set a maximum public-sector pension of £25,000. At the moment senior civil servants, hospital bosses, council chiefs, quangocrats and many others will get tax-free payments of several hundred thousand pounds of our money when they retire and five- and six-figure pensions for the rest of their and their partners' lives. This is unaffordable. The Government should set a maximum public-sector pension of say average earnings, about £25,000 a year. If any public-sector bigwig wants more in their retirement, then they should save up for it in a risky private-sector pension fund just like the rest of us. If all these highly-paid bureaucrats are not happy with such a move, they could always go on strike. Though if they were to stay at home, it's unlikely the country would grind to a halt. Or else they could go on a protest march to Westminster demanding that we all continue to pay their £70,000 to £100,000 a year pensions. It would be interesting to see how much public sympathy and support they would attract. For too long these people have been gorging themselves on our money – it's time to call their bluff and show we don't care if they stay or go, but we're not paying them so much any more.

Force companies to disclose trends in executive pay clearly. Companies should be legally obliged to include in their annual accounts three graphs showing the ten-year trend of the total amounts (including bonuses and share options) paid to executives compared to share price, dividend payments and average employee pay. These three pieces of information would be extremely useful in helping shareholders find out if they're getting value from company executives. For example, shareholders would be able to clearly see if executive pay was rising faster than the share price or dividends. And by tracking executive pay against average employee pay, they would also show employees if they're been taken for a ride by bosses who are forever spouting platitudes like 'our people are our most important assets' while filling their own already bulging pockets at employees' and shareholders' expense.

Regulate so that pension companies have to show their charges. An obligation should be placed on all pension companies to tell each saver in his or her annual statement precisely how much in pounds has been deducted from their savings during the previous year in fees, commissions, management costs and dealing expenses. If you are nearing retirement and have say £450,000 in your pension fund, you might easily be paying £11,000 a year or more in annual charges. That's really quite a lot of money. This information would be pretty useful in helping savers see if they are getting value from their pension company. The same duty of disclosure should apply to unit trusts.

Set a legal limit on charges by pension companies. Pension companies in other countries can make a reasonable living by charging around half a per cent a year. This makes it difficult to see why in Britain they charge one and a half, two, three and sometimes even four per cent a year. Moreover, pension firms take their generous cut of our money however brilliant or more often however dismal their performance. The successor to the FSA should set a limit on pension company charges of say half a per cent a year, plus allow them to take an additional ten per cent of any growth achieved during the year. This would cut charges to savers in bad years and give fund managers an incentive to increase savers' money – an incentive they don't currently have.

Introduce ten-year probationary passports. Anyone born

abroad who applies for a British passport should be made to sign a contract in which they agree that if they or any of their dependents are charged with any criminal offence during their first ten years holding a British passport, then they automatically lose their probationary passport for ten years. At the end of the ten years, they could apply again for a new probationary passport provided neither they nor any dependents had been convicted of a criminal offence.

This could also be extended to people requesting the right to remain in Britain. They too could sign a contract whereby they agree to obey our laws and that they lose the right to remain in Britain if they or any of their dependents are convicted of any crime. These two measures would probably lead to a significant reduction in crime levels and allow us to get rid of undesirables without being repeatedly blocked by the self-serving European Court of Human Rights which is presided over by supposed judges from some of the most corrupt countries in the developed world.

Set a minimum age for providing council housing. Britain has one of the highest rates of teenage single parents in Europe. If council housing and housing benefits were only available to people over the age of twenty five, this might discourage some young people from seeing the production of children as a way to an easy life housed at our expense. If someone below the age of twenty five wants to have children and still has living parents then they should either pay for their own accommodation or stay at home with their parents. Only if both parents are deceased should anyone younger than twenty five be given council housing or housing benefits.

Demand a five per cent per year reduction in the EU budget. When preparing to negotiate its regular budget increases with national governments, the EU always pitches its demands for an increase at unrealistic levels, because it knows that governments will eventually agree to a compromise figure around half of what is demanded. That's how people negotiate. But when Cameron wanted to show he was standing up to the EU, he proposed a budget freeze. That's a ridiculous way to enter a negotiation. If he had really wanted a budget freeze, then he should have demanded the EU reduce its budget by say five per cent a year. Then the eurocrats might have been willing to settle for a freeze or even a one to two per cent a year reduction. Thanks to Blair's catastrophically invertebrate decision to agree to a cut in Britain's EU budget rebate, we now pay far too much into the EU compared to other countries. It's time for our politicians to start negotiating with the EU by showing a bit of backbone rather than already starting as hopeless losers.

Chapter 15

A 'Citizens Spring'?

They're all in this together

Of course, the Government would never even consider any of the actions proposed in the previous chapter. This is because each of these proposals would hurt an interest group with influence over government policy. Tony Blair once promised us, 'a government that will govern in the interests of the many, the broad majority of people who work hard, play by the rules, pay their dues'. Cameron keeps on repeating the same platitude, 'I am on the side of people who work hard, want to get on and play by the rules'. These protestations of being on the side of ordinary people now look more than hollow given that both New Labour and the Coalition have worked hard to protect the elites while right royally stiffing those of us who have been foolish enough to actually 'work hard and play by the rules'.

The Coalition's biggest failure is that it didn't put itself on the side of ordinary people against the vested interests of those who take and spend our money. Instead, like New Labour before it, the Coalition protected the bureaucratic, political, business and financial elites while brutally squeezing the living standards of the majority. So, given that our political masters no longer represent those who vote for them, can ordinary citizens do anything to protect themselves against the greed, dishonesty, hypocrisy and incompetence of our ruling elites of politicians, bureaucrats, businesspeople and bankers?

This last chapter should be the place where the author, having spent the last 70,000 or so words of *Greed Unlimited* lambasting our venal, self-serving elites, comes up with some brilliant proposals as to how we can launch a 'Citizens Spring' rebellion against our rulers.

I wrote my earlier books in the probably naïve belief that I could help cause change for the better. With *Rip-Off: The scandalous inside story of the consulting money machine*, I thought that after the book had exposed many of the tricks consultants use to fleece their clients, businesses would become smarter when dealing with consultants. But I was wrong. Nothing changed. In fact, the consultancy business has gone from strength to strength. Then *Plundering the Public Sector* revealed the Blair/Brown government's enormous waste of money (about £70 billion) on expensive, underperforming consultants and the complete catastrophe of the NHS's new computer system. Result – the National Audit Office (NAO) did a review of the public sector's use of consultants and laughably concluded that in general the taxpayer was getting value for money. The NAO also produced a report on the disastrous NHS computer system and ludicrously judged it as one of the best run public-sector computer projects it had ever seen.

I tried again with *Squandered: How Gordon Brown is wasting over one trillion pounds of our money*. One reviewer wrote, 'it is no exaggeration to say that if the right people read it, take it seriously, and take appropriate action, this book could not only save the taxpayer billions, it could save lives'. It is my understanding that many of the 'right people' the reviewer mentioned did get their minions to read *Squandered* to tell them what was in the book. However, Labour just ignored the book, the Tory Opposition seemed incapable of using the information in the book to attack Brown's waste and incompetence, no action was taken, hundreds of billions more were squandered and many lives were lost unnecessarily. Moreover incredibly, Brown's Labour Party, which was responsible for squandering so much of our money so incompetently and virtually bankrupting Britain in the process, wasn't far off winning the 2010 general election.

Then followed *The Great European Rip-Off* attacking EU corruption and waste and *Pillaged! How they are looting £413 million a day from your savings and pensions*, a book exposing the greed and lies of the financial services industry. Result, nothing much happened and the EU and financial services industry have kept on siphoning off ever-increasing amounts of our money.

At the time of *Plundering the Public Sector*, I contacted one of the most histrionically vociferous members of the Public Accounts Committee (PAC) offering to brief him on the kinds of questions he could ask at a PAC session where the bosses of the worthless and catastrophically expensive NHS computer system project were to be brought before the Committee. I got an extraordinarily arrogant and rude letter back telling me that there was not likely to be anything I could teach him about the project. Sure enough, when I attended the session, I saw that the PAC's questions were feeble, poorly-informed and ineffective in exposing what was really going on with the disastrous NHS computer system project. As for the MP who gave me the brush off, his questions were probably among the most asinine, pointless and irrelevant of all those posed by PAC members – and the competition for being the most useless PAC member that day was pretty tough.

We assume, or at least I assumed, that in our political system we have parties which are genuinely fighting against each other for the benefit of those whose votes they grovel for once every five years or so. I therefore thought that my books could help whichever party was in Opposition hold the Government to account. But most of our politicians are actually playing a well-paid, well-rehearsed and rather enjoyable game. They have much more in common with each other, whichever party they come from, than they have with those who vote for them. They're all part of the same club, the same clan, the same sect, the same greedy, self-serving elite. If you ever attend any meetings of committees like the PAC, you soon see that they're just a charade where politicians pretend to be tough with wasteful bureaucrats and military leaders and those supposedly being held to account just swat away any uncomfortable questions with relaxed, well-practised ease. Then at the end of the session they all congratulate themselves and each other for another fine performance having achieved absolutely nothing for the people who pay their big salaries, expenses and pensions.

The rather depressing conclusion of my latest book *Greed Unlimited* is that there's actually very little ordinary people can do. When the politicians, bureaucrats, business bosses and bankers are all in this together, all enriching themselves while impoverishing the rest of us, how can we fight back against them? Moreover, what choices do we really have? The Coalition Government may be run by a bunch of arrogant, incompetent, shallow, self-serving fools. But the alternative is the return to power of Labour. This is the party which did more than any other to wreck Britain with its obsession with borrowing and wasting our money on its public-sector paymasters; its policy of diluting our national identity by allowing uncontrolled immigration; its attempts to destroy the middle classes, which Labour loathed, by removing any excellence or aspiration from our education system while Labour politicians mostly sent their own children to private schools; and its pandering to the liberal elites through the introduction of human rights legislation which has made human rights lawyers wealthy, has protected criminals and has been used to persecute those who do try to obey the law.

We are at a key moment in our history. The greed, dishonesty and incompetence of the ruling elite of politicians, bureaucrats, businesspeople and bankers will probably lead to a loss of confidence in free market capitalism. Faced with the complete failure of our democratic institutions to control the avarice of our masters, people will turn against free markets and vote for increased state control in the belief that this will protect them from the economic chaos we've experienced since the financial collapse of 2007.

There was a time when the large industrial trade unions ran Britain. Their stranglehold on the country was broken by Margaret Thatcher's crusade against them. If, or rather when, Labour wins the next election, we will probably find that the real power in the country is put into the hands of a few public-sector union bosses who control the Labour Party. They will naturally seek to expand their empires by increasing the public-sector workforce once again and extracting higher salaries and more generous pensions for their members. They will, of course, be completely indifferent to the fact that Britain is to all intents and purposes bankrupt and can't afford another era of Brownian and Ballsian financial incontinence.

These new masters will ignore the dreadful state of our economy and instead set their sights on the £4 trillion we have in savings and pensions and trillions more in the value of our homes. We can be sure that to satisfy its public-sector-union paymasters, the next Labour government will launch a series of punitive tax raids on our £4 trillion in savings and on the value of our homes spouting slogans such as 'British savings for British jobs' and 'fairness' and they will expropriate our money using excuses like 'the older generation, who have seen huge increases in their wealth through rising house prices, should help the next generation'. They will also penalise those who have saved for their retirement to fund those who couldn't be bothered by claiming 'everyone is entitled to dignity in retirement'. But unfortunately for us, the money they take won't be used to boost the economy and jobs. Instead, as happened during thirteen years of Brown and Balls, most of our money will be flushed down the toilet in another orgy of waste and mismanagement with unproductive public-sector jobs increasing and bureaucrats' salaries and pensions once again heading towards the skies.

When Miliband and Balls take their places in Downing Street and launch their great new spending spree, we can expect a loss of confidence in Britain's economic solvency, a massive rise in the interest payments we have to make on our ever-increasing borrowings and a collapse in the value of the pound.

If we are to prevent the people who caused our economic misery returning to power we need great leadership. But given the self-serving, small-minded political pygmies at the top of all our main parties, it's difficult to see where that leadership will come from.

In the meantime, there probably won't be any 'Citizens Spring'. All we ordinary people can do is slightly irritate those who hold power over us. That's a pretty sad note on which to end the book.

How to irritate our masters

British democracy has worked reasonably well over the last fifty to sixty years. There have been a few recessions, but in general we've had almost constantly rising prosperity. And when most people's standard of living is improving, we tend not to look too critically at those who rule us. That has now stopped. We have suffered a huge economic shock, we have looked to our leaders for a solution and have found that they have nothing to offer as they are too busy enriching themselves at our expense. Britain has given birth to powerful international campaigning organisations such as Amnesty International and Oxfam. But we don't have a tradition of grassroots protests like, for example, the French. If we are to fight back against the greed, hypocrisy, lies and avarice of the ruling elite of politicians, business bosses, bureaucrats and bankers, we will have to overcome our apathy and learn new skills of activism and protest. The only alternative is surrender.

Politicians

EU election – vote UKIP

As the EU elections, due to be held in 2014, are based on proportional representation, rather than the 'first past the post' method used in general elections, they provide a real opportunity to give the three main parties a bloody nose. If a large majority of British members of the European Parliament (MEPs) were from UKIP, this would shatter the main parties' credibility when they claimed to represent ordinary people's attitudes to the wasteful, undemocratic and thoroughly corrupt European Union.

General election – vote for the Taxpayers Party

In general elections, Britain's 'first past the post' system makes it almost impossible for small or fringe parties to break through the stranglehold the three main parties have over seats in the House of Commons. But with confidence in all the main parties at a record low, one can always hope that this situation could change. That's why I've formed the Taxpayers Party. At the Taxpayers Party we are looking for supporters and people who want to become candidates in council elections or the general election. For more information, go to www.votetaxpayers.org.uk Just a few Taxpayers Party MPs in Westminster and a few Taxpayers Party people on local councils could cause havoc for the ruling elites, because we could continually and embarrassingly expose the stupidity, waste, corruption, cronyism, dirty deals and greed of our national and local rulers.

Bureaucrats

Demand your 'human rights'

In *Fleeced* I explained how we could use human rights legislation to scupper the plans of our corrupt wasteful leaders. The Human Rights Act (HRA) 1998 received Royal Assent in November 1998 and mostly came into force in October 2000. The Act makes it unlawful for any public body to act in a way which is incompatible with the European Convention on Human Rights (ECHR). Perhaps the most worrying thing about the HRA is that it gives rights without suggesting any corresponding responsibilities. For example, Article 14 confers the right to 'education and to have access to vocational and continuing training'. But it doesn't dare propose that people have any responsibility for ensuring they and their children get the best education they can so they can contribute to society. Article 15 gives us all have the 'Freedom to choose an occupation and the right to engage in work'. But, of course, there is no hint of the possibility that we have a duty to society to work rather than live off the taxes of those who can be bothered to get out of bed in the morning. Article 9 confirms the 'Right to marry and found a family'. It is never proposed that when deciding how many children we want to produce, we should think about whether we, rather than the state, can afford to support them and give them a good upbringing.

Then there's the wonderful Article 41 of the ECHR. This gives us the Right to Good Administration: 'Every person has the right to have his or her affairs handled impartially, fairly and within a reasonable time by the institutions, bodies, offices and agencies of the Union'. Moreover: 'Every person has the right to have the Union make good any damage caused by its institutions or by its servants in the performance of their duties'. It could be argued that Parliament is an agency of the EU and therefore the theft of our money by our MPs is a breach of our right to good administration. Moreover, perhaps all public-sector bodies are EU institutions and they are breaching our human rights by taking and wasting hundreds of billions of pounds of our money.

With a bit of creative thinking, somewhere in the ECHR's fifty verbose Articles many people will find some reason why their leaders are possibly breaching their human rights – and when they find it, they should attack with all guns blazing. In fact, the ECHR is a goldmine of opportunities for ordinary people to fight back against the incompetence, mismanagement, profligacy and avarice of our ruling elites.

Use corporate manslaughter laws

In 2007, I published a book called *Who Cares? One Family's shocking story of 'care' in today's NHS. Who Cares?* tells the story of Paul Steane. He went into hospital for minor surgery, but after repeated mistakes and neglect by inexperienced doctors and overworked nurses in dirty wards, Paul suffered twice from dehydration – not being given enough water to drink. Emerging from hospital a helpless invalid, in constant pain and unable to walk, talk or breathe properly, Paul took his own life. The book was, of course, ignored by the many bureaucracies who should be regulating our hospitals to ensure patient safety and dehydration continues to be one of the major causes of unnecessary deaths in our hospitals.

The Corporate Manslaughter and Corporate Homicide Bill received Royal Assent in July 2007 and became law in April 2008. Previous legislation around corporate manslaughter was found to be difficult to use because of the necessity to link gross negligence to one specific individual. Under the new law an organisation can be found guilty of corporate manslaughter (corporate homicide in Scotland) if the way in which its activities are managed or organised by its senior management amount to a gross breach of the duty of care it owes to its employees, the public or other individuals and those failings caused a person's death. This law is an incredibly powerful weapon that ordinary people can use against the bureaucrats who earn so much money running our underperforming hospitals. A few hospital bosses fined or imprisoned for corporate manslaughter would do wonders in reminding NHS bureaucrats that they get their huge salaries and massive pensions to serve their patients and not just themselves.

Drown the equality industry

The hugely expensive (over £70 million a year) Equality and Human Rights Commission (EHRC) has probably caused this country irreparable damage by making businesses afraid to employ people; by protecting criminals from justice; by guaranteeing illegal immigrants the right to remain in Britain claiming benefits for the rest of their lives; and by ruining our pension system through forcing annuity companies to pay the same annuities to men and women even though women live longer. We should drown this useless organisation with a flood of complaints about being discriminated against. For example, someone who smokes can get a larger annuity than someone who doesn't smoke – that's discrimination against non-smokers. Then there's Club 18-30 with its slogan – 'We know 18 to 30 year olds. Over 80,000 of them spend the most important weeks of their year with us. We know what's hot. We know what's not'. Surely this is discrimination against miserable old people who just want a holiday where they can complain about the outrageous behaviour of young people all the time? And there's Saga – 'Saga offer an array of products and services exclusively for the over 50s, including insurance, home care, holidays and the UK's best selling monthly magazine'. Isn't this discrimination against anyone under fifty? And we have Sheilas' Wheels – 'Car insurance, home insurance, travel insurance and pet insurance designed specifically with women in mind!' Presumably this discriminates against men. There must be thousands of other cases where common sense allows companies and government agencies to provide different services to different groups of people. But in the world of the EHRC, there is no place for common sense – political correctness is all that matters.

Banks and financial services

Only bank with your bank

The main high-street banks (HSBC, Barclays, Natwest, Lloyds etc) want to run our current accounts. They don't make too much money from this. But it gives them the chance to do what they call 'cross-selling' – using their contacts with us and information about us to flog us all kinds of other financial products. These include deposit accounts, mortgages, insurance, pensions, investments and so on. But, apart from some very rare exceptions, you'd be a fool to buy any of these products from your high-street bank. For deposit accounts you'll usually get much better rates from the former building societies. Mortgages – it's normally better to go to a specialist mortgage broker. Insurance – why pay a large commission to your bank, when you can buy more cheaply direct from an insurance company? Pensions – anyone saving with a high-street bank is going to pay so much in charges that they're going to end up awfully poor. Investments – time after time it has been shown that banks (especially HSBC and Barclays) have cobbled together and mis-sold appalling investment schemes which have made billions for the banks and lost billions for their gullible customers. Never ever put any money into any investment being pushed by your high-street bank!

So the lesson is – 'only bank with your bank'. Only let your high-street bank run your current account. If you do any other business with the likes of HSBC, Barclays, RBS, Lloyds, Natwest then the chances are that you are paying for over-priced, poorly-performing products.

Swamp your bank with complaints

The Libor rate-rigging scandal may provide a perfect opportunity to fight back against our predatory banks. Anyone with a savings account in a bank involved in rate-rigging should write to their bank asking for the bank to appoint an independent auditor to investigate what interest rates their savings have received over the last five or so years, how these rates have been affected by LIBOR rates and what interest rates they would have got had the LIBOR rate not been rigged by the bank. They should also demand compensation for any money lost due to LIBOR rate rigging.

A 'Citizen Spring'?

Don't put any money in unit trusts

If you're looking for somewhere for your savings, you'll find a queue of people - banks, financial advisers and many others - all eager to get you to put your cash into unit trusts. Why? Because they care about your wellbeing? Or because they make massive commissions from flogging unit trusts? In Britain we pay an astonishing £59m every working day to unit trust managers and to the people who sold us those unit trusts. That's £59m a day - £15bn a year - being taken from our savings and pocketed by other people. Unit trusts will make you very rich - but only if you're a unit trust manager or salesperson. If you're an ordinary saver, they'll only make you poorer.

Say you put £10,000 into a unit trust. You immediately lose about 5% (£500) just for investing. Most of that goes in commission to salespeople. Then you lose about 3% (£300) a year in management and dealing costs. And when you withdraw your money, you lose another 5% (£500) because the price you sell your units is usually about 5% lower than the price you buy them. So, if you hold your units for five years, you generously give 25% (£2,500) of your money to multimillionaire managers and salespeople. (If you had £100,000, you'd be giving away £25,000 - £5,000 a year!) Of course, you hope the fund managers will make your money grow. But ninety per cent of unit trust managers fail to beat the overall performance of the markets where they put your money. And almost no unit trust managers ever beat the returns on cash. If you put your £10,000 into a fixed-interest deposit account, you'd get about 4% a year - over five years compounded that's 21.5%. Due to their high charges, a unit trust would have to grow by 46.5% (9.3% a year) to beat a safe, no-risk cash deposit. That is just not going to happen.

Protect the banana skin and grave brigade

We British often feel uncomfortable talking about money with our parents, grandparents and other possibly elderly relatives. Perhaps we're afraid of looking like we're on a fishing expedition to find out how much we can expect to get when they finally clock out. But it's precisely our elderly relatives who are the juiciest targets for banks and other financial institutions with dubious savings products to sell and tough sales targets to meet to get their bonuses. We need to overcome our discomfort, ask anyone in our family who is either in or heading towards the banana skin and grave brigade what they are doing with their savings and try to establish who is trying to sell them any kind of financial product – longer-term stock-market investments, supposedly capital-protected bonds or probably toxic equity release schemes. Only by talking openly with family members, can we protect them against the greed and mis-selling of our predatory financial services industry.

Businesses

The protest organisation UK Uncut should be commended for being one of the few groups to actively campaign against some of our most prolifically tax-avoiding companies. UK Uncut's main policy that there should be no public-sector cuts is financially unsustainable. There is a massive amount of waste which could be taken out of our public-sector bureaucracies without having any negative effect on the services delivered. But their efforts to expose the £95 billion or so a year being lost to tax evasion by the rich and leading companies make them probably the only organisation to have dared stand up to our self-serving masters. Their protests against Philip Green and companies like

A 'Citizen Spring'?

Boots and Vodafone have helped draw attention to the massive scale of tax planning and tax avoidance by the rich and powerful. It's a pity that there aren't more organisations like UK Uncut and it's a pity that there aren't more people willing to spend the time and effort supporting such protests.

The post-democratic age

We have moved beyond democracy into a new age. In this new age, our institutions – businesses, politicians, the public sector and the banks - no longer serve our interests. Instead they serve themselves, ruthlessly exploiting us to make themselves richer at our expense. In *Greed Unlimited,* I have tried to show the scale of the problem and suggest some actions our Government should take to help us out of our current economic quagmire. These have included giving our bureaucrats a short, sharp shock with the imposition of a four-day week; scrapping corporation tax; bringing in a False Claims Act; cutting the cost of politics; protecting our national assets; taking on the pensions and unit trust industry and standing up to the EU. But as for the fundamental problem - the fact that our political, commercial, financial and public-sector institutions work against us rather than for us – that is more difficult to solve. So I'm forced to end *Greed Unlimited* in almost exactly the same way as I ended *Fleeced* three years ago:

> It can sometimes seem as if the democratic political process has now passed the point of no return. So the only way we can defend the rights and interests of the majority against the greed, arrogance, waste and incompetence of the small ruling elite of politicians, bureaucrats, business bosses and bankers is by active

campaigning and by using their laws against them. It will be interesting to see whether we can ever successfully fight back to defend our interests against the rapacious, self-serving, new ruling caste.

Endnotes

1   Reuters 18 May 2012
2   BBC News 24 May 2010
3   Speech 23 April 2012
4   BBC News 8 May 2012
5   *Guardian* 30 December 2011
6   *Guardian* 7 June 2010
7   http://www.youtube.com/watch?v=5dRfO-EOOW0
8   ibid
9   AFP 7 May 2012
10   *Daily Mail* 19 July 2012
11   *Chancellor's speech* Brighton Labour Party
       Conference 1997
12   Adapted from *David Copperfield* Charles Dickens
13   *Squandered: How Gordon Brown is wasting over £1*
       trillion of our money David Craig (Constable 2008)
14   Daily Mail 18 *July 2012*
15   *Daily Mail* 4 July 2012
16   *Guardian* 27 February 2012
17   *Financial Times* 5 June 2012
18   *Kay Review of Equity Markets* Final Report 2012
19   *Sunday Times* 3 June 2012
20   *Guardian* 12 January 2010
21   *Sunday Times* 27 May 2012
22   *Sunday Times* 15 July 2012

Endnotes

23   *Guardian* 14 January 2009
24   *Sunday Times* 15 July 2012
25   *Wall Street Journal* 17 November 2010
26   *Guardian* 30 April 2012
27   Norwich Union media team 6 June 2008
28   *Transforming the Organization* Kelly and Grouillart, McGraw-Hill 1995
29   *The Economist* 6-12 May 1995
30   BBC news 26 September 2000, *Independent* 14 April 2000 and http://www.number10.gov.uk/Page5399 24 February 2004
31   Transformational Government Annual Report 2008
32   ibid
33   *Investor and analyst briefing* 9 October 2008
34   *Daily Telegraph* 23 October 2009
35   *Daily Mail* 8 April 2012
36   *Daily Telegraph* 20 April 2012
37   *What Investment* 18 January 2011
38   *Sunday Telegraph* 12 May 2012
39   *The Independent* 9 May 2012
40   *Daily Telegraph* 30 October 2009
41   *Daily Telegraph* 6 April 2011
42   *ibid*
43   *Daily Telegraph* 30 October 2009
44   Daily Telegraph 8 February 2011
45   *Guardian* 25 March 2011
46   *Huffington Post UK* 6 March 2012
47   *Daily Mail, Mirror, Guardian* 19 June 2012
48   *Daily Telegraph* 24 March 2012
49   *Daily Telegraph* 24 March 2012
50   *Daily Telegraph* 24 March 2012
51   *Jarrow and Hebburn Gazette* 2 March 2012
52   *www.theyworkforyou.com*

Endnotes

53   http://www.theyworkforyou.com/mp/simon_reevell/
dewsbury#register

54   *Daily Mail* 30 June 2009

55   *Smaller Government: What do ministers do?* Public
Administration Committee 2011

56   *Smaller Government: What do ministers do?* Further
Report with the Government's response

57   *Daily Mail* 29 June 2010

58   *Daily Mail* 29 June 2010

59   Treasury Annual Report 2010-11

60   Cabinet Office Annual Report and Accounts 2010-11

61   *Daily Telegraph* 30 April 2012

62   http://www.ageuk.org.uk/get-involved/campaign/
preventing-winter-deaths/

63   www.efinancialnews.com 9 January 2012

64   Conservative Manifesto 2010

65   *Daily Mail* 25 January 2011

66   *Daily Mail* 9 March 2010

67   *Daily Telegraph* 25 April 2012

68   *The Great European Rip-Off* David Craig (Random
House 2009) pp 229

69   *Daily Mail* 5 March 2012

70   *EUBusiness* 1 June 2012

71   *Financial Times* 27 April 2012

72   *Daily Telegraph* 19 April 2012

73   *EUBusiness* 1 June 2012

74   Publicservice.co.uk 22 March 2012

75   Publicservice.co.uk 22 March 2012

76   Daily Mail (check!) 12 January 2009

77   *Daily Telegraph* 4 December 2011

78   *Guardian* 7 September 2010 and *Daily Mail* 21
August 2010

79   *Daily Mail* 21 August 2012

Endnotes

80   *Daily Telegraph* 11 April 2009

81   *Sunday Times* 22 July 2012

82   *Publicservice.co.uk* 22 March 2012

83   ibid

84   *Daily Mail* 12 February 2012

85   *Rip-Off: the scandalous inside story of the consulting money machine* David Craig (Original Book Company 2005)

86   *Observer* 12 February 2012

87   *E-Health Insider* 16 July 2012

88   Public Accounts Committee *Major Projects Review*

89   *Defence Reform Liability Review* 18 November 2011

90   *Defence Reform Liability Review* 18 November 2011

91   *Daily Mail* 26 May 2007

92   ibid

93   *Independent* 18 June 2012

94   *Daily Telegraph* 16 May 2012

95   BBC News 26 January 2012

96   BBC News 3 April 2006

97   *Public Finance* 7 April 2006

98   *Daily Telegraph* 17 September 2008

99   ibid

100   *Daily Mail* 25 July 2010

101   *The Register* 26 July 2010

102   *Sunday Times Rich List* 2012

103   *Fleeced* David Craig (Constable 2009) pages 97-130

104   *Sunday Times* 10 June 2012

105   *Telegraph* 1 May 2007, *Guardian* 2 May 2007, *Robert Peston's Blog* BBC 1 May 2007

106   *The Huffington Post UK* 4 January 2012

107   *The Huffington Post UK* 16 February 2012

108   *The Huffington Post UK* 4 January 2012

109   *Herald Scotland* 11 November 2010

Endnotes

110   *Andrew Marr Show* BBC 4 January 2009
111   *Andrew Marr Show* BBC 4 January 2009
112   *Andrew Marr Show* BBC 4 January 2009
113   *Sunday Telegraph* 9 June 2012
114   *Daily Telegraph* 10 June 2012
115   *The Great British Taxpayer Rip-Off* Mike Denham
116   *Daily Mail* 18 April 2008
117   Budget 2010 - Chancellor's statement to the House
118   Budget 2011 - Chancellor's statement to the House
119   Budget 2010 – Chart A3 page 77
120   *The Northern Echo* 26 June 2012
121   *OBR: Britain is bust* Interview recorded for the *Daily Telegraph*
122   *Bloomberg Markets Magazine* 6 October 2010
123   *Investors' Chronicle* 22 March 1996
124   *Daily Mail* 18 April 2012
125   *Channel 4 News* 27 September 2010
126   *BBC News* 26 November 2011
127   *Daily Telegraph* 2 July 2012
128   *Chancellor's Budget Speech* 23 March 2011
129   *Sunday Times* 13 May 2015
130   *Financial Times* 16 April 2010
131   *Daily Telegraph* 6 August 2011
132   *Daily Telegraph* 11 June 2012
133   FSA announcement 31 May 2012
134   *Pensions World* 9 February 2012
135   *Pensions World* 9 February 2012
136   Charlie Bean speech 21 February 2012
137   *This Is Money* 24 May 2012
138   *LAPF* November 2011
139   David Miles speech 1 March 2012
140   www.viableopposition.blogspot.ca
141   *Daily Mail* 19 July 2012